Around the World
by Mouse

Harry Pearson

LITTLE, BROWN

LITTLE, BROWN

First published in Great Britain in August 2005 by Little, Brown

Copyright © 2005 Harry Pearson

A CIP catalogue record for this book
is available from the British Library.

ISBN 0 316 85733 5

Typeset in Baskerville by M Rules
Printed and bound in Great Britain
by Clays Ltd, St Ives plc

Little, Brown
An imprint of
Time Warner Book Group UK
Brettenham House
Lancaster Place
London WC2E 7EN

www.twbg.co.uk

Around the World
by Mouse

Preface

It is very easy to visit foreign lands and write sweeping generalisations about them. It is even easier if you don't go at all.

When I first started work I lived in a shared flat just off the Edgware Road in London. It was in many ways a typical chap-rented apartment. There was ill-assorted furniture in various shades of fungus and sludge, the ghostly odour of long-ago cabbage, a hot-water system that produced barely enough to soak a flannel and kitchen drawers that contained grapefruit knives, asparagus tongs and a cake slice but no can opener or scissors.

I was employed as a receptionist at a luxury West End hotel. One day a Saudi Arabian guest gave me a tip that amounted to a week's wages. When my shift ended I went straight to Hatchards in Piccadilly and bought *The Times Comprehensive Atlas of the World*. On icy winter nights, when the frost got in through the cracks in the windows and froze the water in the toilet, my flatmates and I would force-feed the gas meter with 10p pieces till it was stuffed like a Strasbourg goose, turn the gas fire up to maximum, fill half-pint mugs with a mix of drinking chocolate and Stroh's Austrian rum, open the atlas and point out the places we were going to visit at some unidentified and apparently still distant point when we had money. Some of the longest and happiest journeys I have ever made took place on the third floor of a house in Maida Vale.

Since then I have visited many countries, but as I have got older I have come to like travelling less and less. It is not the destinations that are the problem: to paraphrase Will Rogers, I never knew a place I didn't like (well, except Dubai, obviously); it is getting to them. It is the travel part of travel that I couldn't stand. I had begun to take Dr Johnson's grumpy response to Boswell's comment that the Giant's Causeway was surely a thing worth seeing – 'Aye, worth seeing, but not worth going to see' – as my motto. The situation came to a head when I was trapped at Brussels Airport for seven hours waiting for a flight to Hamburg. I am terribly fond of Belgium, with its museums devoted to the history of washing and its ice lollies called Big Nuts, but Brussels Airport was not a place anybody could warm too. Unless possibly it was on fire. A miasma of tobacco smoke and atomised duty-free perfume samples hovered over the departure lounge, the public address system was running through a five-CD boxed set of power ballads called 'Now That's What I Call Music I Never Wanted To Hear Again 3' and two workmen were ripping up a section of terrazzo flooring with a circular saw that made a noise like the death rattle of a triffid. Brussels Airport that day seemed like some trial run for an EC anti-illegal immigration device. 'This is the heart of Europe', it seemed to say, 'now piss off.'

After that experience, if I could have answered the old wartime question 'Is your journey really necessary?' with a clipped 'No, never' and stayed at home until someone had made the starship *Enterprise*'s teleporter a reality, I would have been very happy.

Luckily, at that point two things happened. Firstly, while

browsing through Abebooks (good for secondhand and rare books, among others) I came across Alex Atkinson's magnificent *USA For Beginners*. First published in 1959 and, shamefully, out of print pretty much ever since, subtitled 'By Rocking Chair Across America' it comes with illustrations by Ronald Searle and an opening paragraph that reads 'Too many books about the United States are written by men who have only spent a few weeks in the country. This book is different: it is by a man who has never been there in his life.'

Shortly after I had read *USA For Beginners* my parents gave me a new edition of *The Times Comprehensive Atlas of the World* and so an idea took shape. It struck me that there was now something quite like the *Star Trek* teleporter: the internet. I would recreate those journeys I made in north London all those years ago using the atlas to plot my route and a computer to visit the places on it. I would travel 600 miles a day on the transport available, circumnavigating the globe in less than two months. I would see the sites via webcams, soak up the atmosphere through homepages and message boards, buy souvenirs, send e-postcards and get food poisoning when I ordered the battered squid balls even though bloggers had warned me they were notorious.

Afterwards I would write a modern version of Atkinson's work, only longer, with fewer pictures and considerably worse jokes. This is that book. I think you will agree that in my aim, especially the latter part of it, I have succeeded beyond all expectation.

Alex Atkinson used tourist literature, film, TV and fiction to form his impression of the United States. I have used only the World Wide Web. Everything that follows happened in cyberspace. The people, situations and places are all virtually real. My criteria for plotting the journey were only to visit places I have never actually been to, to see sights I have never actually seen, so that I could not draw on past experience. Naturally there are many destinations meeting those criteria that do not feature in these pages. This is not through any fault of theirs. I would, for example, have loved to visit Croatia, birthplace of the tie, where the currency is the pine marten and there are thirteen different types of therapeutic mud. I was also drawn to South Africa after my search engine threw out the information that one of the Rainbow Nation's favourite savoury treats is a corn-based snack called 'Salty Cracks'. I would love, too, to say that I had been to Scarborough, Maine, and seen Lenny, the world's only life-sized chocolate moose (he weighs 1700 pounds and he's made of solid milk chocolate!), but the clock was against me. Another time, maybe.

1

To the Vulgar Nations and Afterwards

North Shields to Banska Bystrica

Even a journey of 30,000 miles must start with a single click. One February morning I kissed my family goodbye, checked Macromedia Flash 5 was in place, finished running Fastview and then pointed Netscape 6.2 northeastwards and set off.

I had downloaded music to my Realplayer jukebox specially to mark this occasion but unfortunately I must have pressed the wrong button. So, instead of departing to the Three Degrees' 'When Will I See You Again?', I waved farewell to the theme music from *Rentaghost*.

The day was bright with a moderate westerly breeze and maximum temperatures of 9°C. There was a probability of light showers in the afternoon and the local newspaper featured a story about a fight at a funeral in which one mourner had head-butted another in a dispute over the relative merits of their floral tributes. 'My client had drunk fourteen pints of lager that lunchtime,' defence counsel said, 'and can remember nothing of the incident.'

At the Women's Institute the prize for the prettiest

ornamental sugar spoon was won by a lady from Corbridge.

As I sailed down the Tyne in a canoe I had hired virtually for the virtual purpose, I felt confident of my abilities to survive the journey ahead. I was travelling light but I had been studying a number of survival websites and now had the necessary know-how to fashion a rude shelter from bent branches and cook up a delightful nutritious broth by pouring boiling water over an owl pellet, or 'Mother Nature's stock cube' as it is known to us backwoodsmen.

As I passed under the A69 I felt a tingle of excitement in the pit of my stomach (at least I assumed that's what it was – it may have been a minor urinary infection). It was excitement tinged with nervousness. I had one major worry – the machine on which I was travelling. Others, I know, have crossed the world on camels, donkeys, coracles, bicycles and vehicles made from rough-puff pastry and powered by the simple expedient of playing a blowlamp across the rump of a Berkshire hog, but nobody so far as I know has attempted it on a vintage computer.

My Compaq Presario had been bought in 1998. As far as computer people were concerned this made it an object of such antiquity that its model number, 1680, might as well have referred to the year in which it was made. If a human year is the equivalent of seven years in the life of a dog, it is the equal of twenty-five in the life of software. When I covered the Gaelic Football final at Croke Park, Dublin, journalists from the west of Ireland pointed at my machine, laughed and asked, 'Is it coke or peat you're burning?' I was relying on Windows 95 to power me, a system now considered so prehistoric by the manufacturer that they no longer offered online assistance to repair it. If I crashed in the Gobi Desert I was on my own.

One thought consoled me as I reached North Shields, home to the world-famous Fish Quay Festival and childhood residence of Stan Laurel: the memory of Catherine and my first car. The Fiat 127 Sport had cost us £200 back in the days when £200 was not very much money at all. Its orange bodywork was acned with rust, a fancy matt-black cowl on the bonnet was held on with kitchen string and the exhaust pipe fell off if any of the backseat passengers coughed and farted simultaneously.

Undaunted, we went to Spain in it. The Fiat passed the test magnificently, though my abiding memories are of the time it took to trundle us up the mountain passes of the Picos de Europas. One sunny morning as we crawled up an incline near Potes a snaggle-toothed shepherd actually leant in through the driver's window, bade us good day and commented favourably on the weather as we passed. On another a cyclist, so fat that his stomach bounced rhythmically on his knees as he pedalled, overtook us. It looked like he was playing keepie-uppie with his lunch. It did not take long for him to disappear from sight.

On the information super highway my Compaq was the equivalent of that Fiat. I knew it would be as slow; I hoped it would be as reliable.

North Shields International Ferry Terminal was all abustle as a tiny percentage of the 750,000 passengers who passed this way every year prepared to make the journey across the North Sea to Ijmuiden, a port in the Netherlands that billed itself as Amsterdam, but wasn't.

I paused momentarily to admire the DFDS Seaways Ro Ro berths. The pontoons had a depth alongside of 7.5 metres below chart datum and were capable of accommodating a new generation of seagoing ferries (routinely disparaged by the older generation of seagoing ferries because they had not done National Service and have no sense of values). Then, slinging my duffel bag over my shoulder, I stepped up the gangplank and prepared to board the *Duchess of Estonia*. Before I could do so I had to download Java plug-in 1.3 1_02. While Java run time environment set-up prepared installshield (R) wizard and created Java JAR files, I filled the time by puzzling over life's great imponderables (what is the point of wasps? Why did I sit through the whole of Eric Rohmer's *The Green Ray*? Is there really a French cheese called Bridel Terrior or was it just a spelling mistake on the Tesco online website?) and repapering the spare room.

Eventually the ferry's entrance area appeared before me. It was rather fuzzy and featured much glittering metal and silver paint, like the interior of *Battlestar Galactica* painted by Renoir. In the Columbus Club there was international-class professional entertainment. No details were given save for some photos. The American travel writer Paul Theroux claims the ability to tell a person's name just by looking at them. I can do something similar. The uninitiated some-times call it 'making things up' when in reality it is 'incisive creative insight'. I have only to look at a photo and, not only can I tell what the people's names are, I can also gauge their character and what they are talking about. To me every pic-ture tells a story, though sometimes only under torture, admittedly.

From the photographs I could tell the band was made up of former coalminers from Nottinghamshire called Los Millionaros and backed a chanteuse, who may well have gone by the name of Marti Cinzano, performing a version of 'Evergreen' that would have wrung tears from a rattlesnake.

Later there was disco dancing till the early hours performed by a blonde in a mono-shouldered black dress with gold trim and a bloke with a cap-sleeve T-shirt who was doing that funky white man thing of biting his lower lip and bobbing his head in time to the rhythm of the music, albeit different music from that which was playing. The sea is a cruel mistress.

As I walked along the passenger portside upper deck attempting to catch a glimpse of a school of capering porpoises, a stormy petrel or the flickering lights of a distant oil rig on which men sat in front of TV screens, grunting in frustration at the fact that, under copyright laws, it was forbidden to show home rental videos on them, the 'You got mail' icon popped up.

A man hailed me from my inbox. Irwin was a hearty American fellow and by his prodigious use of exclamation marks I judged him to have a loud voice and a habit of guffawing loudly at the end of sentences. 'Harry-IV-Pearson,' Irwin bellowed. 'Lose weight in the shower? Sound impossible? It's not! Thanks to a new scientifically proven miracle formula! As seen on NBC! Interested? You should be!'

Actually, I *was* interested. Like any man in his forties I am always looking for a way to shed a few pounds without fuss or effort. Not for health reasons, obviously, but because these days in cyberspace you never knew when you might bump into someone you hadn't seen since schooldays. And on such an occasion it was important to look your best. After all, there's nothing more guaranteed to lift a man's spirits than meeting someone for the first time in twenty years and finding that your hair is thicker than his. I may be putting a misanthropic spin on this but it's my belief that the success of Friends Reunited is largely down to the fact that many people have become psychologically addicted to the buzz of finding contemporaries who have aged quicker than they have.

With this in mind I answered Irwin promptly and decisively: 'I most surely would, Irwin!' I said, slipping into what I hoped he would recognise as the peppy speech patterns of a no-holds-barred, straight-shooting son-of-a-gun. 'There's just one slight problem! I don't have a shower! Would the scientifically proven miracle formula work if I sat in the bath and poured water over my head with a saucepan?'

I thought that a man of Irwin's can-do disposition would respond positively to this, but he didn't snap back the instant reply I was expecting. After waiting several weeks I reluctantly took his reticence as a no. Disappointed, I retired to my Commodore de luxe cabin and watched an episode of *Columbo* with Dutch subtitles.

We disembarked next morning. Ijmuiden has the largest channel locks in Europe, but is nowhere near as exciting as that makes it sound. I boarded a coach for Amsterdam. We passed through the Dutch countryside. The Netherlands is a nation like no other. But then again, where isn't? Twenty-five per cent of the land is below sea level, it is the world's third largest exporter of food and there are twice as many bicycles as cars. It is also our planet's most densely populated nation with more than four hundred inhabitants per square kilometre. As a response to the tightness of their surroundings the Dutch have grown to be the tallest people in Europe. They are humanoid skyscrapers. The most popular sweet, 'the drop', is flavoured with salt and liquorice.

The Dutch football league features sides called Go Ahead and Be Quick but that kind of dynamism is no help against natural predators. As I crossed Holland a local non-league side, Putbroek, was locked in a struggle with a herd of wild pigs that kept getting on to the pitch and digging it up in search of worms. The management had now taken the unusual step of covering the playing area with human hair. 'Pigs have a well-developed sense of smell,' a spokesman says. 'As soon as they catch a human scent they run away, never to return.'

Altogether less susceptible to scents was the Bilderberg Group. The Netherlands is the birthplace of the Bilderberg Group, an organisation the exact nature of which occupies a mammoth-sized chunk of cyberspace. Prince Bernhard of the Netherlands founded Bilderberg and its members were variously accused of being a world government in waiting, neo-Nazis, international Zionists and giant lizards from outer space. It was said to be responsible amongst other things for globalisation, forging the European Union, inserting microchips into the buttocks of US servicemen and flying about in black helicopters scaring cattle in Wyoming. Whatever the nature of its other achievements, it was plain from even a cursory scan of the many, many sites devoted to Bilderberg's conspiratorial machinations that the organisation has at least done one thing that has greatly benefited mankind – it has kept fat, bearded geeks with ketchup down the front of their T-shirts far too busy to breed.

At Amsterdam station I spent several hours studying the timetable, largely because Netherland's railway's pop-up boxes were not designed for the random journey and rebelled at the notion of anybody simply wanting to travel one way, to 'The West' at 'about now hours'. Eventually I hopped aboard a 12.06 sneltrain that seemed to be heading in vaguely the right direction.

The world is a large place and plainly I couldn't stop

everywhere. Rather than being clamped in the teeth of tourist traps, or sucked into the swirling vortex of ever changing hip and happening destinations, I elected to stop every 100 miles at some burg I had never heard of, or, when I moved beyond my more customary haunts and that field became too large to choose from, to the place that sounded most like an aardvark sneezing.

Amersfoort (which met both criteria admirably) proved to be a marvellous place that styled itself, accurately, as 'a living work of art'. It was home to the Netherlands school for bell-ringers (with its permanent exhibition on campanology) and the Vocal Challenge barbershop choir, a group who prided themselves on being 'a bit more fanatical' than the rest and whose combined moustaches would carpet the average British sitting room so luxuriously you'd never need to wear slippers. As if this were not enough there was also a large boulder known as The Boulder.

The Boulder is the Dutch equivalent of The Hartlepool Monkey. (The following section is for the benefit of foreign readers; Brits might like to skip on to the next exciting paragraph.) Hartlepool, a port on the north-east coast of England, is infamous for an incident which is alleged to have occurred during the Napoleonic Wars. One day a ship sank at sea and its mascot, a monkey dressed in a sailor's uniform, was washed ashore. Having heard that the French were small, dark and jabbered unintelligibly, the citizens of Hartlepool seized the monkey as an enemy spy and hanged it. Ever since they have been known locally as the Monkeyhangers and taunted mercilessly for their unworldliness and stupidity. Sensing that the best way to deal with the situation was not to deny, but, as it were, to embrace the monkey, Hartlepool now takes some pride in the event that once brought them such shame. The town's rugby team portrays the lynched simian on its crest and Hartlepool United football club has a man dressed in a monkey costume as its mascot. As the result of a vote taken by fans he is named H'Angus the Monkey – a moniker that narrowly defeated the cheekier Spank (the Monkey; come on, keep up). In the 2002 election H'Angus (or at least the man who dressed as him) was elected mayor of Hartlepool on an independent ticket. One of his manifesto pledges was that every child in the town would be given a free banana. In true political style, when he came to office he failed to fulfil this commitment, claiming it was financially impossible and that he had never said he *would* do it, only that he would *look into the possibility* of doing it. Later he found himself engulfed in scandal when he went to a local pub one Sunday lunchtime and watched a stripper. One of the dancers professed to being shocked by the sight of the mayor, though some felt that as she earned a living performing a lesbian dance routine in a pub, she oughtn't to have been quite so sensitive. Back to The Boulder.

Sometime in the seventeenth century a local squire named Everard Meyster decided to play a prank on the townspeople of Amersfoort. He had discovered a large boulder on the heath near the town and set about persuading the inhabitants that it would be a good idea to move it into the main square. It took four hundred Amersfoort men to do it and afterwards they were so delighted with their achievement they had a party with beer and pretzels. Unfortunately word soon got around that Meyster had conned them into carrying out this massively pointless task and before long everybody in Holland was mocking the people of Amersfoort. The

Boulder, which stood in the Varkenmarkt, had made them a byword for idiocy throughout the nation. Embarrassed and outraged, the townsfolk decided to get rid of The Boulder. Reluctant to move it again, they dug a hole, pushed it in and buried it. As can be imagined, this tended only to compound things. In 1903, in a Hartlepool-like attempt at empowerment, Amersfoort dug The Boulder up again and now every year they hold a party in its honour.

One in three people in the Netherlands belong to a sports club. Ten million Germans are nudists. As I crossed the border near Nijmegen I entered a country in which there is a possibility that every eighth person you see will be naked. And those who aren't will not be pulling sour faces and making tutting noises. In a survey carried out in the GDR shortly before reunification 57 per cent of East Germans said they approved of 'nude activities'. Such is the grip that naturism has on Germany that it is now entirely legal for the citizenry to go about their daily lives totally unclad. However, the authorities reserve the right to challenge people in court if they think their nudity may be sexually motivated.

I had not gone far into the Rhineland before I found myself surrounded by German nudists who seemed to occupy every beach, cove and dune. Many of them seemed to spend their time standing and staring off into the distance. At first I took this reluctance to go to ground as a sign of wilful exhibitionism. Then I thought about it and realised that the last thing you want to be doing when you have no pants on is to sit on sand. I tried to get into the spirit of things by casting off my own clothes, but as I started to unbuckle my jeans the postman walked past my office window, so I had a chocolate macaroon instead.

Apart from nudism Germany is noted for being the home of the world's oldest bird fossil and Neanderthal man, who lived just outside Düsseldorf. The country offers more than one thousand unusual venues for meetings, conferences and events, including castles, palaces, disused coalmines and steelworks and a decommissioned nuclear power station near Kalkar on the Lower Rhine.

I stopped for coffee in Remscheid (pop. 120,145). The Ford Capri-owners' club of Germany and the national eight-way formation sky-diving team are based in the town. Remscheid's crest features half a white lion and a sickle, two objects that may not be unrelated.

Heading northward on the ICE I read the *Electronic Telegraph*. The newspaper reported that back home in dear old Blighty Ann Summers had replaced Tupperware in the hearts of womenfolk. What this said about contemporary morality I am not sure but it was certain to liven up lunchtime in the workplace, as hungry welders and ravenous international swaps dealers struggled to disentangle their luncheon meat sandwiches from a spangled thong, or to free a Scotch egg from the clasp of a peek-a-boo bra.

What can I tell you of my next port of call, the Hessian town of Nassel? The answer is nothing. For some reason Nassel had turned its back on the information age and closed its shutters to the computer. As to what lay behind this decision we can only speculate. A personal view is that the inhabitants had never got over the ridicule heaped upon them when they rolled a concrete pillar over a gibbon they suspected of being in league with the Commies. In Wolfsburg the professional football team was coached by Wolfgang Wolf.

And so to Berlin, city of deep-voiced women and men

in stockings, where John F. Kennedy announced, '*Ich bin ein Berliner.*' This was widely believed to mean 'I am a jam-filled doughnut.' Almost as much internet space was devoted to unravelling the truth behind this alleged gaffe as it was to the Bilderbergs. There were discussion groups entirely devoted to it. The overwhelming conclusion was that, contrary to popular myth, JFK got it right and that his pronouncement really did mean 'I am a citizen of Berlin'. So, sadly, when it comes to diplomatic buffoonery, we are left with dear old Lord George Brown, who, during a fact-finding mission to South America in the 1960s, is alleged to have approached a scarlet-clad figure at a reception in Buenos Aires and, as the band struck up, asked for the next dance, only to be rebuffed: 'I will not dance with you for three reasons. Firstly because you are drunk, secondly because this is the Brazilian national anthem and finally because I am the Cardinal of Montevideo.'

My dealings with the German capital were, I'm afraid, not entirely successful. I attempted to visit an exhibition at the Botanical Gardens with the intriguing title 'Sex im Planzenreich – Lust und Frust' (Sex in the Plant World – Lust and Frustration), only to find that I was several months too early. Then my efforts to take in traditional cabaret (hopefully involving transvestites and raunchy jokes about gherkins) at the Restaurant-Theatre Pump, Duck and Circumstances, somehow ended with my wandering into the home of Mike Batt, founder member of the Wombles pop group and Britain's leading songwriter and composer.

'There are only a handful of better ways of spending your time than checking out Mike's latest newsletter,' said the man who greeted me (possibly Mike himself; I'm afraid I didn't recognise him without his giant furry head on). One of these proved to be looking at Mike's picture gallery. This featured a quite extraordinary snap of Mrs Thatcher playing the drums at Abbey Road Studios. From the way the Iron Lady is gripping the sticks it is plain that she is no novice at the skins. One can only guess what might have been had not motherhood and the Conservative Party intervened. She'd probably have formed a supergroup with Eric Clapton, Stevie Winwood and Norman Fowler and built a reputation for drinking massive quantities of whisky and trashing the place. Only this time while playing music.

I was also interested while in Berlin in finding out something about the Situationists. One of my heroes is Noël Godin, a Liège-born performance artist whose work involves hitting famous people with cream pies. Victims are selected because they are pompous or pretentious. Perhaps not coincidentally, most of them have been French. Godin's acolytes and helpers include two other men who deserve wider recognition: Jan Bucquoy, director of the film '*The Sexual Life of the Belgians 1950–1978*' and one-time owner of the Brussels Museum of Underpants, and Plastic Bertrand, punk rock singer of the hit 'C'est Plein Pour Moi'. Godin's autobiography is entitled *Cream and Punishment*.

The Berlin Situationists influenced Godin and I'd imagined they might offer a similar mix of surreal comedic anarchy. Perhaps they would have, too, but every time I inquired about them people said things like 'They were avant-garde not only for what now with mondeanous expression is called the youth revolution', and it wasn't long before I got a headache.

I spent the night at a hotel in which expressive art and

exclusive design created a generous and harmonic ambience. I ate nuts.

The following morning, having spent a restless night in a city that seldom sleeps, I boarded the 9.06 train from the station. It was 1°C with a promise of snow as I headed south into Lower Saxony. 'The beautiful girls are from Saxonia' is a popular German proverb. I have no idea if it is true or not, but one thing is for certain – it is not much of a proverb. I suggest that if this is the tenor of German proverbs then other favourites may well be 'A bird in the hand will fly off unless you keep tight hold' and 'A rolling stone eventually stops in accordance with the laws of physics'.

For sporting reasons I debouched briefly at Chemnitz, home of the Saxonia Globe Snippers. As a child the great Argentine footballer Diego Maradona was saved from drowning in an open cesspit. The uncle who effected the rescue uttering the immortal words 'Try to keep your head above the shit!' This is good advice in any situation, but it is particularly pertinent for English sports fans. For years we have been struggling to keep our chins above the effluent, while our national teams jump up and down on our skulls.

The latest shove back into the manure had come at Tinsley Green in Sussex on Good Friday, when the Saxonia Globe Snippers had beaten off the challenge of twenty-one English sides to become Marbles Team World Champions, or Murmel-Weltmeisterschaften as they pithily put it in Germany, for the second consecutive year. One of the World Championships organisers blamed the poor performance of our native marbles players on all too familiar failings: 'Too much beer and not enough practice,' said Julia McCarthy-Fox.

Possibly so, though a personal view is that the English teams had also undermined their chances by coming up with clever names for themselves such as Bloody Marbleous, it being a well-known rule of sport that the wittier a team's name the worse they will play. As anyone in a local five-a-side league knows a fixture against Surreal Madrid is points in the bag (unless your own team happens to be called Bayern Large, naturally).

Some may feel this defeat for the English was of small consequence. Other Europeans see things differently. When the boys from Chemnitz won the title last time around, one Italian newspaper chose to interpret their victory as revenge for Geoff Hurst's controversial winning goal against Germany in the 1966 World Cup final. The Globe Snippers themselves were thankfully above such hype. After their first victory team spokesman Andreas Haldebrandt pronounced, 'We are very happy' (words that suggested he would be celebrating with a Werther's Original toffee and a small glass of milk) but the damage they have inflicted is real enough. Marbles is an ancient sport. Ovid wrote about it. Breughel painted it. Sussex is one of its spiritual centres. The World Championships began in nearby Copthorne, moving to Tinsley Green in 1932 (fortunately for village pride Copthorne remains at the epicentre of the thriving Sussex stoolball scene).

The region has produced some of the sport's true marble greats. Men such as Jim 'Atomic Thumb' Longhurst, a gardener from Slaugham who, back in the 1940s, would astonish fans by shattering a beer mug from four feet away with a powerful flick of his tolley (the marbles equivalent of pool's cue ball); Sam Spooner, the Sussex cowherd who used the same tolley for forty-five

years and is credited with being one of the first men to
swear on British radio when he blurted out a quick
'bloody' during an episode of *In Town Tonight* in 1946; and
the diminutive Welshman Wee Willie Wright, who won
the world title five times back in the 1950s and always
kept a hot-water bottle in his coat to keep his flicking
thumb from stiffening up between knuckle-downs in the
six-foot ring.

These men were giants of the Sussex style of marbles
known as Ring Taw in which competitors use a tolley to
try and knock marbles out of the ring. Where I grew up
we played a simpler and more brutal game. In this the first
player threw down his marble and the second tried to hit
and move it. If he did he got to keep it; if not, the first
player took his turn to try and hit and budge his opponent's marble.

Fast and furious, it was a quick way of losing your marbles. An unwary child could step into the infant school's
playground with his pocket money's worth of shiny new
glass alleys on Monday morning and find, when the bell
rang for assembly, he had nothing left but the plastic net
bag he bought them in. The reason for this was simple.
While the neophytes came armed with marbles made
from glass or pot, the top boys only used steel ball bearings, or doshers as they were known.

Doshers of any size gave a player a distinct advantage
over ordinary marbles. But while most children were only
able to locate small doshers (known as tipsies), usually by
prising them from the catch on an airing cupboard door
using a screwdriver, those of us lucky enough to have relatives working in heavy industry could get our hands on
industrial ball bearings. I recall having one of these that
was the size of a squash ball. Even a direct hit from a few

inches away couldn't budge it. 'Atomic Thumb' Longhurst in his pomp would have struggled to defeat me.

I haven't had my dosher out for some while now, but I dare say it could still do a job on the Germans and keep our faces above the dung for a little while longer. Sadly, nobody at the Globe Snippers clubhouse was around to accept my virtual challenge.

After Chemnitz I paused a while in delightful Gorlitz, Germany's easternmost town. While there I saw a famous double sundial made in 1550 by Zacharius Scultetus, a monument built on meridian 15°E as a tribute to Yuri Gagarin, and a Hungarian-made Ikarus 263 bus, which is a 12-metre version of the underfloor 260 and features the double-door arrangement that was once standard throughout East Germany.

As I crossed the border into the Czech Republic the temperature rose and the vague offer of snow was replaced by a murmured threat of drizzle. Women in blue and white headscarves sat in sunlit doorways painting goose eggs. Mountain ranges bound much of the country.

The Czech Republic has few natural resources; amongst them are uranium, antimony and offal. They make sausages out of everything. But something was missing from the Czech Republic beyond crude oil, diamonds and a chemical element that forms a key ingredient in the making of liquid soap. The news media was full of politics, economics and world events. It was plain there were no celebrities here whatsoever.

The Czech Republic has a rich cultural and artistic tradition. Karel Capek was the first writer to use the word 'robot', Franz Kafka the first to coin the term Kafka-esque to describe something that wasn't, and then there was Jaroslav Hasek. Hasek, author of *The Good Soldier Svejk*. In

the tradition of Czech artists, Hasek also involved himself
in politics, forming The Party For Moderate Progress
Within The Confines Of The Law. The Liberal
Democrats later stole many of his best ideas. The Czech
Republic was the birthplace of the composers Antonin
Dvorak, Leos Janacek and Bedrich Smetana, who had a
veal dish named after him. Speedway too is popular.

My next stopping-off point was Pardubice, a statutory
town in eastern Bohemia that billed itself as 'one of the
most perspective cities in the Czech lands' and was
renowned for its spectacular late Gothic wainscoting.
Pardubice is known as 'the cradle of Czech aviation'. In
one of the town bars I ordered a cocktail called 'Semtex'
in honour of the celebrated local armaments manufacturer. Gingerbread makes a pleasant gift.

Pardubice was a centre of sport. Here I found the
famous racecourse at which the brutal Velka Pardubice
steeplechase has been run since 1874, the track used for
the Golden Helmet speedway championships and the ice-
hockey rink where Dominic 'The Dominator' Hasek
began his career. The Dominator's achievements are considerable but those of that other sporting son of
Pardubice, Baron Artur Kraus, outweigh them. The
baron was the first man in the Habsburg Empire to ride a
motorcycle and the first to play lawn tennis, having translated the rules himself. Not content with that, he also
opened Bohemia's first planetarium. Four times European
waterskiing champion Frantisek Stehno lives nearby.
There are almost twelve dance clubs in the town.

I continued southwards. In Austria the air was filled
with the music of Mozart and the scent of unseasonable
flowers. People in the national costume of boiled wool,
cowhide, badger hair and Lycra wore smiles upon their

ruddy faces; skiers schussed, white horses waltzed and strapping men called Hans whittled mighty elms into glockenspiels using knives with handles fashioned from the headgear of game beasts. I passed through a landscape of blossoming orchards, winsome cattle and churches that looked as if they might play 'The Happy Wanderer' if you lifted the roof.

Everything in Austria was so perfectly arranged that a particularly meticulous model railway enthusiast might have constructed it. In the canopy of the shady trees a cuckoo clock emitted a churlish cry of triumph as it laid its single egg in the nest of an oblivious quartz radio alarm. You can eat dumplings for starter, main and pudding.

In the Alpine regions they have a magazine devoted to the local fashion stylings – *Dirndl News*. This brings updates on the latest trends and developments in the world of horn-toggled cardigans, leather walking breeches and striped full-length pinnies. The headlines were impressive. I cannot understand German but believe they may have read 'Leaf green is this year's pine green, designers say' and 'Boiled wool wins "test of thorns" battle with micro-fibre in hunting jacket trial'.

The traditional activities to be undertaken when wearing Austrian national dress are: touching your ankle, pointing at mountains and yodelling. In Switzerland yodelling was under threat with the average age at most yodelling clubs topping sixty and yodelling pressure groups pushing the government to fund summer yodelling camps for kids. In Austria they had no such problems. Thanks to the work of pop singing yodeller Anton, yodelling was all the rage with the young folk who dance the night away to traditional hits such as 'Lederhosen Are So Fine' and 'My Pleasure Is A Dog'.

A dark cloud had appeared on the horizon, however. According to pro yodeller Herman Haertel, 'To yodel one needs all of one's energy. It is a powerful cry that comes from the soul. It is addictive.'

Plainly yodelling addicts are a menace to any society, especially one that values its sleep. In Switzerland, where it is illegal to flush your toilet after 10 p.m., it was hard not to conclude that the collapse of traditional Alpine pastimes was actually part of a government plot. (Even the venerable Alpine horn was reportedly threatened with extinction, hunted by blastenhunds, small and agile dogs from which its only means of escape is to hide by posing as a tobacco pipe viewed through the wrong end of a pair of binoculars.)

The yodelling habit is a hard one to kick. Austrian health authorities are believed to be experimenting with synthetic yodel patches based on the ones Michael Douglas used to help treat his sex addiction. Yodelling is also popular in Kentucky, China and amongst the forest pygmies of Central Africa. The Welsh word for yodelling is *iodolo*.

In Vienna there was less yodelling and more psychiatry. I sped through an inner suburb of five-storey apartment blocks, the sort of street-corner European bars in which a lone middle-aged man in a maroon V-neck will be smoking king size and staring into his lager and shops selling orthopaedic underwear in shades of pinkish fawn, and into the intellectual maelstrom at the heart of the old city. The coffee shops of Vienna were pulsating with ideas and calories. Men with dark beards knitted their brows with concentration as they pondered the nature of id and ego or tried not to burp, or both. In the spirit of Klimt and Schiele their female companions sat with a bestockinged fetlock cupped coquettishly behind one ear, smearing lipstick across their cheeks with bold and wanton strokes.

It sometimes appears that no famous person or action in Austrian history has gone without a cake being baked in commemoration. You half expect to come across an *Anschlusstorte* or a *Waldheimschnitten*. That Austria's most famous living son, Arnold Schwarzenegger, has gone so long without having some suitably bulging gateaux named after him is a mystery. Perhaps they have yet to invent a pastry wooden enough for the task.

In Vienna I bought several boxes of Sissi Thaler chocolates. These were named after Empress Elizabeth, expert horsewoman, poet, beauty and pioneering weight watcher whose life was so filled with disasters it reads like a grisly regal version of Monty Python's four Yorkshiremen sketch. Her only son, Crown Prince Rudolph, committed suicide with his teenage mistress in the hunting lodge at Mayerling; Maximilian, her brother-in-law, was shot by Mexican patriots while his wife, Charlotte, went mad; her cousin, King Ludwig of Bavaria, was declared insane then found dead along with his attendant in suspicious circumstances; her sister was killed in a fire at a Parisian charity bazaar; her husband, Franz Joseph, having infected her with syphilis, deserted her for a woman named Schrat and she herself was murdered by a knife-wielding Italian patriot while boarding a pleasure steamer in Switzerland. Luckily she didn't live to see her nephew, Franz Joseph, assassinated at Sarajevo, an event which plunged Europe into the Great War. Strangely, this life of woe was seen as ideal material for an animated series for children called *Princess Sissi*. To this day I can still sing the theme tune all the way through, though my family throw turnips at me when I do so.

It may seem a frivolous thing to have a cake named
after you. Not so! The Austrians treat cakes with gravity.
In Linz the local news agencies reported that a four-year-
old boy had recently phoned the police to complain about
his grandmother's plum dumplings. Local man Adolf
Hitler had planned to make Linz the capital of The
Thousand Year Reich, but things didn't work out.

Slovakia is roughly twice the size of New Hampshire,
which is approximately two-thirds the size of Finland or
Scotland plus Rutland and the top half of the Royal
Borough of Kensington. In Slovakia flat prices continued
to rise, Jana Kirschner had once again carried off an
armful of awards at the local equivalent of the Grammies,
President Rudolf Schuster stood accused of acting like a
dead bug and twenty-one train lines were about to be shut
down in a government economy drive. Luckily 66 per
cent of households had cable or satellite TV so there was
no need to go anywhere.

Some famous Slovaks are Jesse 'The Body' Ventura,
who was born in Minnesota, and Canadian film-maker
Ivan Reitman who was definitely *not* born in the Czech
Republic; have you got that? There is also Milan
Markovich, talk-show host, political cabaretist and star of
the stage show *You Can Leave Your Shoes On (Please Don't Take
Your Shoes Off Please)*, and a Wonderbra model.

In Banska Bystrica I dined in a traditional Slovak shed
that served regional specialities on a grate. In Kyjesvskie
Namestie the sky was the colour of Communist cement.
Street lights glowed sulphurous yellow, the road was a
ribbon of sludge. Buildings that looked like broken teeth
huddled in the darkness. Inside the citizenry watched
Mary-Kate and Ashley Olsen while the local political parties argued about which of them was going to be most

horrible to Hungarians or rottenest to the Romany. I spent the night in a pension garret with a white sheepskin rug laid on lino in a shade of goat's lung grey. Foreigners paid twice as much as Slovaks. The whole place was frankly loathsome. People who have visited Slovakia will probably say this is wildly unfair and inaccurate. Be that as it may; I can only speak as I find. And as far as I am concerned it was one of the most unpleasant places I have never set foot in. And I intend to keep it that way. I was happy to leave. I would have been even happier if I hadn't known where I was going next.

2

Land of the Midnight Teeth

Banska Bystrica to Meghri

The Germans have a word for it: *schadenfreude*, the pleasure
we take in the misery of others. Yes, there is always someone worse off than yourself. And before you say 'I'd like to
meet him I could do with a laugh', think about it.

You may be stuck in a ten-mile tailback in an overheating
car with a jiggered cassette player and a radio that can pick
up just two stations, one of which is hosting an all-day tribute to the music of Judas Priest while the other offers a
two-hour phone-in on female circumcision; you've just
crawled past one sign reading 'Next services 15 miles' and
can see another one coming up that says 'Mm, bet you
wish you hadn't drunk all that coffee now, don't you?' And
all the while you know at the other end of the journey are
the snapping tills of the planet's second largest shopping
mall. You've got a bladder the size of a basketball, you're
surrounded by lane-switching junior management with
baked-bean-coloured skin and shiny suits hanging in the
rear windows of their fleetmobiles and the other occupants
of your vehicle are wearing 'I shop therefore I am' T-shirts
and clutching your credit cards. But at least you're not

trying to make a living as a Michael Jackson lookalike. You can take comfort from the fact that at no point in your life have you ever felt you looked sexy in cycling shorts. And, of course, you're not on your way to the Ukraine.

First, though, I had to get out of Slovakia. Up until now I had been using the railways, but the swingeing cutbacks by the Slovak government made that impossible. International coaches ran to everywhere, from Sofia to Copenhagen, but none went into the former Soviet Union. There were local buses, of course, but nobody liked to talk about them.

I decided to rent a car instead. The car hire company I approached in Bystrica was reluctant to allow me to have one, however. The reasons were twofold. Firstly, the terms of their rental agreement precluded the driving of a car across an international boundary, and secondly I didn't have a driving licence. I pointed out that both should really provide no impediment because I was only seeking to virtually hire a virtual car and virtually drive it across a virtual border. At this point I sensed they had got rather fed up with me and gone back to work.

Unable to rent a car I was faced with only one choice – I had to steal one. I found an inconspicuous looking twenty-year-old Lada Vaz 2106 in a fetching shade of concentrated orange which, from the two-lettered prefix at the start of the number plate, I knew had been registered in Kosice. Hotwiring a car is a simple business – if you access *The Anarchist Cookbook* website – especially if it is a simple car, and since the 2106 doesn't come with any extras much beyond a glove compartment it fits that description perfectly. It's just a case of looking under the dashboard, finding the two matching wires and splicing them together.

The 2106 packed a 1.3-litre engine capable of taking it from 0 to 60 in a breathtaking twenty-one seconds. I stuck to first gear. I had no desire to hurt anyone and, besides, I can never remember which is the clutch and which is the accelerator. Once outside the city limits I gunned the beast up to 25 kph and headed east. If anyone was in pursuit I felt confident they'd overtake me and disappear into the distance long before the border. And if they caught me, well, as long as the arresting officer was registered with Paypal I was confident I could buy my freedom using the large number of dollars I had accrued by auctioning forty-year-old die-cast car catalogues to retired US military personnel. A man's got to make a living.

I crossed the border in relatively good spirits. The Lada was a fine vehicle. It had advanced safety features including a driver's air bag. Actually it wasn't an air bag, it was a balloon and a bicycle pump. When you think you're about to have an accident you blow the balloon up with the pump. To do this you have to take both hands off the wheel and steer with your knees. So when you think you're about to have an accident you're usually right.

In Slovakia the temperature had been hovering around zero but when I crossed the border the mercury in the thermometer shot upwards. In Lvovskaya Oblast it was 22°C with partial cloud cover and a scattering of showers. The sudden leap in the temperature was alarming. At first I worried that it might have had something to do with the fallout from Chernobyl, but on closer inspection I discovered that a less sinister reason lay behind it – CNN hadn't updated the weather for going on six months.

Using the stealth of a hunting cat and a considerable bank balance, Ted Turner has gradually acquired control of 35 per cent of the world's virtual weather and 99 per cent of the time he does a damn fine job of keeping it shipshape. Every once in a while, though, there's the inevitable glitch. Luckily the warmth and light rain in the Ukraine were ideal conditions for local farmers, but things hadn't always worked out so happily. It was widely believed in some quarters, for example, that the severe flooding in Central Europe during 2002 was caused by a programmer failing to gradually reduce precipitation levels in the Danube basin as instructed because he was too busy monitoring the price of some Metallica memorabilia he'd just put up for sale on eBay.

The city of Lviv holds the record for having the most number of names for any major metropolis. It is also called Lvov, L'viv, L'vivs'ka, Lwow, Lwiw, L'wiw, L'wow, Lemberg, Leopoli and Leopolis. The locals call it 'home'. The Ukraine has changed hands many times, having been variously owned by Poland, Lithuania, Austria, Russia and a big man in a Hugo Boss suit and Ray-Bans. All these great empires have left their mark on the place. The Lion City is an open-air museum in which every street is a legend. There is architecture in abundance, ranging from the Renaissance through Baroque to something that looks like a truckle of cheddar wearing a Tyrolean hat. Picturesque filigree street lights stand sentinel over cobbled squares and babbling water fountains, while fierce old ladies in gaberdine macs guard the gateways to all public buildings and the air is refulgent with their caustic remarks as they harangue the hundreds of American religious salespeople who throng the streets offering free Cup-a-Soup to any native who lets Jesus into his or her heart. Most Ukrainians are already Christians, of course, but they follow the orthodox faith, which is big on spirituality but low on crunchy garlic croutons.

In the Ukraine there were many finely decorated bus shelters and strangely shaped haystacks. The women all look either like Anna Kournikova or vintage medicine balls. The men wear leather jackets and so many jumpers they can't bend their elbows. If they can bend their elbows they reach for a semi-automatic or a balalaika. There is gunfire and music everywhere in the Ukraine. It is jaunty, thigh-slapping, jump-in-the-air stuff accompanied by yells of 'Hoy!' and 'Hah!' and filled with the kind of sponta-neous glee that only comes with months of practice. The music is much the same.

The Ukraine has a few problems. It is the UN's third largest debtor. An estimated forty thousand state and private businesses are owned by organised crime gangs. Seventy per cent of all business is transacted on the black economy. Between 15 and 20 billion dollars has been smuggled out of the country illegally. Mafia gangs loot archaeological and religious treasures, traffic in drugs, sell women to the European and Asian sex trades and weapons to nationalist death squads. Banks feed client information to armed extortionists so that they can iden-tify their targets. Major international businesses shy away from investment. The deputy prime minister was recently accused of stealing $1.2 billion worth of gas and oil. Sometime in the late 1990s the Ukraine zipped past Indonesia to gain the number one spot in the league table of the world's most corrupt nations. The main occupa-tions are agriculture, murdering journalists and marrying Western businessmen.

In any Ukrainian town you can shop for brides online. Thirtysomething divorced dental assistants with teenage children look out at you from under just about enough make-up to cover their desperation. The agencies' assessments of their proficiency in English read like a school report: 'Nataliya's oral comprehension is fair. May need help with longer written sentences.' Bust sizes never fell below 36 inches.

'I am tender, merry, loyal and modest,' the women said. 'I like culture, sports and cooking romantic dinners.' There were indications that the concrete sarcophagus placed over the smouldering ruins of Chernobyl was starting to leak. Between fifteen and thirty thousand people had already died, wheat had mutated, cancer eviscerated communities. HIV rates were rising by 20 per cent per annum, the sharpest increase on earth, there were regular cholera outbreaks, needles littered the gutters, prostitutes the pavements, homeless children the streets. The President, Leonid Kuchma, sent eighteen million New Year greetings cards at an estimated cost of $350,000, while the opposition parties formed a coalition pledged to rid the country of the menace of Freemasonry. 'Only love,' the women said, 'can make a fairy tale of an everyday life.'

After Lvov I drove across an open landscape of pale acacia trees, sunflowers and pinkish-green buckwheat. The air buzzed busily. Beekeeping is a mainstay of the agricultural sector and has been for many years. The first man to undertake apiary on a truly large scale was a Ukrainian, Peter Prokopovic, who had ten thousand hives between 1800 and 1810. A further breakthrough for Ukrainian beekeepers was the invention of the bee treadmill, a device used to measure how far a bee will walk to get nectar, but one that could surely be harnessed as a renewable energy resource. Sadly since those pioneering days the Ukraine's beekeeping has stalled. The hives are sometimes built to resemble little wooden dachas complete with painted doors and windows. In winter they are wrapped in woollen blankets against the frost. It is like the 1880s, a visiting American observed. Beekeeping is mentioned twice in *War and Peace*.

South-east of Kam'yanets-Podil's'skyy, amongst fields of tobacco and the caramel scent of sugar-beet refineries, I left the Ukraine heading for Moldova, said to be 'a country in the way of all disasters'. Down the years it has been ravaged by Mongols, Huns, Turks and radio funnyman Tony Hawks. Yet despite that, earning an average $400 dollars annually and being subject to night-long power cuts, the population are full of originality, cheerfulness and brilliance.

Moldova is flat with a stately row of poplar trees to the east, a river to the west and far to the south an indeterminate smudge of corrupted pixels. In rural areas life is played out to the sound of the dulcimer and the bagpipes. The men wear embroidered, puff-sleeved shirts and trilbies with wampum bands, while the women wear expressions of suppressed amusement. Wallpaper is not their strong suit.

I knew little of Moldova's charming capital Chisinau beyond the fact that the local football team was called Zimbru Chisinau. Since Zimbru is a type of antelope this put the team amongst a select body of European sides named after animals. Other notables included Chamois Niort of France, the Finnish side Wild Cats of Tempere and Wootton Bassett FC.

I parked the Lada in a deserted boulevard close to a Stalinist apartment block. I had decided to abandon it and get the train. The Lada was so noisy I couldn't hear myself think. In the Ukraine that had been an advantage; thinking about the Ukraine was like watching *Camille* with the barrels of a loaded shotgun in your mouth.

In Chisinau (sometimes called Kisiev to confuse invaders) I was warmly welcomed. 'We do not know who you are or what you are looking for,' I was told. 'Perhaps you lived here long ago and the wind of time blew you away, but your heart has kept a dear afterglow. We are delighted to share with you the warmth of our hearts.' Moldovan is a Romance language.

The city looked like an architect's drawing, with pristine tower blocks, wide tree-lined boulevards and vast open squares in which no crisp packets or super-lager cans bounced or tumbled and the strident flowers of socialist horticulture were permanently in bloom. In urban areas the populace favours a different dress style from the rustic folk. In the streets of Chisinau (and doubtless of other Moldovan cities such as Beltsy and Bender) the women wore mini-skirted twinsets while the men favoured the shirt-sleeved order of young draughtsmen who had just nipped out of the office momentarily for an Embassy Regal in 1968. The productions of wine, wood and skins are pillars of local industry and the capital city's submersible pumps are also widely appreciated.

Yet, despite that, all was not rosy. Moldova had once been governed from Bucharest and many feared it might be drifting that way again. 'They want to make us to become the fifth leg on the emaciated cow of the Romanian economy,' protested one winemaker vividly.

I passed the night in a hotel that may have been a converted telephone exchange just around the corner from the Organ Hall. The lampshades were papier-mâché eggs, the tablecloths were transparent and the rooms looked like something you'd see in video footage of a police raid.

After breakfast a charming American lady named Joan Carey approached me via my inbox and asked if I would be interested in an effective low-cost teeth-whitening product. She showed me photos of young people who, thanks to cabamide peroxide gel, now had teeth so white and even they looked like they were wearing gum shields. I would get to the USA eventually and I was looking forward to it. From the many sales pitches I received from that great land across the water I had formed an image of a place peopled by vigorous folk who pursued teenage farm sluts with a gleaming smile and a bottle of male potency spray endorsed by adult movie star Ron Jeremy.

I took the train to Tirasopol and there boarded another bound for Odessa. For two hundred years this young Ukrainian city has been surrounded by popularity and love. Kandinsky once lived here. So did Pushkin. Private car parks have been eliminated.

The foundations of Odessa were laid in 1794 at the behest of Catherine the Great, the original teenage farm slut, by General Suvorov, that rarest of beasts, a forward-thinking Russian army officer. Duke Emmanuel de Richelieu succeeded him. The duke was a French émigré who decided to create a city more beautiful than Paris. He might have gotten away with it too, if meddlesome locals hadn't insisted on digging the street up to steal copper cables.

That night I took myself out to one of Odessa's many sparkling nightspots. At first I had sought advice on where to go from someone who ran a website devoted to the joys of the Black Sea port, but she was unable to help, having moved to California in the 1990s and not returned since. I suspect that was for the best. Odessa was the sort of place you could only really get romantic about if you were 5000 miles away.

The club I eventually settled on – largely because it

was the only one I could find a picture of – had melted candles on the tables, the bum end of barrels nailed to the walls and colourful bowls of wax apples arranged for decorative effect. The only other customers were a bearded man and a girl with chunky biceps who were intensely not talking to one another. To a soundtrack of old Ukrainian favourites such as 'Ruzia Drove The Ducks To The Pen' and 'The Eye Of The Tiger' I ate meat in onion and honey sauce washed down with chilli vodka.

The Ukraine is famous for its vodka, much of which was invented in Belgium. It comes flavoured with many different things including honey, lemon and something with a vague metallic twang that could be cordite. These are all traditional flavourings. Attempts to introduce new ones such as smoky bacon and prawn cocktail was stifled during the Soviet era. 'Nothing noteworthy took place in the distillery till the 1990s,' noted a spokesman for Ivanov Vodka sternly. Ivanov's Old Kiev brand 'was ranked best of all vodkas of the Old Kiev brand name, produced in the Ukraine, by Tasting Committee for Quality Control of Ukrspirit Concern'. And praise doesn't come much higher than that.

I left the club before things could get out of hand, or the bearded man began to eat fondue, and went off in search of a pram to push down the Odessa Steps. Unfortunately I found the way to this cinematic milestone barred by a raft of statistics about fine-sand production in Krasnodar. Krasnodar is capital of the Kuban Cossacks who are much like normal Cossacks only with marimbas. The Ukraine is a lawless place and Odessa (pop. 1 million) is its biggest port; violence is therefore to be anticipated. As I tried to step around a pile of pie charts detailing the proportional input of cement production into the

Ukrainian GNP, I heard a slight creaking noise off to my
left. I looked up. Immediately the warning signs began to
flash. 'Your computer is broadcasting an IP address,' they
said. 'With this address someone can instantly begin
attacking your computer!!!'

Suddenly a vast man with a head the shape and density
of an anvil, his big salami fingers tapping away at the key-
board of a looted Powerbook tune-up, loomed menacingly
on the Compaq's starboard bow. As he prepared to let rip
with a volley of fully automatic worm viruses cunningly
disguised as a naked Britney Spears I ducked into
Amazon.com and took cover behind the soul boxed sets.
The software melting slugs ricocheted off *The Scepter Records
Story* and disappeared into the blackness of cyberspace.
With a grunt of frustration my adversary followed them.

I ran scandisk on all drives to check for damage. The
reports came back negative. Relieved, I bought a Chilites
compilation and vowed to get out of the Ukraine as fast as
I could. The next afternoon I cautiously travelled the few
miles to Ilyichevsk and boarded the six o'clock Ukr ferry
for Varna. I wasn't followed.

At 184 metres the *Geroi Odesy* was one of the biggest rail
ferries in Europe. Built twenty-five years ago at the Pula
Ulyanik yard in Yugoslavia, it had the greasy, solid, no-
frills look of a hod carrier after a big fry up. The one-way
fare for the overnight trip to the Bulgarian Riviera was
seventy-five bucks plus a $10 'lading fee'. I paid the money
and went in search of a shower.

The fact was I was running dangerously low on mints
and deodorant. Spending time in cyberspace has a terrible
effect on human scent glands. I estimate that spending
six hours on the internet has the same effect on bodily
odours as drinking ten pints of brown ale, eating a curry

and then running a marathon in rubber pants filled with cheese. Why this should be I do not know. Scientists can put a man on the moon but on this topic they remain strangely mute.

The Black Sea looked blue, but that was just an optical illusion. It was black. This was due to the fact that below a depth of 150 metres it was totally anoxic, a state of affairs that ensured that much of the Black Sea was as lifeless as Eastbourne the night before pension day. The bits that weren't were home to many breeds of rangy fish with pointed noses, side whiskers and the general appearance of John Carradine playing a Wild West gambler, and anchovies.

Life in the Black Sea was not easy for these fish. Apart from the anoxic wastes, there was the hazard of pollution and the mayhem caused by various rogue species that had smuggled themselves in via the ballast water of foreign ships. First off came *Rapana thomasiana*, a predatory Japanese snail with the appetite of a sumo wrestler which gobbled up most of the native oysters without pause to consider if there was an 'R' in the month or not. Then in the 1980s the bilges of a freighter discharged a slick of comb jellyfish, a fist-sized glob that normally resides off the East Coast of the US. With no predators willing to slurp them up, the comb jellyfish population of the Black Sea increased at such a prodigious rate that, within six years, it was estimated to have a combined weight of 900 million tonnes. The jellyfish gobbled up fish eggs almost as fast as they bred. By 1990 the annual harvest of anchovies had dropped by 90 per cent. Fortunately, around this point the jellyfish reached critical mass and more or less imploded. Now the anchovies were back in numbers and being fished to the verge of extinction again. It was hard not to feel sorry for this plucky little piscine. It overcame jellyfish, raw sewage, pesticides and marauding sturgeon only to end up in the box on the back of a pizza delivery boy's moped.

From the deck of the *Odesy* I watched the bobbing lights of the fishing fleets. To the west, dark beneath the setting sun, was the Danube basin where spoonbills, egrets, pelicans and pygmy cormorants were bedding down amongst the crack willow and bulrushes, troubled perhaps by the mournful howling of a wolf, the irritable growl of a bear woken from his winter slumbers and the knowledge that every time anybody within 300 miles flushed the toilet they would end up sticking their heads in the result.

The Genovese lighthouse winked a greeting as we passed Constanta, the old port that was Romania's wide gate towards the world. Once Dacians and Macedonians had fought there, but nowadays it was quiet save for the occasional mournful tolling of a church bell and the heavy crash of local currency.

In Varna luscious forests surround golden sands. During the day thousands of umbrellas form pointillist patterns on the beaches. After sundown there is an endless fiesta of light, sound and night entertainments where visitors join in a party under the stars dressed as Carmen Miranda and the man from *The Love Boat*.

In the Sunny Day resort the Palace Hotel was entirely populated by women in bikinis. Outdoor activities included sailing, volleyball, waterskiing and bananas. The Grand Hotel has its own bowling alley while the Dallas Business Club offers the spirit of America under a Bulgarian roof complete with leather TV loungers, elephant tusks and carpeting so busy it has been diagnosed as

workaholic. My attempt to get into the Spartacus Private
Mix Club was rejected as a bad request. US haircare
products are in limited supply and fluffy toilet tissue is a
whispered rumour.

After taking in the collection of festive loaves at Varna's
Ethnographic Museum I visited the Botanic Gardens.
The Botanic Gardens boast an 'astonishing collection of
cacti', the most astonishing thing of all being that anyone
should collect so many cacti. Despite the cacti the Botanic
Gardens were a place of rare loveliness. Bee-eaters flut-
tered amongst the scented box trees and terraces stretched
down to a sea that glimmered like silver.

The Botanic Gardens surround a palace that once
belonged to Queen Marie of Romania. Queen Marie was
British, daughter of the Duke of Edinburgh, grand-
daughter of Queen Victoria. A famous beauty with a
passing resemblance to Gillian Anderson of *The X-Files*,
she was known as Missy and had three sisters: Ducky,
Baby Bee and Sandra (how Sandra came to be so dully
nicknamed is a puzzle. I can only surmise that her real
forename was Pumply-Nugget). As a young woman Missy
won the heart of the future George V. Granny approved
the match, but Missy's mother was a Russian who, from
prolonged exposure to the morbid sourness of the British
court, had come to despise her adoptive land. So instead
Missy was married off to Kaiser Wilhelm II's cousin,
Ferdinand Hohenzollern Sigmaringen, Crown Prince of
Romania.

European princes of that era were either boring and
lugubrious or mad and rapacious. A common thread of
stupidity ran through them all. None could shake his head
without spraying the servants with saliva. Ferdinand was
one of the dull ones. Missy's life might have devolved into

an endless grinding routine of social functions and affairs
with cavalry officers. Luckily two things prevented that
from happening: frequent outbreaks of war and her son
Carol, who specialised in the kind of febrile nuttiness that
would make even a Habsburg archduke sit up, put his hat
on backwards and go 'Whibble!'

That night I dined in a rustic tavern on sweet medlar
plums and fine sparkling wine. Outside a man in a fur fez
played plangent Thracian tunes by squeezing a goat and
blowing up its left foreleg. Beauty is part of the Bulgarian
heart and soul.

At the port of Varna East grumbling container ships
disgorged their cargoes of wood pulp and fertiliser as I set
sail aboard the *Geroi Sevastopol* bound for the Black Sea's
eastern shore. As we plotted our course across the unctu-
ous water I scanned the horizon for the rare monk seal
and the fabled towers of Trabzon. I could see neither and
so contented myself with the knowledge that somewhere
over the horizon in Turkey there was a town called
Batman.

In Batumi it was the time of clouds and sun. Visibility
was 1.6 miles. Though further north there was an area
nicknamed 'The Black Sea Urinal' because of its high
rainfall, the climate in Batumi was subtropical. It was
nowhere near as subtropical as it is in Northumberland,
however.

Here on the cusp of Asia there were palms, cypresses,
magnolias and oleanders. Girls in turquoise spaghetti-
strapped shifts wafted beneath the orange and lemon trees
and past the strange ersatz Greek ruins of the shore.
White yachts that gleamed like US teeth cut the waves and
red powerboats bucked the foaming surf. My attempt to
check into a couple of hotels was thwarted when I crossed

the threshold to find they were actually shops selling cut-price DVDs. Luckily I was able to procure a de luxe room at the Tennis Club. Soon I was sitting beneath the thatched rooftops of the Bungalo nitespot, sipping the local tarragon syrup and experiencing a selection of international dishes surrounded by nice nature and high quality rattan furnishings. My fellow guests sporting all-over tans and Cacherel Pour Homme tapped their toes to the Latin-tinged music. Sunglasses were worn as hats. Batumi, in short, looked like some wild and wacky guy had decided to host a *Miami Vice* theme night. And that wild and wacky guy was the President, Aslan Abashidze.

Batumi is the capital of Ajaria, a semi-autonomous republic that is nominally part of Georgia. The country is sometimes sarcastically referred to as Aslandia in honour of the leader of the All-Georgia Revival Party. Aslan is a slight, balding man with the narrowed eyes of a gunslinger. His party's publicity machine described him as dynamic, patriotic and visionary – three adjectives which ought to strike fear into the hearts of anyone with even a vague knowledge of European history. Ajaria was viewed by many, including, it seemed, Aslan himself, as his personal fiefdom. The President lived just 500 yards from the presidential offices but every morning he drove to work in a seven-limousine motorcade that practically stretched from door to door. His daughter Diana ran the Black Sea's glitziest disco, named, with characteristic family modesty, Dianaland. His son Giorgi made speedboats.

Aslan boasted that he had created a little paradise in this corner of the former Soviet Union. Maybe so, but it was a paradise of high-tone gun shops and five-star brothels. There was a kind of magic in Aslandia, but it had little to do with C. S. Lewis.

I had planned to take a plane from Batumi to Armenia, but when I visited the airport I found that, while you could fly to Moscow on Wednesdays and Kharkov and Kiev on Sundays, the rest of the week was shrouded in mystery. So I took the early morning bus across the border to Gyumri instead. The trip lasted eight hours. We passed through a landscape of crag, forest, ancient monasteries and elderly electricity pylons trailing a cloud of bitter dust. On board the bus children whimpered, Gameboys pinged, Walkmans chinked, old ladies gave detailed accounts of the workings of their bladders to anyone within earshot – several received responses from Istanbul and Moscow – and the air was filled with farts and accusations. A woman in front turned suddenly and offered me the chance to buy a Mother's Day gift of lingerie at an unmissable 50 per cent discount. I asked if I looked like the sort of pervert who would give his mother a sateen basque and matching suspender belt. A frosty silence descended.

The bus disgorged us in Gyumri in mid-afternoon. The city is nearly 4000 feet above sea level. The climate is dry, the air clean and healthy and the drinking water soft and sweet. Gyumri is the second largest city in Armenia. It has been populated since the stone century. These days the only people remaining are a small man with an elaborate cape and a sculpture of Charles Aznavour. I went to the railway station, which looks like a Mexican feed store, and boarded the Gnastsk train to Yerevan. The toilets on Armenian trains are notoriously filthy and you are advised to bring your own.

In Yerevan the climate is continental and the streets are littered with Parisian-style bistros. Like Turkey, Armenia appears to be in denial about the fact it is in Asia. I debouched from the diesel to find women in ankle-length skirts and men in straw boaters bustling about cobbled streets that echoed to the flinty ring of horses' hooves. Everything was in black and white. This was because the first website I'd arrived at was devoted to Edwardian photographs. Luckily the twenty-first century was just around the corner.

Armenia was the first republic of the Soviet Union to be given permission to open a café. I sat in one near the singing fountains of Republic Square, sipping one of the renowned healing waters, gazing upon the snowy dome of Mount Ararat and occasionally jumping with alarm as one of the tables nearby erupted into a traditional dance, intoxicated in all probability by the pure mountain air.

Yerevan gives off a rosy glow thanks to the pink volcanic stone of its buildings. Its citizens are sophisticated with a rich tradition of pantomime. They like to joke about the stupidity of the people from Abarantsi. One joke ran like this: an Abarantsian man was on holiday and had his photograph taken riding on a donkey. He sent it home to his mother with a note: 'Dear Mum, Here I am with a donkey. With love your son. PS. I am the one on top.' The range of fruit and vegetables is astonishing. Potholes are plentiful, but pickpockets few.

In Gyumri they had a local hero in Charles Aznavour. In Yerevan they had the eighteenth-century bard Sayat Nova Khachatour Abovia. Aznavour sang 'She' and canoodled with Edith Piaf. Abovia revolutionised the Armenian language and climbed Mount Ararat looking for Noah's Ark. There are an estimated twenty-three rock 'n' roll bands in the country. The city is running out of room for cemeteries.

I checked into a superior tourist hotel where the other guests cruelly snubbed me. The conference tables had a small swimming pool in the centre of them, which had been drained and filled with a vase of garish lilies. In the Eastern bloc gardeners had specialised in breeding plants that looked as if they had been shot in Technicolor as a counterpoint to all the concrete.

The next morning, after breakfasting on paper-thin flatbreads and sour plum purée washed down with a glass of crunchy Nescafé, I boarded the bus for Meghri on the Iranian border.

We rumbled through the Biblical Valley and into the Zangezur Panhandle, stopping every few hours at some convenient roadside bush. The landscape was as parched, rugged and mean as Lee Marvin waking up after a three-day bender. Weirdly formed rocks leered at us as we passed, dried riverbeds croaked and the shrubbery tried to hide behind boulders as it heard us approach. Once in a while we passed a lonely shepherd who waved at us with the distracted look of someone who has woken from a disturbing dream and can't quite remember where he is. The only town of any size we went through was Kapan. Kapan had once been a Red Army base and a mining centre. Now the army had gone and the mines had closed and all that was left was a large boarding school that exuded institutional violence.

It was after dark when we reached our destination. Meghri was noted as the hottest place in Armenia. It was famous for its figs and pomegranates. I spent the night in a Soviet-style rest house. Invaders had plundered all the town's lavatory seats and the hotel corridors smelled of cockroach repellent, frying lamb and Stalin. Exhausted, fuddled by the rattling of the bus, I crawled into bed. I was asleep before my feet hit the pillow.

3

The Organ of Love Stalks Unaccompanied

Meghri to Bukhara

I had sent e-postcards to friends from Ajaria. In Meghri as I sat staring bleakly at a breakfast bowl of sheep's hooves in onion broth I received a reply to one of them. 'You are a bit like Lionel Jeffries in the film *Chitty Chitty Bang Bang*' it read. 'He keeps saying he's going to Alaska and disappearing into that funny little shed.' This was true in a way, although a personal interpretation of Grandpa Potts's behaviour was that the shed in question was actually a privy and the expression 'I'm off to India' was a euphemism for a bowel movement.

Unlike Lionel Jeffries, whose virtual journeys from the shed involved the accumulation of much suitable paraphernalia, I was travelling light. In an effort to simulate the rigours of travel I had not changed my jeans since I had set off and they had now reached a level of saturated grubbiness that made my thighs itch. I had also stuck to the same pair of underpants. Literally. In the interests of hygiene I had washed them every night first using shampoo and body wash gel snaffled from German and Austrian hotels. When this had finally run out in Moldova

I had switched to the kind of green marbled carbolic soap old northern women keep in the scullery for washing out the mouths of swearing children. I hoped this gave a reasonable approximation of the sort of thing you might find in the former Soviet bloc. It certainly brought crunch to your gussets.

The bus from Meghri took some time to cross the Iranian border. The Islamic Republic of Iran was very careful what it let through customs. On the banned list was *Hello!* magazine, satellite dishes, Celine Dion CDs, evangelical Christians and men's shorts. Still, I expect the Khameini regime also had its down side.

We travelled through Persian Azerbaijan, a land of wide meadows and fertile valleys split in twain by formidable mountains that yet have fostered a vital culture. Carpets, crochet work and piston heads are local products of renown.

I took lunch in Tabriz, City of the First Ones. The historical background of Tabriz is lost in a halo of ambiguity. Suffice it to say that during my brief visit I was exhilarated by the gardens, aroused by the pungent odours of the spice bazaar, excited by the news that Islamic scientists are called *foghahas* and saddened by the fact that the Sweet River had dried up.

Tabriz had been capital of the Little Medes, part of the Persian Empire of Cyrus the Great. Cyrus was depicted riding in a peculiar winged chariot – the sort of image that for many internuts was proof positive that aliens had visited earth. That wasn't the main thing about Iran that exercised overheated imaginations in cyberspace, however. The national dialling code for Iran is 119. 11/9 is the way the British write 9/11. The digits in 119 add up to 11. The two digits in 11 look like the Twin Towers.

The more times I read this the more the shivers began crawling up my spine like maggots sensing rotten horse-flesh. Because it was clear quite a lot of people actually believed it.

In a restaurant in Emmam Khomeini Street I was served a filling soup of beans and cowmeat, which the menu informed me helpfully I should eat with a spoon and a small hammer.

It was becoming obvious to me as I travelled the inter-net that something strange and wonderful was happening to English. People across the globe with no knowledge of the language of Shakespeare, Milton and George W. Bush were feeding stuff into their computers, clicking on 'trans-late this page' and posting the results with no idea what it looked like. Translation is a subtle skill and no machine has yet mastered it. Faced with the range of options on offer for each word, the computer with almost unfail-ing accuracy picked the wrong one. If you took the phrase 'The interiors are decorated in a shade of rich madder', translated it into Italian, then German, then back into English again you ended up with 'The insides are medalled in shadows affluent and more crazy'. Which made no sense but was decidedly poetic. Cyberspace, it seemed to me, was producing a new English that was gnomic, florid and elliptical. As the days wore on I became more and more fluent in the hyperlanguage until, when I turned a corner and found myself confronted by 'angry and non-domestic opinions', I knew I was actually seeing a wild and untamed view.

Thus fortified by the cowmeat, I went in search of a toyshop. The Iranian authorities had recently made a concerted attempt to purge the country of Barbie dolls. One government minister was reported to have denounced the 12-inch-tall blonde and her sometime boyfriend Ken as 'A Trojan Horse' (well, it sounded like 'horse' anyway). Religious police had been visiting stores and confiscating the curvaceous plastic teen queen and her assorted sisters, buddies and ball gowns. 'Barbie,' said one relieved retailer, 'is more dangerous to Iran than US missiles.' Sentiments with which any parent who has ever stepped barefoot on one of her tiny stilettos will heartily concur.

Mindful of the vacuum this would create in the world of Iranian girls, the government had designed its own replacement dolls. Sara and Dara were a pair of eight-year-olds dressed in modest Muslim clothing who promoted traditional family values. The dolls' robust Islamic heritage was undermined somewhat by the fact that they were made in godless China. The original Iranian-made versions had been so crap even the mullahs had rejected them.

I found Sara and Dara in a department store. They were endearing in a podgy sort of way. Thanks to secure online ordering and air mail, my daughter was playing with them three weeks later. When last seen Sara was sporting a figure-hugging Lurex mini-dress while Dara explored his feminine side in floral bikini briefs and a fur-trimmed satin cape.

Souvenirs secured, I boarded another bus, this time one of a superior stamp, complete with air conditioning. It also had a VCR. I had heard that Iranian cinema had become poetry bearing a message of liberty. Unfortunately there were no video cassettes on the bus so I was unable to judge. It seemed plausible enough. Iran had started to relax a bit since the days of the Ayatollah Khomeini. The ban on chess and billiards had been lifted and it was said that in the fast-food restaurants in Tehran men and women wantonly queued at the same till.

We passed across the high country of the Qusheh Degh where Armenian ewes and wild pigs made their homes, and the domed yurts of nomads blistered the dun-coloured land. Here was mile after mile of sheep-grazing ground. It was treeless and such hamlets as there were clung to cover, lonely fugitives from the howling wind. The powdered snow from frosted drift pockets swirled across the three-lane highway. We paused briefly in Ahar for a change of driver, a restock of pomegranates and to admire the large billboard that bore the Islamic Republic of Iran's unofficial motto 'Israel Must Be Destroyed!'. Ahar ought to have been twinned with Dazit (Poland) and Eureka (Kansas) but it wasn't.

Lorries, ancient US Mack and White trucks that dated from the days of the Shah, lumbered past as we rumbled along the highway, their cabs decorated with scripture from the Koran where normally you'd see Linda Lusardi or a football scarf. Every 100 miles we came across the debris of those whose injunctions to the Almighty had gone unheeded, blackened and mangled upon grey ice.

The area around Ardabil was famous for mineral water and sludge therapy – the latter efficacious in the treatment of 'diseases of the bearing implement device' and 'diseases with infringement of a hair cover'. The Mausoleum of Shikh Safi is magnificent, so intricately tiled that from a distance it appeared it had been rendered and then sprinkled with hundreds and thousands. Iran is the world's number one importer of rice.

A kindly Iranian who lived up to his nation's billing as the Land of Nobility and Gallantry had earlier assured me that in Ardabil there were 'many restaurants and gusthouses'. In the latter case he proved singularly accurate. It was probably the cowmeat and beans.

Guilan Province boasted lush forest on its northern skirts and a moderate Caspian climate. The border with Azerbaijan was in the town of Astara where wooden houses roofed with thatch that sprouted madly like the coarse hair of a warthog stood sentry over the glistering mulch of paddy fields. From here I picked up the Tehran to Baki bus and headed north, my progress interrupted only briefly by mustachioed Iranian customs officials eager to check that I had not exceeded my personal carpet allowance of six square metres.

As soon as we forced our way across the bridge into the former Soviet Republic the bus driver tuned into Radio Araz. A burst of what sounded like a Dutchman speaking Russian was followed by the dramatic swirl of Azeri pop music. Azerbaijan has many musical stars. Amongst the brightest were Aygun Kazimova, who looked like Christina Aguilera with more tyre pressure, and Rostropovich, who didn't.

Other illustrious Azerbaijanis include chess maestro Garry Kasparov. Kasparov had recently been defeated by a computer, news that was greeted by millions of people across the globe shrugging their shoulders and mumbling, 'Join the club, mate.'

The most famous Azerbaijani of all, though, is, of course, Tofik Bakhramov. The national sports stadium in Baki is named in his honour. Tofik's great achievement, the moment that propelled him on to the international stage, came at Wembley in 1966. He was the celebrated 'Russian linesman' who ruled that Geoff Hurst's shot had crossed the line and so gave England victory over West

Germany in the World Cup final. At Lankaran I raised a glass of warm beetroot juice in his honour.

Azerbaijan takes its name from the Persian word for fire. There are four hundred mud volcanoes in the country, each of which explodes every couple of decades, shooting flaming hydrocarbon gases a thousand feet into the air. Crude oil oozes from the rock; natural gas seeps from the ground and burns with an eerie blue glow. A popular local dish is boiled hoof with garlic vinegar.

The weather was refreshingly cool with more sun than clouds as we ground our sluggard way through Masali, Bilasuvar and Sahar. On the fringes of Pirsaat I caught sight of the Caspian Sea island of Bandovan Birnu. The island was inhabited and yet officially recorded at 92 feet below sea level. Luckily for people who lived on them the Caspian Sea was officially recorded as being nearly 100 feet below sea level, so their homes were safe, if somewhat paradoxical.

The bus took an eternity to get to Baki but even that was too quick for my liking. As if nature had not done enough to create a sci-fi landscape in Azerbaijan, mankind had added to it. Scientists rated the area around the capital as the most ecologically devastated on earth. Water, air and soil were rendered noxious thanks to a mephitic cocktail of petro-chemical spills, DDT, pesticides and the defoliants used by the local cotton farmers. The only thing that kept oil slicks from running aground on the beaches was the belt of raw sewage and animal carcases that ringed the shoreline. 'Cheap meat never makes good soup' is an Azerbaijani proverb.

The fiery lands had a fearsome reputation. Western embassies warned that corruption was endemic, the roads horrific, the amenities basic, the driving barbaric and assaults on foreigners routine. This plus the oilfields made me think it must be a lot like Texas. Only without the added menace of gridiron, spare ribs and Garth Brooks.

Eleven international companies were working on the country's oil and gas fields. BP, Exxon and Amoco were here, so too were Saudis, Norwegians and Japanese.

Azerbaijan had hoped to become a new UAE. In downtown Baki five-star all-suite hotels reared up above the rotting concrete blocks of the Soviet era and the foyers were full of the self-important babble of international entrepreneurs. Unfortunately the Baki oil boom had been more of a pop. For most of the 1990s Azerbaijan had been the centre of the world's biggest strikes, then at the turn of the millennium drillers in Kazakhstan hit a reserve so mighty it made the Azeri deposits look like puddles. People said that by 2030 Kazakhstan would be the world's second biggest oil producer after Saudi Arabia. The petroleum circus had moved on leaving behind its legacy of pollution and listless, worn-looking women with peroxide hair and chipped nail varnish. Life expectancy for men is fifty-eight.

I checked into an old Intourist hotel where I could tell from the photos the man-made fibres of the carpet crackled with static. Touching the door handles without putting rubber gloves on first resulted in a shock that made your teeth chatter like castanets. The public areas were filled with yelps and the smell of singed eyebrows, while the electro-conductive powers of underwired brassieres meant that smoke rose in signalling puffs from the refulgent cleavages of the loitering concubines.

As I tripped gingerly across the lobby a nice Azeri man approached and offered me 'participation in fishing sturgeon breeds fish on motor boat in high sea (fish out through nets) with maintenance of safety measures (favourable windless weathers permitting)'. This was tempting even though the chances of actually seeing a sturgeon were, as the inestimable Don King (whose hair suggested a passing acquaintance with Soviet floor coverings) is fond of remarking, 'Slim to nil and slim just left town'.

The sturgeon is a lumpy simpleton with barnacled skin and the tiny, staring eyes of the terminally confused. It first appeared in the days of the dinosaurs and can live to be a hundred years old and weigh 1500 pounds. Sadly, that kind of longevity is unlikely these days. Poaching and filth have wiped out 90 per cent of the Caspian Sea's stocks in less than a decade.

The shortage of sturgeon had grossly inflated the price of caviar, which was now so expensive even the Queen had been forced to take it off the menu. Every English schoolboy knows that caviar comes from the virgin sturgeon, that the virgin sturgeon is a very rare fish and that the virgin sturgeon needs no urgin', which is what makes caviar a very rare dish. Like much of what English schoolboys know, this is rubbish. Fish lay eggs. Virginity isn't an issue.

Perhaps the confusion stems from the fact that caviar – which means 'cake of strength' – in common with any foodstuff that is expensive, smells of fish or looks vaguely like a dick is widely regarded as an aphrodisiac. Beluga was currently selling at £200 per 50 grams. This was considerably more than male potency spray endorsed by the aforementioned Ron Jeremy, though the flavour was similar.

That night I dined on Norwegian seafood and exotic game entrées to the accompaniment of music that was a mature creative expression of humane and moral wit. I made my bed beneath an aurora borealis of electrical sparks and my dreams were filled with the bump, grind and squeak of meshing computers.

At dawn next day, still jittery, I boarded a ferry bound for Turkmenbashi, 336 kilometres across the Caspian. The ferry, *Mercury-1*, was a Dagestan-type built in Kalingrad on the Baltic in 1998. Hunkered down low in the water, it had the appearance of a murky blue toad.

We slipped out through the grease-spotted, stinking waters of Baki past the silver tubes and cylinders of the oil refinery, an area of quays, container bridges and yards where steel cuboid containers from China, Turkey and Kazakhstan were stacked up like Lego bricks. A Libyan freighter, so battered it should have been condemned, was laden with huge bundles of scrap timber. An ageing Maltese-registered ship, pockmarked with rust, its bilge pumps spewing murky water, had a hull of two vast, merging blocks of salt-faded colour – dull red and grey-green. It looked like a gigantic Rothko canvas, though it was worth considerably less, obviously.

An hour later we sighted the Oil Rocks. The Oil Rocks were a monument to a particularly mad kind of Soviet determination. It was a city in the sea built on pillars and landfill and it had more than 200 kilometres of streets. There were tower blocks, bakeries, a cinema and a school. Five thousand people lived out there, pumping crude up from under the seabed so that it could be turned into plastic drink bottles and tossed into the hedge at the bottom of my garden by passing motorists.

It would have been easy to get depressed, but the internet exists to distract us from despair. No sooner had I begun to wonder at the torturous ways of the global economy than the following uplifting message dropped into my inbox: the match between Brazilian giants Botafoga and Gremio ended in controversy when three minutes from time, with the score 1-1, a goal-bound shot from Botafoga forward Fabio was deflected past the post by a lapwing. 'Had the damn bird not crossed the line of the shot I would have scored the winner,' Fabio fumed. Asked if the bird was hurt in the incident Fabio's teammate Ademilson snapped, 'Unfortunately not.' The Portuguese name for the local breed of peewit is *quero-quero*.

I arrived in Turkmenbashi on Carpet Day. Carpet Day was a national holiday in Turkmenistan. The country also took time off work for Melon Day and A Drop of Water is a Day of Gold Day. Carpets are important to Turkomen both male and female. According to local lore, 'Water is a Turkomen's life, a horse is his wings and a carpet his soul'. Even the national flag had an elaborately patterned runner down one side of it.

The streets of Turkmenbashi were stink-bombed with the stench of the sulphur mines. Local nomads, faces dark and wrinkled as pickled walnuts, wore lambskin hats that looked like Sylvester the Cat's fur after dynamite has exploded in his face. They sang songs of love, sheep and weaving, plucked at idiophones, tootled on stone chickens and wrestled one another with sinewy gusto.

Turkmenistan was home to 4.5 million people and 6.5 million fat-tailed sheep – both were outnumbered by images of the President, Saparmyrat Niyazov. Niyazov was a beefy man with the massive, meaty head and smiling eyes of Hoss from *Bonanza*. He had seized the reins of power six years before Turkmenistan gained independence and gripped them so tightly ever since they might have been the windpipe of a dissident. He styled himself Turkmen-Bashi, Father of the Turkomens. Streets, villages, airports and towns were named in his

honour (the port of Turkmenbashi had formerly been
Krasnovodsk); so were a star and crashed meteorite. His
portrait hung on all public buildings, large billboards
carried samples of his wisdom, two state-controlled
TV stations did little but report on the many wonders
he performed and his doctrinal masterwork *The Book of the
Soul*, which hammered together the apparently diametri-
cally opposed philosophies of Islam and Lenin, had
recently been declared a sacred text by the country's
parliament.

Turkmen-Bashi's achievements were manifold and
extraordinary. He had, for instance, renamed the month
of April in honour of his deceased mother; passed a law
that old age did not begin until eighty-five (he was sixty-
two), that adolescence lasted until twenty-five and that
anyone under thirty-seven was a youth; and commissioned
a 14-metre-high gold-plated statue of himself that
revolved on a motorised plinth so that it always faced the
sun. Melon Day was his idea, so was giving the entire
population free salt. Aside from these machine-pistol
bursts of despotic whimsy Niyazov mainly confined himself to doing the standard things that dictators do:
suppressing press freedom, confining protesters in lunatic
asylums, building palaces and dyeing his hair.

The best news of all was that the CIA was reportedly
advising Turkmen-Bashi on internal security because the
White House regarded him as an important bulwark
against the spread of fundamentalist Islam. When I discovered this information I immediately tried to get a £100
bet on that British troops would be fighting him before the
end of the decade. I couldn't find an online bookmaker
who'd give me anything better than 5-3 on.

I boarded the Trans-Caspian railway, a piece of transport

history that had been completed by the Russians in 1888.
The carriages and corridors were thronged with multi-
farious humanity. Australian backpackers and Ohioan
Bible salesmen jostled with zinc-extraction engineers,
camel herds, disco-dancing Russian babes, bourbon-
slugging Gonzo journalists from NYC, Peace Corps
volunteers and widowed African princesses who were
soliciting financial help to retrieve $35 million worth of
gold and precious stones from a bank in Togo. I found
myself sitting next to a lively American youth named
Garry who had a tan like a tandoori chicken and said that
for 40 dollars US I was welcome to watch him really have
sex with real women who really wanted to have sex with
him. 'This is not porn,' Garry assured me good-heartedly.
'This is *real!*'

I pointed out to Garry that even if it was real it was still
porn unless, of course, the women who really wanted to
have sex with him were French, in which case it was erot-
ica, or extremely unattractive, in which case it was
obscene. I don't make the rules; I'm just reporting them.
Garry withdrew to think about what I had said. From the
stifled sobs, groans and whimpers I would later hear
coming from the buffet car I sensed that either Garry or
one of his companions was taking it hard.

This last joke was brought to you courtesy of Risqué
version 6.9 Double entendre software. To download free
of charge go to www.eyheyhey.com.

With the chugging rhythms of the locomotive counter-
pointed by the skittering syncopation of red-hot cinders
skittering across the carriage roofs we pressed on into the
rainbow-coloured deserts of the interior. Mile after mile of
rolling dunes that moved at a rate of 20 feet a year (only
marginally quicker than the train) was broken by the odd

ruminative quadruped and the occasional group of women clad in fuchsia pink who stood arms outstretched in a manner that suggested they were miming the act of holding aloft a tray of beer mugs while simultaneously fending off an amorous drunk. There were also hundreds of statues of a chunky man in an ill-fitting Soviet suit. What did Communism have against tailoring?

Two women sat across the aisle from me. The youngest of the pair wore steel-framed spectacles and an I-told-you-so look. Her companion was a lady of a certain age whose brindle-coloured hair crumpled sadly about her ears like an unsuccessful soufflé. Their words were as alien to me as the hairbrush is to Telly Savalas so I had to spend time adding my own English subtitles.

Older woman: Did you do anything last night, then?

Younger woman: Our Bob rented that video *Shakespeare in Love.*

Older woman: What's it about?

Younger woman: Dunno. We switched off after ten minutes. It was crap.

Ashgabat, 'City of Love' and capital of Turkmenistan, was like Disneyworld with Turkmen-Bashi playing the roles of both Walt and Mickey Mouse. Here there were myriad unexpected wonders that reflected the *joie de vivre*, artistry and sense of beauty of the leader. The world's largest carpet (commissioned by Turkmen-Bashi); the world's largest shopping-centre-cum-fountain (a bizarre modernist pyramid in front of which, flanked by topiary tornadoes, stood a bust of Turkmen-Bashi); the Arch of Neutrality, a mighty white stone trivet, supporting a concrete coffee grinder on top of which was the revolving and gilded image of Turkmen-Bashi; the Earthquake Memorial, a huge sculpture of a black bull balancing between its horns and hunched shoulders a dark globe on which perched the golden figure of Turkmen-Bashi; the presidential palace, a brutal, angular version of the White House with shinier cladding and a dome the colour of an egg yolk which was the home of Turkmen-Bashi.

Turkmenistan's most popular brand of washing powder is Barf. Statistics show that that boxes of Barf are the nation's most popular souvenirs for visiting Americans. If you want to make money from the tourist trade market a range of bar-b-q cheese-flavoured snacks called Puke.

Seeking respite I visited the Tolkuchka Bazaar, said to be the finest in Central Asia. Tolkuchka means 'a lot of elbowing' and the scene was indeed crammed with shoppers in rich and colourful native garb eagerly snapping up camels, horses and Adam Sandler DVDs. I had gone into my office early that morning and hadn't seen my partner Catherine for several hours, so to relieve the pangs of homesickness I popped into the local branch of Benetton, held a dress up in front of myself, said 'Call this a size 14? Who are they kidding?' and stomped out again.

The lights of Ashgabat sparkle throughout the night, though nobody much is around to marvel at them. I dined within earshot of the record-breaking waterfall – about 800 yards – in a restaurant in which a manikin dressed in a gas mask formed an attractive feature. I feasted on corn-meal porridge and mung beans washed down with vodka named after Turkmen-Bashi and returned to my hotel, which, surprisingly, wasn't.

Turkmen-Bashi had used whatever wealth his county's considerable natural gas supplies had created to set about westernising the little oasis town of Ashgabat. Hotels had been high on his list of priorities. Like the Gulf Arabs, Turkmen-Bashi saw the cornerstones of Western culture as shag pile carpets and twenty-four-hour room service (if democracy was on the list it was down near the bottom, somewhere between mini-bars and those 'Sanitised for your protection' toilet strips). Get these in place, the message seemed to be, and all else will follow automatically. Turkmenistan was a nation of shacks and Sheratons.

The next morning I was unable to wash because running water was only available between 6 a.m. and 9 a.m. This was either because the rest had been diverted to the waterfall or that putting my jeans in at the hotel laundry had overloaded the system. I breakfasted on the local fizzy drink, Orange Yupee, reboarded the Trans-Caspian and headed off across the southern skirts of the Kara Kum Desert.

Here amongst the dusky, voluptuous dunes the spiral-horned goat made his rude home; at dawn wild tulips pushed forth their velvet crowns embroidering the desert to a many coloured tapestry that bloomed but briefly before it was chargrilled by the pitiless gaze of Rebus, its funeral remains interred once more by the molasses-dark sand – that damned infernal sand which tripped about the stirring air, skittering hither and yon like a carefree young nymph born aloft on the eddies of love's first tender glance. I don't know what was in that Orange Yupee, but I could do with more of it.

I alighted at Mary. Mary had once been Merv. In this day and age you've got to accept that kind of thing. In 400 BC Merv had been conquered by Alexander the Great; if it had been called Mary back then he'd probably have left it alone. In Mary I lunched on beef in cottonseed oil, was briefly arrested by the artefacts in the town museum but released without charge and bought a postcard featuring an Akheltek stallion, a gas pipeline, a radar tracking station and Turkmen-Bashi.

My next stop was Chardzhev, which, after the fashion of the locale, had recently changed its name to Turkmenabad. Turkmenabad had a prison colony, a capricious stream, a high percentage of weather and nothing much else I could put my finger on. I crossed the border into Uzbekistan an hour later. I was glad to leave Turkmenistan. The statues of Turkmen-Bashi were starting to get on my nerves. Besides which having to deal with a single female Turkomen challenged all notions of grammar and severely confused my computer spellchecker.

There are only two doubly landlocked nations in the world. One is Liechtenstein, the other Uzbekistan. Apart from that the pair have nothing in common. Uzbekistan is like a diamond in a sand setting. There are four thousand architectural monuments; the vegetarian and animal kingdoms are vivid and colourful, while passing caravans have predicated the historical richness of the region and the talents of local artists created much to attract the traveller's eye. In Liechtenstein there are banks.*

A quirky demographic means that 60 per cent of the population of Uzbekistan is under nineteen. No official reason is advanced as to how this happened, though the fact that the population explosion began in the same year that *Body Heat* was released on video is surely not coincidental. Whatever the cause of it, one in four people in

*A gross slur on Liechtenstein, which has much more to offer than just banks. This, after all, is a country that didn't give women the vote until 1984 and whose national anthem begins with the stirring phrase 'Up at the spring of the young Rhine'.

Uzbekistan is a teenager. I therefore braced myself for a country of slamming doors and spot cream, that had a national motto of 'That is sooooooo unfair', bathrooms you could only get into at four-hourly intervals and which functioned under a mushroom cloud of deodorant, masculine talc and the tangy vegetable-soup whiff of congealing hormones.

That the country proved to be nothing like this at all owed much to the placid nature of Uzbeki teenagers, a generally docile group from what I could see, much given to wearing dark socks in combination with baggy khaki shorts and white tennis shoes and sitting around the lurid flower beds maturely discussing the relative merits of top Samarkand rock 'n' rollers Tip and the hip-hop stylings of leading local rapper DJPiligrim (or Maggok as he preferred to be known these days).

Uzbekistan is one of the world's biggest producers of cotton, which is known as 'white gold', though only by people who don't know the price of bed linen. Other important local activities are silkworm breeding, livestock rearing and sheep bleeding. It is to be hoped that the latter is a spelling mistake, but I wouldn't put money on it. The national sport of Uzbekistan is the ancient martial art of kurash, an indigenous form of traditional upright jacket wrestling also popular in Canada, Bolivia and the Dominican Republic. Bingo costs approximately 2p a card.

In Bukhara I checked into a hotel of rare and simple loveliness. Converted from a nineteenth-century house, it had open balconies, carved wooden shutters and woven wall hangings, the owners having singularly failed to grasp the idea that the sophisticated international traveller demands at least one pay-per-view channel that will be recorded on his bill as 'extras'.

After marvelling at the fabulous tiling of the madras-
sahs and mosques, I visited the well down which the
British spy Stoddart had been held by the Emir Nasrullah
until he went stark staring mad and was executed. Emir
Nasrullah, like many of the emirs of Bukhara, fulfilled the
role of eastern potentate with a relish that suggested the
words stereotypical and cliché had never entered his
vocabulary. Probably there was no room for them because
so much space was taken up with synonyms for cruelty
and dissipation.

The last emir had the afternoon habit of standing on
the balcony of his palace watching the ladies of the harem
bathing and then, when the mood took him, throwing an
apple down into the pool. The woman who caught it got
the signal honour of spending the night with him. The
emir was a portly man with the obscene jutting lips of a
grouper fish. My guess is he got to hear the phrase 'Oops,
butterfingers!' more often than most of us.

When Soviet troops arrived in 1919 the emir scam-
pered off to Afghanistan leaving the harem and its
attendant eunuchs behind. The Red Army's attempts to
liberate them were thwarted, however, by their refusal to
leave. This is not so surprising. There are some sad sights
known to man, but there are few more poignant than that
of a redundant eunuch.

I took my ease in a café in the central square, lounging
on silken cushions, sipping green tea, smoking a Turkish
cigarette and attempting to project an air of mystery. After
a while I got tired and settled for looking a bit odd instead.
As the pomegranate sun slowly surrendered its hegemony
of the sky to an obsidian moon, the muezzin began the
ululating call to prayer. The commercial centre of the
Great Silk Road is a city of such spirituality it was said

that light ascended from Bukhara to heaven rather than vice versa. This is probably not the place to bring it up, but, frankly, if over the preceding three weeks I'd accepted every incredible offer to make my penis up to three inches longer without pain or surgery you'd be stepping on it.

4

'Haunts of the Whistling Thrust'

Bukhara to Ulaan Baatar

The train rattled through the Kizil Kum Desert past a massive iron-ore extraction plant that sat in the sand, covered conveyor belts stretching out from its pulsing centre like the tentacles of a giant octopus, its lights winking in a gloaming of dust clouds. Apart from that the only signs of life were foraging caravans of Bactrian camels; two-humped and shaggy haired, they looked like beatnik versions of the regular dromedary.

Bactrian camels have bushy eyebrows, a drunken gait and a digestive system so remorseless they can eat rope. They are named after a part of Afghanistan they don't come from. When the Bactrian needs to replenish its water supplies it can drink 114 litres of liquid in less than ten minutes. This will sound very impressive to anyone who has not spent Saturday night in a pub in Middlesbrough.

Digression. A polite note to the compilers of computer spellcheckers: Middlesbrough is spelled Middlesbrough. There is no second 'o' in Middlesbrough. There is no need to keep underlining Middlesbrough with a wavy red line because that *is* the correct spelling. I hope that is clear. Middlesbrough. Now put your copy of *Chicks in Chainmail* down, dust the taco chip crumbs off your front and go and sort it out. And while you're on, there isn't a hyphen in fuckwits either.

During the mating season the male Bactrian camel attempts to attract a partner by drooling, spitting and urinating copiously. Surprisingly this works. That it does is all down to what zoologists call the 'handicap principle of selection'. By discarding the precious commodity of water the male camel is sending out a message about his self-confidence and fearlessness. He is effectively saying, 'Come on, desert, if you think you can take me, have a go.' It appears that females of certain species are genetically attracted to male traits that are counterproductive to survival. There will now be a short pause while male readers slap their foreheads and mutter, 'So that's why she left me for that tattooed nutcase with the motorbike.'

To see Samarkand once is to be enchanted by its magic forever. The exterior of every building is covered from pavement to azure, shining dome with tiles, geometrically patterned with lavender, kingfisher blue and mallard green, spotted with madder or picked out in black. No precise figures exist but it is my belief that Samarkand has a greater density of grouting than any city on earth. MAPC is Cyrillic for Mars bar.

Sitting on rugs of affluent antiquity beneath the dappled shade of ghostly trees I watched the variegated swirl of the passing city. Old fellows with snowy beards cresting like waves about their rocky cheeks walked with the discernible spring in the step of those who know that back home the wife is preparing a tasty supper of spiced sheep-tail fat in dough; round-faced girls with cheekbones so high they seemed in imminent danger of disappearing under their eyebrows danced with fluffy willow buds entwining their raven hair; young women in wreaths of pale blue damask clutched ornamental flowerpots to their bosoms and cast modestly coquettish glances at the groups of youthful hawkers peddling lacquer boxes, ceramic gnomes and video cassettes. Since time immemorial the people of Uzbekistan have lived according to the timetable of sun, moon, water and earth. Now they have the *TV Guide* too.

The talk on the cushions surrounding me was of Uzbekistan's President Islam Karimov. A dead ringer for Peter Lorre, Karimov had held office for more than a dozen years, fending off all attempts to depose him by the Progress of Motherland Party. So far he had manfully resisted becoming the centre of the kind of personality cult that Turkmen-Bashi had created next door, but there was still time. At the moment, however, he was too busy proving the truth of the popular Uzbek adage 'Every man has a fool up his sleeve'.

The dolt concealed in Karimov's jumper was not so much himself as his daughter, Gulnara. She had married an American and was currently involved in a messy divorce case in New Jersey. Unfortunately for Ms Karimov her husband won custody of their two children, which meant that in order to set maintenance payments the judge demanded a full disclosure of her assets. These proved to include $4.5 million in jewellery, $3.3 million in cash, $11 million in various Swiss, US and Russian bank accounts, a Moscow penthouse valued at $4 million, a Tashkent recording studio, nightclub and spa complex worth $6 million, various other businesses and shares worth in excess of $20 million and a $7000 piano. The annual per capita GDP of Uzbekistan is $2500.

Since Karimov effectively controlled all the mass media in the past, he might have prevented most of the citizenry from receiving word of the scandal. The internet made that impossible. Anyone with a PC, a modem and a printer could run off thousands of copies of the news report from Russian newspapers and distribute it. This was *samizdat* on a global scale. Cyberspace was unpatrollable. It offered the chance to bring hope and freedom to the world. Unfortunately the world tended to get distracted and start looking at the homepages of men who refought the great battles of medieval times on a living-room floor in Michigan using thousands of Playmobil figures instead.

Angered by their inability to bury Gulnara-gate, the Uzbek authorities reacted in random yet Draconian fashion – they denounced billiards as a public nuisance and a hazard to health and morality and banned it. 'We are frustrated,' said the president of the Uzbekistan Billiards Association. 'We have devoted our entire lives to billiards.'

Tiring of tessellated tiling, I tried to visit a supermarket. It was my intention to carry out important research on the local varieties of breakfast cereal and budgie feed and to ascertain whether I could get Orange Yupee online, or preferably intravenously. Unfortunately when I went through the portal entrance I was overwhelmed by such a blizzard of drop-down adverts for off-track betting and cheap credit cards that I staggered out again for fear of becoming involved in a virtual version of that scene in *Brazil* when Robert De Niro disappears under the whirling newspapers.

Instead I went into a restaurant called Foodtechnoplus that was nowhere near as bad as it sounded, but only just. I drank black tea with salt and pepper, ate *plov* and eavesdropped on a pair of young folk who had popped up in front of me unbidden. The couple had been brought together that very evening by an agency specialising in love and friendship. The chap had a Zapata moustache and the intense, cross-eyed expression of Joseph Fiennes trying to pass the Amersfoort boulder. 'Hi!' he said. The girl, looking sideways through a sheet of honey-blonde hair, responded, 'Hi!'

'I have been seeking you all my life,' the chap announced dramatically.

'Me too . . .' the girl murmured gnomically.

There was a pause. Perplexed by the cryptic nature of her reply (did she really mean she had been seeking herself all her life? Was it some sort of 'I've Never Been To Me' thing?), the chap could only offer back a weak, 'Hi!'

'Hi!' the girl said.

'I have been seeking you . . .' the man began again. If this was the way they had been carrying on no wonder they couldn't get a date. Placing your bread on the table flat side up may cause offence.

The next morning I visited the mausoleum of Tamurlane the Great. A direct descendant of Genghis Khan and the last of the great nomad emperors, Tamurlane's sculpture had gradually replaced those of Lenin and Marx across Uzbekistan as the locals sought a return to the more traditional economic philosophies of sack and pillage. Born near Samarkand, Timur the Lame began life as a sheep rustler and ended up master of an empire that stretched from Anatolia to the Tien Shan Mountains of China, from Delhi to Moscow. At the age of seventy he was on his way to batter the Ming Chinese when old age caught up with him and he died.

In between conquests Tamurlane found time to invent a boardgame, Tamurlane chess. This was like ordinary chess except that a prince replaced the queen and there were a number of extra pieces including a vizier, two elephants, a pair of siege engines, a brace of camels and a couple of giraffes. In the lee of a sixteenth-century mulberry tree, to the accompaniment of honking geese, hawking children and offers of a debt-free future from an Atlanta credit agency (debt-free and credit: how does that resolve itself, I wonder?), I sat down to play against a computer from Utrecht.

The annals of warfare contain many bizarre uses of animals to unsettle an opponent, including the employment of flaming pigs, but as far as I know the giraffe has never played much part on the battlefield. This is because it is a timid and gentle creature with limbs that might have been drawn by Salvador Dali and a head arrangement that is the mammalian equivalent of sticking a tin helmet on a stick and waving it above the parapet to attract enemy fire. A giraffe is about as threatening as Lego. Not so the version in Tamurlane chess which gallops about the board decapitating knights, flattening camels, swatting elephants aside with one blow of its mighty throat and throttling bishops with its 18-inch tongue. I was destroyed in ten moves.

Disgusted, I went into a bar, drank some gassy beer and watched a fuzzy TV that carried reports of a local man who had just won a world title for Thai boxing. Even hares may pull the beard of a dead lion.

Every Uzbek who owns a car is a part-time taxi driver. I have no idea what the man who took me across the

border and into Tajikistan did for the rest of the week
but from his swashbuckling style behind the wheel I would
judge he was working in the kamikaze sector. To Billy
Ocean red light spelled danger. To this man it spelled 'put
your foot down now for free cakes'. His shroud of choice
was a Ukrainian Gaz Volga M21 saloon in funereal black.
It looked like Montgomery of Alamein's staff car and had
the shock absorption of a cluster bomb. There are many
potholes on the highway from Samarkand to Khojand
and we were soon intimately acquainted with most of
them.

Otherwise the journey was a source of multifaceted fas-
cination. Peasants in their rubicund and bejewelled pomp
gathered along the roadside selling crops of green
radishes, yellow carrots, plump melons and reconditioned
spark plugs and the lush valleys were a patchwork of vine-
yards, mulberry, cotton and corn broken by the odd
traditional display of fire eating.

The Uzbeks had recently mined the border with
Tajikistan but the road was still open. We crossed through
the army checkpoint. Uzbekistan was a strictly Islamic
state. The Tajik government welcomed all denominations,
though their preference was $10 bills.

Tajikistan bordered Uzbekistan, Kyrgyzstan and
Afghanistan. It was the poorest republic of the former
USSR. Eighty per cent of the population were so poor
they needed to form a human pyramid even to reach the
poverty line. In the eleven years since the country had
gained independence it had had three changes of government and five years of civil war. Armed clans patrolled
the countryside seeking trouble as the squirrel seeks nuts.
In the urban centres gun battles erupted like pimples.
Assault, drug trafficking and kidnap were commonplace.

If a Tajik had a fool up his sleeve you sensed he'd slit his throat. 'Talk makes talk,' the Tajiks said. 'Three men may keep a secret, if two of them are dead.' The Boy Scout Association of Tajikistan had been replaced by a casino.

The British government said not to go, the Canadian government said not to go, the US government warned that your regular health insurance might be invalid. Tajikistan was rough, tough and lawless, but so was my daughter's fifth birthday party and I had survived that, so on I pressed, spitting, drooling and urinating regularly in an attempt to impress onlookers with my macho reckless-ness.

Tajikistan is a proud and exclusive land where vast and craggy hummocks hover over the shimmering surface of wind-wrinkled lakes, the road is straight and empty and a man standing solo in the surrounding meadows wears yak-hide boots, a candy-striped robe and the put-upon look of a lone tree in a land of dogs.

To add local flavour I tuned the Volga's radio to a music station in the capital Dushanbe (formerly Stalinabad) and listened as a woman who sounded like Alanis Morissette on helium keened over the loose, psychedelic twanging of a sitar, outbursts of non-specific whistling and a percussion section that appeared to consist of somebody beating a wet towel against a breeze block. The average song lasted for 32 miles. He who talks without thinking dies without getting sick.

Khojand (formerly Leninobad – you can say what you like about Soviet Communism but it kept signwriters in work) was noted as the safest place in Tajikistan. The bullet holes in the public buildings were several years old. Body armour was optional. There were many old people around. I suspected this was because Death was just too scared to visit Tajikistan. Word was that last time he'd turned up here someone had hit him over the head with a length of scaffolding pole, stolen his scythe and sold his bony steed to a glue factory.

The city's situation in the fertile Fergana Valley had earned it the nickname 'The Pearl of Asia'. It is home to the biggest statue of Lenin in the East. Vladimir Ilyich stands gazing towards the mountains looking even more like Ming the Merciless than usual and characteristically touching his left shoulder with his right hand as if he has gone to brush away a few specks of dandruff and found a suspicious lump near his collarbone he hadn't noticed before. According to a tourist website, 'Finishing in the Syr Darya River is a pleasant local hobby.'

I strolled through the Thursday bazaar admiring silks, goatskin slippers and KGB listening devices and casting sideways glances at the locals. Tajik women wore embroidered caps, one-piece dresses and knickerbockers. When they left the house they donned a veil and carried a dinner plate of freshly sprouted chives. The fashionable look for men was grizzled.

I bought some stamps commemorating the birth of Marilyn Monroe. Minting collectable stamps was a minor industry in the former Soviet Republics. Turkmenistan had issued sets celebrating Led Zeppelin and Queen, while the Uzbeks had done one on the theme of Space Fantastics.

I wanted to find out more about life in Tajikistan but my guide Rustam seemed intent on showing me the FBI's ten most wanted list instead. At number two was a seventy-one-year-old racketeer, murderer and drug dealer who looked like the sort of children's magician who'd turn up on a cut-price cruise ship. According to the FBI profile he liked walks on the beach, animals, culture and travelling. In the US this man was rated as armed and dangerous. In Tajikistan they'd have dressed him in frills and called him Jessica.

There were no hotels in Tajikistan to speak of. Luckily I had my survival skills to fall back on. I used branches and moss to erect a rude shelter. I woke next morning feeling as if I'd been abused all night and took the northbound train.

I had originally intended to cross Kyrgyzstan. On balance, though, that did not seem wise. Kyrgyzstan was so troubled and belligerent it made Mike Tyson look like Papa Smurf. Even space fantastics swerved to avoid it. Instead I went up through Tashkent and into Kazakhstan on the Turkistan-Siberian railway.

Kazakhstan is noted for its limitless steppes and whimsical canyons. Steep chinks add immeasurably to the inimitable beauty of the landscape. The terrain is flat and dun coloured with the occasional frail, green sprinkling of wormwood, tamarisk and feather grass. Viewed from a distance it looks like a mildewed Ryvita.

The most frequently asked question about Kazakhstan is 'Does it have anything to do with the Cossacks?' The answer is no. The Kazakhs are a nomadic people of Turkic origin whose name means 'wanderer'. Cossacks by contrast are, well – whole books have been written on the subject and come nowhere near to providing an answer. A polite stab at it might be that they are probably stationary nomadic fighting farmers who are mainly Slavic but not entirely and Orthodox Christian except for the ones who aren't. Simpler then, all in all, to say what Cossacks are not. They are not Kazakhs. Except for the odd one or two, obviously.

Kazakhstan gained independence in 1991. It started out as Kazakstan. The additional 'H' was a sign of mounting self-confidence, like a provincial hairdresser who greets the opening of his second salon by commencing to pronounce his forename in the continental manner – *Ber*-nard, with the 'D' silent. The oil boom and a government that was by regional standards verging on the sensible had helped Kazakhstan to become a bit of a success story. Annual economic growth was in double figures; nobody seemed remorselessly intent on killing anyone else. If you could ignore the unusually high radiation levels, the outbreaks of self-mutilating protest in the prison colonies and the institutional prejudice against non-Kazakh speakers it was, all things considered, rather jolly. There are horses everywhere. Mainly on your plate.

On average women in Kazakhstan live eleven years longer than men; this may be because the pain of childbirth inures them to the food. Kazakh cooking is a mirror in which are to be found reflections of the nation's soul. Guests of honour are served the pelvic bone, or a sheep's head specially prepared. Indigenous specialities include dried horse rib sausages boiled in a broad vessel, wind-dried hip flesh and horse neck fat smoked in dew. Some readers may not like the sound of this and I must say I wasn't too keen either. But I have developed an infallible system when confronted with unappetising dishes. I simply translate them into French. *Cou gras de cheval fumé à la Kazakh*. Now, doesn't that sound tasty?

South Kazakhstan Oblast has its own history. During the time of the ancient Turks cities rose impetuously. I alighted at one of them, the regional capital Shymkent. Shymkent is a leisurely paced burg where women with ruddy cheeks and shining corselets greet the weary traveller with a brimming smile and directions to the dendro-park. I checked into a hotel with mint-green awnings and the unnerving look of something about to stagger and fall.

Shymkent had large lead processing and cement works and a vast complex of chemical factories. Though there was pleasure aplenty to be had from the zoo, children's railway and fantasy world, and it was possible to dance until dawn in the café bars of the techno-park, my main reason for being here was to visit the Museum of Karakul Sheep Breeding.

Karakul sheep are a broad-tailed, fat-rumped breed. I should say that these are technical terms rather than insults, though whether Karakul ewes take them that way is another matter. A sheep so ancient that it features in the wall carvings of Babylonian ruins, the Karakul has a Roman nose, pendulous ears, a rope-like fleece and the deranged eyes of a billy goat. It thrives in rugged environments and fights with dogs. Wool from the Karakul is used in carpet and felt making, but it is the pelt that is most valuable. It is from young Karakul lambs that the sheepskin known as astrakhan comes.

Astrakhan hats are a bit of a Kazakh speciality and I decided to buy one. I visited a splendid hunting shop that offered a nice range of Soviet generals' *padakayas* in soft grey with red felt tops. It also had a number of other fascinating products to offer. These included stocks of medicinal materials such as bear's gall, beaver glands and badger fat and a corset handmade from natural dog's fur that was said to cure muscular pains and illness of the joints. Reluctantly I decided to pass on these and, having determined my head size using a foot-long steel ruler and some chalk, loaded my shopping basket with a $150 hat. When I reached checkout, however, I suffered a fit of nerves. Call it prejudice if you will, but even to a man as cavalier with his credits cards as I am it seemed just a little too unwise to pass the details on to some bloke 2000 miles away in a country where you could buy a house with my available-to-spend balance (yes, they were that cheap). So I skedaddled and got one from a shop in Los Angeles instead. As if in protest, the Museum of Karakul Sheep Breeding was shut.

I took refreshment in a typical teahouse amongst proud and independent people and wrote an e-postcard to a friend. 'Shymkent twinned with Stevenage,' I said. 'Wonder how they found one another.' Later that day I got a reply. 'Thanks for postcard. Mayor of Shymkent probably typed 'Shithole' into his search engine.'

On leaving Shymkent we passed through the Betpak-Dala Desert and thence into the endless flatlands. I stared out across the vast, featureless steppes searching for signs of life. Here there lived the Durante-nosed Saiga antelope and the Bukhara deer. Hunting wolves is a necessity as well as a pleasure.

There are many rare beasts in Kazakhstan but none is rarer than the tractor. This may strike you as passing strange since the Soviet Union was famous for producing tractors. Indeed, no visit to the country was complete without a guided tour of a tractor factory. I had hoped to go on one. Kazakhstan had once been a mainstay of tractor production. There was a plant in Pavlodar that employed fifty thousand workers. It sounded like a splendid place. I imagined myself being escorted round it by a head-scarfed, heroic female worker with the healthful sex appeal of the young Kelly McGillis and her own set of torque wrenches. I would admire the DT75 Vladimirez Katerpillar with its tank-like bodywork and cab that resembled a Portaloo, and chat knowledgeably about the pulling power of the Traktor T40 and how favourably that compared with American makes such as the McCormick International and the Nuffield Universal. There would be a meal in the canteen and a tour to see the proactive schemes that were in place to help forge a sense of community amongst the workers (swimming pool, sports complex, crèche, four-hour queue to buy a cabbage) followed by fraternal speeches and vodka. Afterwards we would all embrace one another and I would go away feeling that if only we were given the opportunity, the time and enough alcohol the people of the world could live together in peace and mutual understanding.

Alas, it transpired that during the sweeping privatisation that had followed Kazakhstan's independence a Turkish company had bought the factory. They had stripped it of all its assets and shut it down, leaving a hangover and bitter resentment. In 1991 there had been 221,000 tractors in Kazakhstan. Now an area larger than the whole of Western Europe was home to fewer than forty thousand. Other important industries include cotton ginning, shoemaking, tanning and bellows. None has quite the same resonance as tractor making.

In Taraz the ancient mausoleums were covered in terracotta enigmatically engraved to make them look like they were made of straw. In Shu I chatted with a splendid Kazakh falconer who approached on a bay stallion with a slightly unconvincing background of mountains affixed behind its golden tail. The falconer had a fur-trimmed hat on his head, a golden eagle on his arm and Reactolite sunglasses on his nose. 'Here there are enough fair games, black cocks, ducks partridge and pigeon,' he said, 'and hares and foxes also may be taken.' Though according to his lights I was yet a virgin to nature, he generously offered me the opportunity to spend time with him in his shooting box enjoying ecologically pure products and a good kitchen. He said he could also show me some wild ass. This was the seventeenth such offer I had had that day, but in this case I guessed he was speaking of the kulan (*Equus hemionus*) rather than the red-hot momma ('She's old enough to be your mom, but horny enough to be an xxx-rated slut'). On the rebound from the tractor factory I agreed to join him.

The falconer – whom I shall call Tlekbek because he looked like a Tlekbek to me and since this is my book I feel entitled to call him whatever I want – was warm hearted, sincere and hospitable. Summer was his season for merry-making, but even in early spring he wore the sly grin of someone who has just been handed the bill in a restaurant and noticed that they've missed off the desserts. His laughter was as infectious as verrucas.

Our day was spent in horseback pursuit of hazel hen, willow grouse, tufted duck, fiddler bird and whistling thrust. We quested through luxuriant larch forests, paludal troughs and valleys seldom and secretive. Here were beauty meadows and grandiose waterfalls by which I was not left indifferent. Above us Tlekbek's faithful hunting companion, the tawny *birkit*, wheeled and dived across voluminous, chambray skies. In quiet moments by the huge mirrors of dreaming meres Tlekbek educated me in the ways of the hunter. 'He who advises the bear deserves to be beaten up,' he intoned sagely. 'Despise not the serpent because he has no horns, for lo he may become a dragon and rise up against you.' The *birkutski* had lived long amongst the intricate rhythms of nature, but had plainly found time to watch a few 1970s Chinese TV programmes at some point too.

In the evening we repaired to his shooting box, a traditional aul, set amongst pure air and inexpressible sensations. We ate spit-roasted marmot saddle basted in its own liquids. Then, as the steppe winds began to sound their mournful lament, Tlekbek reached in amongst a pile of brightly coloured pannikins, embroidered palls and pointed bridal headdresses and produced his two-stringed dombra. Soon he was plucking the horsehair strands and regaling me with improvised Kazakh ballads. The music had the drumming metre of cantering mustangs and the dark, echoing timbre of the lonesome prairie. At one point I was sure I heard the words 'I shot a man in Reno/ Just to watch him die' but it may only have been the effects of the fermented mare's milk and the fact I was struggling to concentrate. This was ill-mannered but unsurprising. I had just received word from a friend in Australia. He told me some shocking news. Guinness World Records had determined that the only creature on planet earth capable of uttering a higher note than Mariah Carey is the bottle-nosed dolphin. Even here in the primal wilderness civilisation had a way of jumping out and duffing you in the slats. The spell was broken. The next morning I took leave of my fur-trimmed host and renewed my journey.

Almaty is a blooming city perched between two cultures and numerous cooling fountains. It was founded in 1854. Overlooked by the snowcapped Tien Shan Mountains and facing steppes that stretch to Siberia, its name means 'Father of the Apples'. Almaty had long been the capital of Kazakhstan but around about the time that the 'H' was added the government upped sticks and moved to the more centrally located Astana instead.

Despite this demotion Almaty remains universally favoured as Central Asia's most cosmopolitan resort.

Amongst its tree-lined streets you find casinos, sophisticated nightlife, tower blocks and a vast, domed monolith,
which is one of the world's largest mosques and incorpo-
rates 13,000 square feet of marble. The ice rink is of
equal grandeur while the Monument to Fame is a must
see, whether you like Irene Cara or not.

The natives are athletic people. Apart from winning
Olympic gold in cross-country skiing, Greco-Roman
wrestling and weightlifting the country also boasts world
champions in arm wrestling, underwater orienteering and
ship engine sports. The national bandy team is justly fêted.
The Kazakhs invented polo. But don't hold that against
them.

I journeyed for some days into the Ayak Kalkan Desert
to hear the famous singing sands. Passers-by picnicking
amongst relict ashen trees warned me that in the presence
of an audience the dunes were often seized with stage
fright and failed to utter a single note. I was in luck, however, and accompanied by a group of Japanese travellers
who had spent their lives cataloguing the various noise-
making beaches and deserts of the world (including the
barking sands of Hawaii and the harp sands of their own
country) I was privileged to hear a rare public performance by the sands. In truth it must be said that it was more
of a basso profundo moan than a song or even a yodel.
Indeed, the uninitiated might easily have mistaken it for a
foghorn. In fairness to the singing sands I should say that
I was listening to a selection from 1995. It may well have
added a tribute-to-Howard-Keel medley since then.

Back in Almaty I planned the next part of my journey.
I had to cross the border into China and then turn north
into Mongolia. Buses and taxis were a possibility, but some
harsh-breathed Americans I had met on the train had

confidently told me that I could buy a motorbike in Almaty for 100 bucks. The following day I went to the autoplatz in search of a hog, or, if that seemed a bit too scary, a piglet.

I had my heart set on a Ural M72 Cossack, the Russian version of the shaft-driven BMW R71 they had been knocking out from the factory at Irbit since the Second World War. The M72 had a 750cc side-valve engine and was by all accounts the sort of noisy, oil-spewing beast that anyone who has never actually ridden motorbikes dreams of. And I had never ridden a motorbike.

Another advantage of the M72 was that even someone with modest mechanical skills could easily maintain it. My own mechanical skills were not so much modest as chronically shy, but I had recently had some success raising the handlebars on a micro-scooter and my confidence was high. As it happened I couldn't get an M72, but amongst the Voskhods, Dneprs and beach towels laden with starter motors and carburettors I did find a Chang Jiang, its rugged Chinese counterpart.

I paltered long and hard with its vendor, a wall-eyed Buryat with a manner that was about as reassuring as a rook with a gobbet of road kill in its beak. There was much toing and froing in our respective languages, frequent foot stamping, fist waving and nose blowing. Many moons ago in the carpet bazaars of Istanbul I perfected a technique of elliptical bartering, countering the salesman's every claim about his product with a piece of incomprehensible trivia in an attempt to break his spirit. I employed the same psychological technique now. The Buryat bike seller pointed out the Chang Jiang's interior tool box. I reminded him that Croatia was the only country with no mountains over 3000 metres ever to produce an Olympic downhill ski champion. He drew my attention to the low mileage. I drew his to the fact that Nederland, Colorado, is the home of the Frozen Dead Guy Day celebrations. He indicated the fresh tread on the tyres; I informed him that keeping ferrets is illegal in the state of California. Thanks in no small measure to my finely honed tactics I eventually knocked him up to $350. Any less and he'd have been robbing myself.

An hour later I was heading north, tearing across dirt with the wind in my hair, the sun on my back and flies splattered across my cheeks like winged blackheads. Beneath me the Chang Jiang growled, gurgled and expectorated viscous blobs of grease as she galumphed towards her top speed of 60 mph. She was old enough to be your mom, but noisy and unhygienic enough to be an XXX-rated Bactrian camel.

5

'Feather Gust of the Romping Chat'

Almaty to Ulaan Baatar

The A5 autoroute cleaved through countryside as flat as a
Frisbee and the colour of dried dung. At Sayovesk there
was a military base and a missile elimination facility where
the ICBMs the Soviets hadn't got around to detonating
on the steppes were being decommissioned. Throughout the Cold War the Russians had used Kazakhstan
for target practice. Over five hundred warheads had
been exploded here, more than a fifth of them *above*
ground. The uranium that formed them was mined
locally and then depleted more or less on site in a chain
of reactors operated by the Red Army. As if that was
not enough, Lop Nor, where the Chinese had carried
out forty-four nuclear detonations since 1961, was just
400 miles away. Radiation levels were so high around
Sayovesk that after the sun went down the landscape
must have glowed as if viewed through night-vision
goggles.

I stopped for gastronomic refurbishment close by the
Chinese border in Panfilov. Panfilov's name had recently
been changed to Zharkent. Renaming was a hobby

amongst the politicians of the former USSR. Since 1991, 109 towns and cities had adopted a new identity. Whatever you called it Zharkent was a pleasant spot. There were fresh apricots in the shops, trees lining the streets, broad-faced women busily decorating felt and broad-backed men singing 'For All The Girls I Loved Before' at the karaoke machines. In 1438 there had been a Catholic cathedral here. The bishop was the Duke of Burgundy. Within a decade of its construction Tamurlane had flattened it. Now the main attractions were a nineteenth-century prison and a rare species of tiger-striped dragonfly.

I bought bread and jam of green nuts and sat eating them and reading the *Sydney Morning Herald* beneath the rippling boughs of a camphor tree. In Victoria, Australia, two alpacas had been introduced as a break-time attraction at an elite business and conference centre. They were available for petting, feeding and photo opportunities. Said the centre owner, 'They are an excellent tactile meetings circuit breaker. They generate a lot of fun amongst delegates and provide us with a novel medium for follow-up communications.'

Twelve-foot-high fences of barbed wire separated China from Kazakhstan. Crossing them was like stepping forward in time. Literally. The Chinese government had decreed that their country was all one time zone. The clock was set by Beijing, 2000 miles to the east. People in the west of the country got up before the sun rose and went to bed in daylight. Those who lived on the border could walk across the frontier and reclaim several hours of their life in a hundred yards.

After the border point the road climbed steeply to 9000 feet. The Chang Jiang proved equal to it. The engine's 23 hp was more mountain pony than thoroughbred. I passed the turn-off for Lake Bortala, scene of the annual Nadan folk gathering, a shaking constellation of horse racing, girl chasing and lamb tussling which the Chinese authorities officially categorised as 'friendly and enjoyable'.

I thrummed along the northern fringes of the Taklamakan Desert. Taklamakan means 'If you go in you don't come out', which makes it sound like a nightclub in Scunthorpe. In fact it's nowhere near as inhospitable as that, though night and day temperatures are very different and you must adjust your clothing to prevent wind.

The oasis settlements were a vast sea of peach blossom and willow. At Yili there were many mosques, at Hatan paper was made from mulberry bark. Now, as for much of my journey through Central Asia, I was following the route of the historic Silk Road. Along it through the centuries men of fame had left their footprints behind them. Judging by the jarring of my spine the road crews still hadn't filled them all in yet. Significant buildings like a string of pearls sparkled brilliantly along the ancient highway. Thanks to medically approved vitamin enriched dermatological cream the dream of a bikini-beautiful body after childbirth had just become a reality.

The sun was a pancake on the ceiling of an azure yurt. The scenery had a vaguely familiar look. This was because the Japanese TV series *Monkey!* had been filmed on location here. *Monkey!* told the story of a Buddhist monk, Tripitaka. Tripitaka was played by actress Masako Natsume, a casting decision as strange as that of giving Horst Buchholz a part in *The Magnificent Seven* or Madonna a part in anything. He/she travels across China to collect some sacred scrolls protected on his/her journey by a band of characters including the eponymous Monkey (armed with a magic wishing staff given to him by the

Princess of the Western Ocean), Sandy (armed with a Joey Ramone haircut and a voodoo necklace) and Pigsy (armed with a fat stomach and a pair of ludicrous false ears). There was also a dragon that had turned into a horse and a theme tune with words that began 'Born from an egg on a mountain top/Funkiest monkey that ever popped'. Apart from that it was all a bit bizarre.

I was in the semi-autonomous province of Xinjiang Uygur, a place of peaceful settlements, scenic gullies and mountains of statistics. Xinjiang occupied one-sixth of the total landmass of China. It had 500 rivers, 9700 square kilometres of lake, 18,600 glaciers, 258 million cubic metres of ice, the world's second largest shifting sand desert, the highest per capita water resources in all of the People's Republic and its lowest and hottest zones. The province was home to 23,000 mosques, 12 religions and 47 different ethnic groups. According to officials these different peoples lived together in an atmosphere of 'mutual study, mutual confidence, mutual respect and mutual assistance'. And every once in a while the government shot a few people just to make sure they did.

The largest ethnic group were the Uygur. Uygur men wore felt four-pointed caps. Young girls wore a dozen pigtails. Women wore tiny witches' hats in shades of cerise and crimson and used make-up to draw their eyebrows into one continuous line. Uygur males apparently find such mono-brows sexually alluring. It is probably best if Liam Gallagher never visits Xinjiang.

I stopped to refuel at a Sinopec rest stop. In the diner, from what I could gather Mongolian truckers slurped drawing noodles and mixed stew and watched Hong Kong slasher porn on wall-mounted VDUs. Through a door behind the counter you could glimpse the dark, dank bunkhouse where the workers lived on their two-week tours of duty. I have visited motorway services across Europe and regard them as the most depressing places on the planet. The ones in Xinjiang were much the same only with a slightly lower density of unsightly shell suits.

As I sat dipping baked maize cakes into milky tea I was approached by a twinkling chap in a kaftan made from fabric left over from covering a deck chair. 'We are twins,' he exclaimed gleefully. 'One of us lives on one side of the mountain, the other on the opposite side. What are we?'

The obvious reply was 'An irritating pair of bastards' but I shook my head and feigned intrigued bafflement. 'Ears!' the jolly old bird exclaimed with the unfeigned delight of a child discovering it is allergic to broccoli. Though wise and industrious, Uygur people of all ages shared a gift for optimism, humour and riddles. They love nothing better than to bang sheepskin tambourines and perform the 'Bowls-on-the-head-Dance' to celebrate the happy feeling of a bumper harvest. The Uygur had produced an opera that encompassed 340 songs. Hopefully its use has been banned under the Geneva Convention. The heart of the father and mother is on the son and daughter. The heart of the son and daughter are on the mountain and the rock.

On my arrival in Shihezi I was greeted with pleasant songs and dances and by orchards of apricots. The pomegranate trees were sulking. Shihezi had recently been designated 'A Pearl on the Gobi Desert'. Surrounded by snowcapped peaks girdled with clouds and corseted by forested valleys colourful in fish, musical birds, hoarse-throated beasts and so on and so forth, the city fully vindicated that decision. After feasting on Xinjiang baked full goat, a dish that stands equal with Peking duck and

Guangzhou cracking pocket in the Chinese culinary pantheon, I strolled around Entertainment Square. Amongst
green plum blossoms and spurting fountains, I paused to
admire a complimentary sculpture entitled 'The First
Plough in the Army Reclamation'. There was also a statue
of revolutionary General Wang Zhen. In 1989 heroic
Wang Zhen had ordered a squadron of tanks into
Tiananmen Square where they single-handedly defeated a
group of mutinous students armed with offensive slogans
and dangerous scarves. All the harm in the world, as
Monkey observed, is done by people who are certain of
something.

.I would have liked to have bided a while longer
amongst Shihezi's fathomless charms, perhaps paying a
visit to the People's Park where the children's pavilion
draws kids eager to play with the auto-control planet and
the customs cottage is unforgettable, but I needed a place
to sleep. Reluctantly I left town, heading on to the bangs
of the desert. That night the sky would be my quilt, the
sand my bed, the tinkling camel bell my early morning call
and the yelping foxes the couple in the room next door
who seem to have no idea how thin the walls are, or that
somebody is trying to get a night's rest in here for Christ's
sake.

Urumqi is a big city with a small suburb, most of which
is a vegetable basket. In Mongolian its name means 'beautiful pasture' or 'wrestling'. This seems to point to a
certain imprecision in the language. It is as well this does
not exist in English. If World Wrestling Federation fans
turned up at a stadium and found the ring full of rich
grass and grazing cattle, who knows what havoc they
would wreak in their frustration.

Urumqi is the capital of Xinjiang Province. It blends a

folkloric look with burgeoning industry. The latter is largely thanks to the far-sighted socialist economic policies of Premier Deng Xiaoping who had designated Urumqi as a keystone of his 'All open, incline to the West' strategy.

Since 1992, Urumqi had risen to twenty-fourth in the list of 'China's 50 Strongest Cities of Synthetic Growth'. It had consistently fulfilled total output values and the brilliant achievements of the recent past are now stones on the path to a glorious future. People who have studied Chinese government jargon will recognise this as being a synonym for 'smouldering crap-stack'.

However, even a starving camel is bigger than a horse and my time in Urumqi was not without its pleasures. The city had a revolving restaurant, though given the quality of the fare there might well have been a 'T' missing from the descriptive verb. I loafed amongst the potted landscape of the People's Park and visited the Museum of the 8th Route Army in which the lives of many revolutionary martyrs are commemorated with an exhibition of dining chairs and two-seat sofas.

I visited the illustrious carp ponds in the People's Park, but did not venture too near. The Chinese had been experimenting with carp. They had increased their growth rate by up to 20 per cent and produced monster fish that weighed upwards of 150 pounds. They had done this by implanting them with cattle genes. The effect this tampering had on the appearance and attitude of the carp was not reported, but my guess was that anyone planning to fish for them should pack a sword and cape along with the usual tackle.

On my way back from the roller rink, red taxis and blue lorries strafed the pavements. China has more billboards than any other nation on earth. Suddenly two adverts popped up in front of me. One asked if I would like to perform in bed like a smouldering hunk of love, the other reminded me not to neglect my home's septic tank. It doesn't do to overstate these things, but it seemed to me this was pretty much the dilemma of manhood in a nutshell.

Xinjiang Province is famous for the production of jade. Jade protects from bad luck, evil spirits and danger. It can also be used in the treatment of female incontinence. Please don't press me for further details. In an Urumqi factory I was able to view craftsmen carving the stone into intricate and pointless microcosms. I spent nights at the roller rink and the Electric Power Guest House, which I found to be an oasis of tumult amongst the city's calm.

I continued on towards the rising sun, through Turpan and Shanshan. The Chinese government was cracking down on 'Chinglish', corrupted English that they worried would make them an international laughing stock. They had been systematically eradicating signs reading 'Collecting Money Toilet' and 'To Take Notice Of Safe, The Slippery Are Very Crafty' and it was said that 'Fried Crap' had all but disappeared from the fish section of menus. It was good for local self-esteem but murder for foreign postcard writers. Still, at least we can draw comfort from the fact that to the Chinese Coca-Cola sounds remarkably like the phrase 'bite the wax tadpole'.

I have no allergies and a cast-iron stomach. Amongst the European and American travellers I had encountered en route via homepages, message boards and blogs I could sense that this was a black mark against me, a sign of an unwillingness to muck in and really involve myself. Fulminating guts and the occasional gluten-related coma were, it appeared, essential facets of The Experience.

So in pursuit of acceptance I worked up a virtual tape-worm and severe lactic intolerance. I lost cyberweight so dramatically that soon I could play my ribcage like a glockenspiel and slice salami with my buttocks. I related terrible tales to anyone willing to allow me space of how, unbidden, a waitress ignorant of the latest developments of Western culture poured UHT milk on my morning gruel. Of the morning in Qiktim when, after two days of colonic eruptions brought on by an ill-advised dinner of braised gemmy and goat's hoof, I collapsed on the pavement with low blood-sugar, sunken-eyed and raging against a nation in which it was impossible to buy a tin of soya-milk rice pudding and how I was rescued by a sub-stantial pensioner from the Potato State named Cora-Beth. As luck would have it, Cora-Beth's digestive tract rebelled against wheat. And so we were able to share a carryout pizza, she feasting on the cheese and tomato and I upon the base.

Cora-Beth, I would add, was travelling by ergonomic tricycle from Seoul to Paris-Charles De Gaulle, the start-ing and stopping points chosen for no other reason than because they rhymed. So far she had passed through seven countries where she had found proud and independent people living amidst a kaleidoscope of sights and sounds. She was looking for things to tell her grandchildren about and a decent cup of coffee. We swapped dysentery anec-dotes and exchanged addresses. Unfortunately my business card was printed on bleached paper. When I left her, Cora-Beth's chubby mitts had puffed up like a porcu-pine fish and she was trying to prise a tube of emollient cream out from the pocket of her cargo shorts.

It is better to travel alone than with a fool. But the fool who travels without company does both.

In Hami I reluctantly decided to part with the Chang Jiang and take the bus north into Mongolia. I sold my faithful four-stroke friend to a wily Han Chinese quantity surveyor who wore the constipated look of a man with six daughters and only one bathroom. I pointed out the Chang Jiang's tyre tread; he reminded me that walnuts contain seven times as much protein per gram as beef fillet. I told him of the bike's durability and toughness; he told me that the world's first public library was in Poland. I drew his attention to the upgraded electrics; he drew mine to the fact that there is a city called Rome on every continent. I let him have the bike for $150 and reckoned I'd got off heavily.

The bus to Mongolia left in June at 9 a.m. The exact spot in Mongolia to which it was heading was not specified on the timetable. It was entirely possible that it was actually going to the Chinese province of Inner Mongolia rather than the sovereign nation to the north, but I refused to countenance that idea and told the driver as much when I got on. Ahead of us was a dotted route across the Balikan grassland above which the skies were buzzing with dust clouds as convoys of wealthy Spanish gunmen eager to shoot Tien Shan ibex and goitered gazelles rumbled into the Yinu River Valley.

By now I was genuinely sick, some kind of snarling cold picked up amongst the vapour of steam and sneezes at a truckers' stop in Yiwanguan, or more likely brought home from her primary school by my eight-year-old daughter. This is one of the perils of virtual travel that real travellers escape – you are constantly prey to unvirtual interference. Wilfred Thesiger never had to quit the Empty Quarter in mid quest to remove the corpse of an electrocuted mouse from inside the toaster. A real traveller may be trapped by the rising floodwaters of The Mighty Mississippi, but at least they are free to concentrate on their peril without somebody shouting 'Can you just give me a hand changing the disc on this pad-sander?' at them every time they've remembered a good adjective.

Sanding and colds, I should add, do not go together. After several hours abrading brown woodstain off ceiling beams, the mucus and dust had formed MDF in my nostrils. By the time I got back on the bus you could have built a fitted kitchen with the contents of my hankie. My top lip was alive with persistently encroaching slime. My sinuses pinged and rattled like a drum machine. My head felt as if someone had placed a tin bucket over it and invited Barry Bonds to beat on it with a baseball bat. As the bus bumped and ground its way through Nanshankou I fell into that unhappy, delusional state halfway between wakefulness and sleep. I dreamed I was trying to catch a plane but could not find the check-in desk at the airport. I was wearing odd shoes and my eyes couldn't focus on the information screens. I ran across a concourse of lawns, neo-Georgian follies and naked housewives who had sex with their husbands' best friends and found the departure gate. When I showed him the ticket, the airline employee smiled and asked 'Do you want women to go "Wow!" when you drop your pants?' Somewhere along the way I had lost my hand luggage, all my money and souvenirs. On board the plane the man sitting next to me turned and asked, 'So what is taking you to Antigua?' I screamed, 'I don't want to go to Antigua. I want to go home' and then jolted awake basted in my own liquids and with a rawness in my throat that suggested I'd spent the previous night gargling with Nitromorse.

We crossed the border into Mongolia. At a felt village

yaks' milk cheeses dried on the roofs of gers and an old woman at the roadside tossed tea into the air as an offering to heaven. Shortly after starting my computer I did a similar thing with my breakfast, though for different reasons.

Mongolia is the world's largest landlocked country. Seven-eighths of the nation is sky. Mongolia's human population is outnumbered twelve to one by livestock. There are just 3.5 telephones for every thousand people. The queues at payphones would be very long indeed, if there was anyone to call.

I left the bus at Bayan Ovoo. This frontier village, overhung by the Al Boga Uul Mountains, was reputed to be the birthplace of Mongolia's most famous export, Genghis Khan, or Chinggis Khaan as he is now known. In the thirteenth century Chinggis led an army of one hundred thousand cavalry on a campaign of occupation that left him with the biggest empire ever conquered by a single man. His method combined speed, cunning and brutality, with brutality predominating. Not until seven hundred years later did any other despot get around to killing quite as many people. What Bob Beamon was to the long jump, Chinggis Khaan was to mass murder. Towards the end of his rule Chinggis issued a famous proclamation: 'If you do not pay homage to us we will take your property. If you do not have property we will take your children. If you do not have children we will take your wife. If you do not have a wife we will take your head.' It became the blueprint that tax officials worldwide have followed ever since.

In history, however, no debt goes unpaid and seven centuries later humanity took its revenge on Chinggis Khaan when John Wayne played him in a film, *The Conqueror*, which is widely regarded as one of the biggest turkeys of all time.

The part of Temujin (Chinggis's original name) had been written for Marlon Brando but he turned it down. Because Brando had made a name for himself in a Broadway production of *Julius Caesar* the script was written in what in Hollywood was considered to be the language of Shakespeare. 'The Tartar woman is in my blood and my blood says, "Take her!"' Big John exclaims at one point. The Tartar spitfire in question was Susan Hayward who looked about as oriental as Dundee cake. 'Is Temujin so wanting of a woman that he will quench his fire with ice?' she inquires sassily. The ludicrous dialogue would probably have drawn more widespread ridicule but Wayne heroically distracted attention from it by sporting a droopy false moustache and Sellotaping the corners of his eyes to give them a Far Eastern slant. Utah did a better job of looking like Mongolia.

Like all nomadic people, the Mongolians have a tradition of hospitality, generosity and setting fire to crop fields. I soon found myself invited into a pallid canvas yurt. When I had first set out on my journey I had thought I might have to extemporise a little to create the right ambience. That if I visited a Parisian bar, for example, I'd have to slip a Vanessa Paradis CD into DisqPlay, sauté some garlic on a primus stove and dump a smouldering tractor tyre in the corner to simulate the Gitanes smoke. As it was I didn't have to bother. The internet is such a marvellous resource that the atmosphere of anywhere you visit simply jumps out and sucks your face like a calf at a salt cake.

In the yurt I sat by a tin stove amidst the friendly crackle of burning horse dung, the rattle of aluminium kettles and the snake hiss of fermenting yoghurt. The yurt was clean, cosy and wind-tight; the air a baroque overture of long-ago meals, fondly remembered dogs and straining babies.

The head of the family, an apple-cheeked grandfather with skin the colour and texture of kippers, offered me a pinch of snuff. Passing the snuff bottle is a formal occasion and sleeves should be rolled down. I snorted deeply of the proffered bottle and then sneezed suddenly, serially and without warning. The combination of a heavy cold and snuff is not a happy one, although if you are looking for a cheap alternative to Artex it is worth a try.

A yurt in Bayan Ovoo is about as far from a fish and chip shop or a pub as you can get and yet I felt distinctly at home. The Mongolians are a reticent, taciturn people who cover their embarrassment with smiles and are reluctant to talk about unpleasant things. They eat food that lacks spice, flavour or variety and wash it down with milky tea. How they and the English became separated is not recorded.

I was awoken at dawn by the distinctive, mournful snort of hungry yak. The yak is a hump-backed heavy-metal cow. It is also known as the grunting ox. Those who farm the yak describe it as an intelligent, personable, good-humoured and affable companion that, when roasted, tastes like beef. The yak describes the people who farm it as two-faced fuckers. Contrary to popular rumour yak milk is not pink. Hair from the belly of the yak was once used to make pubic wigs, which are called merkins.

I was taking the post lorry from Bayan Ovoo to Ulaan Baatar. This meant spending several days in the back of an open truck travelling across high plains where the temperature could drop to −50°C. For such conditions you need special clothing. Luckily, having spent a lot of time in Newcastle I know what is required in such a brutal climate – a clean shirt and an extra dousing of aftershave.

The post truck rumbled from the edges of the Gobi Desert where the sands were alive with hopping jerboas and scurrying hamsters, to the high steppes, a vast treeless landscape of platinum-blond grass crested by waves of frosted rock and punctuated by tent towns with names such as Moron and Bumbat, where russet-clad monks and women dressed like Queen Amadala from *Star Wars* practised archery. Near Moron a single set of tyre tracks left by a teal-blue truck ran fastidiously towards, and over, a distant horizon. From far off across the sagebrush came the delirious yelps of ginger hunting dogs pursuing Altay argali, punctuated by the rifle fire of Canadian sportsmen who were paying £20,000 each for the privilege of killing the world's largest sheep.

The journey was long and arduous and there were no toilet stops. I imagine I had many a scrape and adventure along the way, most of them the result of trying to relieve myself from a moving lorry in high winds. The Mongolians are a phlegmatic people but they draw the line at some things. It is well known, for instance, that women must never sit cross-legged in a tent and it is unwise to whistle indoors. Spraying urine on people's heads is also frowned upon.

By the time we arrived at Ulaan Baatar my cold had abated. The Mongolian capital is home to seven hundred thousand people, many of whom live in yurt suburbs. The suburban yurt differs from the regular one in having net curtains and a carport. Mongolia was the second country in the world to turn Communist. Since the arrival of democracy the capital has become a cosmopolitan place where you can drink skinny latte, eat burritos and listen to local media types discussing the important topics of the day such as 'Is camel the new yak?'

As he walks the wide boulevards the first thing that strikes the visitor is likely to be the range of headgear. Actually, that's not strictly true. The *first* thing that's likely to strike the visitor is an olive-drab Yaz 4WD driven by a swashbuckling nomad with a Marlboro in the corner of his mouth, but we'll ignore that. There are more than a hundred different types of hat in Mongolia and most people have several of each. Damon Runyon remarked of his character Rusty Charlie, 'He was apt to shoot a man because he did not like the way they wear their hat. And Rusty Charlie is mighty particular about hats.' In Mongolia Rusty Charlie would have found himself among kindred souls. Headgear here is taken very seriously. An old Mongolian proverb says, 'Better to break your head than your hat'.

I checked into the Genghis Khan Holiday Inn. This was, I freely admit, not a place of much local flavour, but I knew it would have the amenities I craved. A personal view is that rough travel is overrated when set against the delights of free shower caps. In fact I am already planning my next book. It will be called *In the Footsteps of Conrad Hilton*. Besides which, by now I was tiring of the diet of pilaf and petrified curds. I had managed to buy some Kraft cheese slices and a white sliced loaf from a stall in the Russian bazaar and knew that within minutes of getting into my room I'd have made myself several sandwiches and toasted them in the trouser press.

My first port of call in Ulaan Baatar was the Palace of Wrestling. I was not sure what I would find here – grappling or grass growing, but it turned out to be the former. Mongolian wrestling is one of the triumvirate of 'manly sports' (the others are horse racing and archery). The

competitors wear skimpy silk briefs and an upper garment
that is best described as topless sleeves. This singular costume was introduced centuries ago after a woman
disguised herself as a man and beat all-comers, thus bring-
ing ridicule down upon the heads of all Mongol
masculinity. It is worn so that females cannot take part. Or
at least to ensure that if any do the spectators get to see
their breasts – one thing that is always likely to make a
man forget any amount of humiliation.

One of the most famous local grapplers is Davaa
Batbayar, 'The Mongolian Falcon'. Batbayar is a professional sumo wrestler in Japan where he fights under the
moniker Kyokushuzan. His nimble, crafty style has
earned him the nickname 'The Supermarket of Tricks'.
Batbayar's memoirs have become a bestseller and his
forthcoming marriage to his Mongolian sweetheart is
eagerly anticipated. (Not least, one suspects, by the
wrestler's accountants. When the 350-pound Samoan
sumo champion Akebono got hitched in the 1990s he is
said to have picked up around $1.5 million in cash
gifts.)

According to *Mongolia Today* the Ulaan Baatar-born *rikishi* has 'won the hearts of Japanese fans with his cheerful
personality, his renderings of traditional songs and his
sniper golf strikes'. It is likely the latter is a mistranslation,
but even the minute possibility that Kyokushuzan spends
his spare time taking potshots at golfers is enough to
endear him to me.

Given the local reputation for being phlegmatic, it is
perhaps unsurprising that *Mongolia Today* rejected the
opportunity to crow about Batbayar's achievements.
Bragging, though, is certainly in order. For this is indeed a
bright age for Mongolian sumo wrestling. That January

Kyokushuzan's fellow countryman Dolgorsuren Dagvadorj, better known as Asashoryu (Blue Dragon of the Morning), was elevated to the status of *yokoza*, or grand champion, one of only two currently still active. At the year's prestigious New Year basho in Tokyo, Mongolians carried off three divisional titles, indigenous wrestlers only one. In professional sumo the Japanese outnumber the Mongolians by around 20 to 1 so that is clearly some achievement.

One factor cited as the reason for Mongolian success is their inner resolve. The life of the professional sumo wrestler is hard and it seems very few young Japanese youngsters can handle the discipline and training. Not so the Mongolians. But then, when you come from a country where temperatures can drop to −50°C and the most widely available alcoholic drink is fermented mare's milk, you learn to cope with most things.

The arrival of the Mongolians could not have come at a better time for sumo. The sport is in crisis. It has been beset by rumours of drug taking, mafia involvement and orgies. The last Japanese grand champion, Takanohana, who retired at the start of the year, stomped from one scandal to another, culminating in a series of strange public outbursts that led to accusations that he had been brainwashed by his chiropractor.

Accusations of bout rigging first surfaced in 1996, but quickly disappeared again when the two whistle-blowers, a retired wrestler and a well-known trainer, failed to show up at the press conference at which they were going to spell out their accusations. Both men had suddenly died due to what the local GP described as 'a mystery illness'. No autopsies were carried out. The involvement of Japan's feared underworld gangs, the Yakuza, was whispered, but only so quietly that nobody could hear.

Recently match fixing has again raised its head. This time the accusers have not been so conveniently silenced.

Older aficionados moan about the influx of foreigners from Russia, Brazil and Bulgaria, the bushy sideburns favoured by the younger *rikishi*, and lament the fact that there are no longer characters in the game such as Mitoizumi whose sky-high salt flinging once delighted the crowds. Ticket prices have been slashed to try and woo the public back, but still seats are empty.

US imports, such as the gigantic, recently retired Konishiki, have not always met with the approval of the Japanese who discount their fighting styles as one-dimensional – not a description often applied to somebody who weighs over 30 stone.

Born Salevaa Atisono'e (Konishiki is the fighting name given to him by the master of his sumo stable. As if to prove the Japanese have a sense of irony, it means 'Little Trophy'), Konishiki rose from humble beginnings in Hawaii to become an *ozeki*, the second highest rung on the sumo ladder, all the time fighting the kind of ingrained prejudice which saw the Japanese Sumo Association deny him the top rank of *yokozuna* because they felt that as a foreigner he didn't have the requisite dignity (though the fact that Konishiki had lately recorded a rap album with Layzie Bones from Bone Thugs-n-Harmony may count in their favour on this one).

Konishiki weighs around 600 pounds. How he gets around the globe is rarely discussed though it is a safe bet he doesn't fly economy. People with charisma, the great US sportswriter George Plimpton once noted, fill a room. The amiable, self-deprecating Konishiki does that quite literally. While other sportsmen and women answer questions about diet with cheerless talk of amino acids and metabolising carbohydrates, the man nicknamed 'The Meat Bomb' and 'The Dump Truck' simply smiles and says, 'One of the good things about sumo is you don't have to be too concerned about what you eat or drink.'

Once at a press conference after his retirement, when he was quizzed on whether he was considering shedding a few kilos now he no longer needed to keep himself in fighting trim, Konishiki replied, 'Since I retired I've been too busy to sit down and really think about losing weight.' It was an answer that drew murmurs of approval from the hall. What sounded like a ripple of applause was actually the noise of middle-aged hacks patting their stomachs.

Konishiki became a Japanese citizen. He married a Tokyo supermodel and is in big demand from the media. He hosts his own chat show, advertises everything from whisky to airlines, and has recently begun marketing his own range of clothing aimed, surprise, surprise, at the larger male. The world of sumo is still ambivalent about his legacy, however.

The Mongolians are treated differently. Asashoryu, 'The Supermarket of Tricks' and their compatriots are lighter on their feet for one thing. According to one Japanese newspaper the Mongolian wrestlers have revitalised the flagging sport with their panache, elegance and balletic poise. Apparently 'They project a nostalgic sense of wind blowing off the steppes'. It is just the breath of fresh air sumo needs.

6

'The Footless Path Has Many Leghorns'

Ulaan Baatar to Suifenhe

I had spent most of my time in Mongolia in Japan. Sometimes virtual life is like that. You log on one morning to find out quickly the capital of Sarawak and the next thing you know the house is dark, the dog is howling and the enzymes in the yoghurt in the fridge have evolved to the point where they are hunting in packs. You still don't know the capital of Sarawak, but you can now sing the theme song from *Top Cat* all the way through *and* a 1:72 scale cardboard model of the Moomin house is on its way from a gift shop in Helsinki.

It happened to me all the time. I'd go into my office to find information about child-friendly hotels in Sweden and when I came back out hours later Catherine would say, 'So, did you find anything nice?' And I'd say, 'You bet I did. Santiago Canizares, the goalkeeper for the Spanish national football team, is going to miss the World Cup after he injured his foot by dropping a bottle of aftershave on it. An incident which, I have to say, is a rather stylish Latin version of the famous one involving Southampton goalie Dave "Lurch" Beasant who suffered similar damage when a jar of salad cream slipped from his grasp. England's netminder David Seaman has so far escaped bottle-related injury, but he did miss several matches this season after damaging a shoulder while trying to land a 28-pound carp.'

And Catherine would say, 'So we'll take the tent, shall we?'

Ulaan Baatar railway station had the fascia of a Victorian library. Behind it lurked concrete cuboids in various shades of grey, from sickly to terminal. The platforms were as wide and empty as the steppes, bereft even of a place to sit, never mind a vending machine dispensing peanuts in a variety of ill-advised flavours. The train to Russia arrived with a creak and wheeze reminiscent of an elderly manatee sitting on a concertina. Romantically numbered after the Soviet pattern, it was painted olive drab with bilious yellow seams and crimson cornicing. The interiors were no less inspiring.

I travelled north in a second-class compartment with what was becoming the regulation agglomeration of Prozac hustlers, Peace Corps volunteers and retired suburban train buffs called Reginald who had spent a lifetime severely underestimating the value of silence. There were also several dozen exchange student bloggers, easily recognisable by their well-rehearsed arguments attacking globalisation, Vietnamese-made Californian humour T-shirts, their tales of wild nights in the Irish pubs of South-East Asia and their Norwegian backpacks so stuffed with noxious laundry that a blue flame permanently burned above them.

Not, I might add, that my own clothing was in a much better state. I had travelled 3000 miles in the same underpants. When I took them off at night it sounded like a hungry man opening a bag of crisps.

I was pleased to see that most, if not all, of the students had absorbed an important lesson I learned during my own student days. When visiting a restaurant or café back during those days of penury I would always make sure to spill plenty of food down the front of my shirt or jumper. In times of nutritional shortage I then simply had to bring the top to the boil in a pint or so of water to create a nourishing bouillon. For most of us this would be a stop-gap. But I believe there are IT professionals who have developed the technique to such a degree that they can live off a hooded sweatshirt for three months or more.

According to the local administration the autonomous Russian republic of Buryatia 'covers an area of 351.3 square kilometres, roughly the same as Germany'. Either this figure is a misprint or somebody has been lying to the government about the size of the Bundesrepublic.

The tiny country of Buryatia snuggles in a friendly cleft between boggy taiga and rolling flats. The paradoxical Lake Baikal, which washes the republic's northern threshold, is the oldest, biggest and deepest freshwater lake on earth. It is the bottomless udder upon which Siberia suckles and nurtures a peculiar culture that teeters on the cusp of East and West.

We chuntered on through the wild mosaic of the Siberian countryside, where fudge and white cows nuzzled amongst larchy vegetation that was raked by troughs, capped by snowy tops, veined by sweetwaters and freckled with pineries. The climate is sharply continental. In Buryatia the sun like the diamond is not niggardly with his sparkling fire. There are three hundred sunny days a year. Predictably, when I alighted at Ulan Ude, it was raining.

The capital of Buryatia is calm and mellow. Rich with nature and recreational opportunities it is a hidden jewel and likely to remain so. Traces of primitive people are everywhere while breeds frozen for many years are evenly distributed. The city was founded by Cossacks – who certainly weren't Kazakhs, in all probability. They arrived in the middle of the sixteenth century, set up *ostrogs* and began demanding *yassack* from the locals. In such a way the indigenous races and the immigrants lived side by side in cheerful incomprehension for many centuries, until the Soviets arrived and set them to work building helicopter gunships.

The single largest ethnic group in Buryatia are the Buryats. The Buryats are a Mongol people. They have canny nut-coloured eyes, stocky chops, sturdy pins and extremely furry hands. They work hard at extracting ores and apatites from base rock, fur craft, forage processing and knitting cosies. The vast majority of them have never heard the Gospel preached in a culturally relevant way. Horns are never given to the butting cow.

I made my bed in a grand hotel of sombre disquiet. It was the sort of place where I guessed the lifts jerked and rattled like break-dancing skeletons, the plumbing needed renewing and so did the odours. The windows were as opaque as a smoker's cough. The TV was a blinded Cyclops. The sheets fidgeted. Hunchbacked staff interpreted 'service' in the agricultural sense and flinched from eye contact as if fearing disease. I demanded *yassack*, but had to make do with an empty mini-bar that emitted zombie groans in the small hours. There were hotels in Ulan Ude of considerably more elegance and charm, but where was the fun in that?

After slapping the bed linen with a towel until it ceased to twitch I took a stroll about the city. My walk took me past a Korean car dealership, the Sputnik supermarket, which boasted 'we work daily without interruption for dinner' and offered a comprehensive range of cosmetics, household tools, head hats and notions, and a shopping centre of brick where birch-bark souvenirs were proffered in abundance. The citizenry, ancients and baby-dwellers alike, were a happy breed much given to celebration and ballet. After loitering o'er long in the decorative home arts section of the Buryat Republican Art Museum, I took my ease on a restaurant terrace where I dined acceptably on endemic fish and dried fruit. The local Aquaburs mineral water was an uplifting tonic. Energised, I speculated about the local nightlife, concluding that it was probably bats.

The next morning I visited Ulan Ude's main square. At one edge, at the entrance to a steep, cobbled street the world's largest capitate of Lenin, measuring fully 60 feet from beard tip to balding crown, stood like a bowling ball at the top of the chute. Nearby a crowd of lady Old Believers in ankle-length crimson skirts banded with vivid hoops of untold colours gathered around food stalls determinedly munching US chicken drumsticks. The Russians had got a taste for American chicken thanks to the food aid programme of George Bush senior. They called them Bush's leglets and ate $600 million worth a year. Mindful of the damage the importation of a billion cheap poultry shanks was doing to the balance of payments, Vladimir Putin had recently tried to ban them on health grounds. According to the Russian Agriculture Minister, the US poultry contained growth hormones, antibiotics and salmonella. 'Russia is not a dumping ground for poor quality food,' he said, information that would come as a surprise to many visitors.

Twisting and dancing about the legs of the chicken

munchers were numerous curly tailed dogs. These were the indigenous Siberian breeds of samoyed, husky and laika. They had been used for sled pulling and reindeer herding around these parts since records began, and possibly before wax cylinders too. They were stocky, bustling hounds with thick fluffy coats and eager, grinning faces. Everything about them, from their forthright stance to their sparkly eyes, suggested they were getting a real belt out of life and were eager for the next round of hi-energy capers. Their owners looked exhausted. 'Husky-type breeds get bored easily,' dog experts warned sternly, 'and a bored husky causes a lot of damage.'

The most famous laika of all time was Laika, the Space Dog. Laika wasn't actually a thoroughbred laika. She was a crossbreed in which laika predominated. She wasn't a Laika either. Her real name was Kudryanka ('Little Curly'), but Westerners muddled her breed type with her name so frequently and with such determination that eventually the new moniker stuck. Laika was found wandering the streets of Moscow and was made part of a trio of cosmo-canines with fellow strays Albina and Mushka.

The first animal into space had been a rhesus monkey named Albert who'd been fired into the stratosphere in a modified V2 rocket in New Mexico in 1948. The Americans would go on using monkeys throughout the early years of the space race, but the Soviets always favoured dogs. By the time Laika began her astronaut training nine other mongrels had already been on non-orbital flights. Some had made it back safely, others had died and some, such as Bobik ('Big Bull'), had escaped into the forests surrounding the launch site and never been seen again.

On 3 November 1957 'experimental dog' Laika was

placed into her compartment in Sputnik 2 and launched into outer space. She became the first creature to orbit the earth and world-famous. At the time the Russians claimed she had happily circled the planet for a week, feeding on jellied food and barking at the occasional passing asteroid before dying peacefully when gas was pumped into her cell as part of a prearranged and humane plan.

Sadly this turns out to have been a bit of a fib. A former Soviet scientist who worked on the space programme recently revealed that in fact poor old Laika, unwitting hero of the Revolution, died within a few hours of blastoff from a combination of terror and overheating. Horrible though this is, it is hard to know whether it was a worse fate than that which was planned for her – revolving around our small blue planet, lonely and confused as she watched her weightless urine floating about like amoeba. Some of the Russian scientists who worked on the project obviously feel the same way. In 1998 one of them, Dr Oleg Gazenko, confessed, 'The more time passes the more sorry I feel about it. We did not learn enough from the mission to justify killing that dog.'

Laika's space coffin spun around the planet 2570 times before it burned up in the earth's atmosphere on 14 April 1958. There will now be a short intermission while I blow my nose.

The Trans-Siberian Express from Moscow arrived at Ulan Ude station just before nine o'clock. It disgorged visitors from Irkutsk. Irkutsk billed itself as 'The Paris of Siberia'. Given Siberia's reputation this was a self-defeating claim, like announcing yourself to be the Nicole Kidman of Tellytubbyland, or the least belligerent man in Serbia.

On board families who had been cooped up together

for five days played fractious games of Monopoly, army guys swigged vodka and tried to forget Chechnya, and the conductors passed up and down the corridors distributing tea and sensual squeezes to new arrivals. I took my place in a second-class compartment with a woman from Tomsk who was travelling to Beijing to swap poodles for silk. She wanted the silk to sell in her shop. What the Chinese wanted the poodles for I didn't inquire.

The other passengers in the compartment were a middle-aged couple. They were both in a state of mortal drunkenness. I had noticed the man in a previous photograph. He was walking down the station platform with his feet wide apart, sailor-style, as if bracing himself against a swell. His face was roughly shaven, he had watery eyes and a smirk that said, 'I'm plastered, but I'm getting away with it'.

His partner, by contrast, was one of those jolly drunks whose unabashed attitude towards inebriation comes from believing that being rat-arsed is a state to which all mankind aspires and that he or she is therefore currently the envy of sober people across the globe.

The two of them had collapsed on to seats like a couple of crows landing in a gale and were deep in conversation. I had no idea what they were saying so I had to dub them. The woman said, 'So, when we get in, what d'you want to eat, Russian or Turkic?'

The man tilted his head to one side: 'I'm not sure I'm in a fit state to answer a question of that magnitude,' he said. 'Well, put it this way,' his partner continued, 'you're on Death Row, right? And it's the night before your execution and you can have whatever you want for your final meal. Do you pick beef stroganoff or shish kebab?'

The man pondered this for a while. 'It's hard to say. I

mean, it would depend what mood I'm in, wouldn't it?'
The woman rolled her eyes and cackled. 'You're being
executed in twelve hours,' she said, her voice rising. 'What
kind of mood do you think you'd be in? You'd be
depressed, wouldn't you?'

The man smiled his secretive smile. 'Not necessarily,' he
said, 'I could be pleased . . .'

'They're going to tie a noose round your neck, stick a
bag over your head and drop you through a trapdoor,' the
woman roared. 'How can you be pleased?' The man held
up a finger, wagging it triumphantly. 'I could be pleased,
right, because death, painful though it may be, will free
me from the infinitely worse torture of the guilt I feel for
my horrendous crimes.' He smiled again. Impressed with
himself.

The woman was resilient. 'And what if you'd been convicted of something you *didn't* do?' she asked.

'Well, then I'd be fucking depressed, obviously.'

'All right,' the woman cried, 'so let's take that as the sce-
nario, right? Do you choose Russian or Turkic?' 'Are we
having a drink first?' the man said.

The train crossed the Khilok River, a swirling thor-
oughfare on which rafts transported salt and nuts from the
water-filled bellybutton of Baikal to the foothills of
Manchuria. In the surrounding terrain opulent ruby-red
cowberries ripened in the sun, while orange lilies and the
pink flowers of rhododendrons bobbed in the breezes.
Amongst the cedar trees nervous musk deer and suicidal
lemmings sheltered and the Siberian sable quivered whenever paintbrushes were mentioned. The landscape was
dotted with nature reserves and prison camps.

One species of local rhododendron had been named in
honour of its discoverer, Baron von Ungern-Sternberg.

The botanist's son was also to make an indelible mark on local history, though in ways more florid than floral. Baron Roman von Ungern-Sternberg is perhaps better known as 'The Mad Baron of Mongolia'. Born in the Gulf of Finland towards the end of the nineteenth century, Ungern-Sternberg was a small-brained, megalomaniac sadist. In normal circumstances there would have been little choice for him in life than to marry an Austrian princess. Fortunately the Russian Revolution spared some poor girl that awful fate. The baron had no military knowledge, refused to budge without consulting his personal shaman and was plainly a lunatic. As far as the White Russians were concerned this was more of a boon than a handicap to a military career and he quickly rose to the rank of major-general in Semanov's army. In 1920 he led the Asiatic Cavalry Division – a motley crew of Tibetans, Cossacks and Buryats, most of whom were actually on foot – into Mongolia, defeated the Chinese garrison, butchered the inhabitants and pro-claimed himself Emperor of Russia. Ungern-Sternberg declared that he would build a line of gallows from Ulaan Baatar to Moscow and hang the Bolsheviks from them. He invaded, was beaten back, his own men attempted to assassinate him with a heavy machine gun, he galloped off and ran straight into the Red Army who finished the job. The man who rides a calf will never reach camp.

Sixty-four per cent of Chitinskaya Oblast in eastern Siberia is forest. There are only 2.9 people per square kilometre. Most of them are huddled together in hamlets of nicotine-coloured wooden shacks, where old folk sit on benches staring toothlessly at passing locomotives and shoe-hungry children fill aluminium pales with water from the local well. The more I looked from the window the more I recalled Chekhov's words: the traveller through Siberia, he said, felt himself gradually eaten alive by the landscape. What I could feel oozing into the train from the dismal landscape was not so much a slough of despond as an entire urban Berkshire of despair. Luckily, at that moment a perky American named Barbara popped up and offered me the chance to advance my personal CV with an instant degree from a prestigious non-accredited university based on my current qualifications and experience. Barbara showed me the details of the scheme. I told her I felt its credibility was undermined by a failure to spell intellectual correctly. She took it *baldly*.

I alighted from the train at Chita, capital of Chitinskaya and a place of clapboarded buildings and clapped-out vehicles. Unemployment was high, money was tight, the city looked the worse for wear and so did most of the population. It was reported in the local press that gangs from Chitinskaya had been riding across the border into Mongolia on horseback, brandishing AK47s and stealing cattle. I have no wish to endorse criminal behaviour, but somehow I couldn't help but find the news that there was still a place for mounted, rifle-toting rustlers in the world hugely gratifying. Chita is twinned with Boise, Idaho.

I stayed in the Panama City Motel, a comely cluster of wooden dachas in shades of Dufy blue. The staff were keen to show me traditional Siberian hospitality. Having read *One Day in the Life of Ivan Denisovich*, I politely declined.

I visited the old timber church that housed the Decembrist Museum. The Decembrists were a secret society of Russian army officers who had fought against Napoleon and absorbed some of France's revolutionary ideals along the way. In 1825, seizing the opportunity created by uncertainty following the death of Alexander I, they led a revolt in St Petersburg. According to the Decembrists the ruling elite of Russia were stupid, backward and half-baked. Unfortunately the Decembrists' own rebellion pretty much confirmed this opinion. Disorganised and shambolic, it lasted less than twenty-four hours before forces loyal to the newly crowned Tsar Nicholas suppressed it. To add to the prevailing wind of imbecility, the authorities' attempt to execute the main ringleader turned to farce when the rope snapped and he ended up breaking a leg instead of his neck. 'In this country,' he quipped acidly, 'we can't even hang a man properly.'

Another 120 of the Decembrists were deported. Eighty-five of them ended up in Chita. Amongst them was Pauline Gebel, a young woman of rare beauty to whom Alexandre Dumas dedicated his novel *The Fencing Master*. The exiles gave a boost to the local scene and set Chita on a path as a hotbed of revolt. In 1905 the city, prompted by the Japanese, who had just taken on the Russians at Port Arthur and, to borrow a phrase from Hunter S. Thompson, thrashed them like a red-headed stepchild, rebelled against the House of Romanov and declared itself a republic. The Tsar's troops arrived soon afterwards and, smarting from their reverses at the hands of 'The Prussia of the East', handed out a few hidings of their own. The Buryats' involvement with the Mad Baron also ended badly.

After a meal of hand-held mutton and Siberian Legend beer, I returned to my motel. A visitor might interpret the anaemic look of Chita's population as a sign of bad diet, lack of sunlight and the ravages of strong drink, but that is only because they have never left the cabin door open at night and then switched the light on. A split second after doing so the mosquitoes appear.

The Siberian mosquito is not to be confused with any other variety. It is a beast of an entirely different stamp. It comes towards its victim at high speed, humming the theme from *Top Gun*. It is so big the locals hunt it with hounds and shotguns. Its proboscis is a depleted-uranium-tipped smart weapon capable of locating a vein through layers of clothing, its body a suction pump. If the Siberians look bloodless it's because they are. Chekhov had talked of Siberia eating a person alive psychologically, emotionally and spiritually. These bastards did it literally.

I had watched the shaking alcoholics appearing in the cafés of Ulan Ude for their vodka breakfasts with some pity. But considering how awful it would be to find myself swatting at my attackers with the frantic and futile determination of a Sunday tennis player receiving serve from Pete Sampras, I could see that the drunks enjoyed one advantage at least over the sober. When a mosquito drained an armful from one of them, they at least had the pleasure of watching it swirling tipsily about the room before crashing in a Peckinpah-esque splatter of gore against wall or window.

The next day, looking pale and uninteresting, I breakfasted on salted *omul* and Pivka Sport, the award-winning energy drink from the Krasnoyarsk brewery, before boarding the Trans-Manchurian Express southbound for Harbin, hub of China's alpine ski industry. The journey took me through the autonomous *okrug* of Aginskiy Buryatskiy, about which information was coming soon.

I alighted at Mogoytuy and took a ramshackle Yaz through prairies of bashful dianthus, tender saxifrage and brash delphiniums to the capital of Aginskoye (pop. 9300) where Buddhist lamas in wine-dark robes commenced a low and rumbling chant and girls in shimmering dresses swayed like the flowers of the steppes. Aginskoye has a rich gold deposit and a rotary club.

The rest of the train journey through Siberia was catatonically tedious. An endless vista of moribund forest and soggy dell interrupted by garrison towns and nuclear missile facilities. I attempted to interest myself in reports that the County Roscommon Gaelic Football Club had been disbanded after the players were caught on CCTV cameras playing pool naked in a Derry hotel (insert your own eight-ball joke here), but to little avail.

At Zabaikalsk on the Sino-Russian border we walked through customs and into Inner Mongolia, while the train had its bogies changed to fit the different gauge Chinese track.

Manzhouli is a bright jewel in the golden crown of the People's Republic of China. Through history it has been known by many names including 'Pearl of the Grassland', 'Place of the Wild Leek' and Lubin. It is the only city in China with mounted policemen.

For thousands of years Manzhouli had been a no-account burg, regularly batted back and forth between China, Russia, Mongolia and Japan. In 1992, however, its fortunes changed. In that year Manzhouli had been named one of China's four open-border cities. Premier Deng had flung wide the window to free trade and a fresh spring breeze had blown in, filling the lungs of the local population. 'Diligence is the foundation of development' was the phrase on every citizen's lips as they worked twenty-four hours a day trading waste steel, refining potato starch, milling garnet sand or proudly busying themselves at the largest wood-importing plant in China.

The city was now the PRC's key land port on the European-Pacific land bridge. Its streets thronged with vehicles of various propulsion systems, its pavements lively with many-skinned folk, its air tickled ecstatically by a multiplicity of tongues. The Manchurian menfolk wore gaudy sailor hats. Their moustaches were long and drooping largely because the sleeves on their gowns were so long it was impossible for them to shave. The women kept themselves to themselves.

Occupying fully 10 square kilometres, the Sino-Russian Exchange Market was the hub of all pecuniary interchange. Here Han, Hui, Korean and Daur bartered and tiffed, while white-faced Russians scoured the flourishing scene in search of *kuai*. Manzhouli is 13,116 kilometres from Los Angeles.

Inner Mongolia is China's biggest producer of ice cream. I bought myself one and then hired a rickshaw, travelling as far as his elastic-band legs would allow. Manzhouli's surrounding countryside was remarkable, a vast green plain, sliced in two by a serpentine river. At nearby Hulan Lake bovine carp jumped and reeds rustled. There were seventy types of wind birds, many wild economic vegetables and frequent greenhouses. For the nature lover it was a place to submerge in a mirage of misty thoughts, while for the businessman the region was a fairyland of oilfields, coal seams and precious deposits. Truly could I say that this was a boundless land in economic balance.

The rail journey south from Manzhouli was not without hazards. Three hundred millimetres of rain had fallen in sectors of Fujian Province and the line between

Nanpingnan and Yangdanzai had been blocked by tons of soil and boulders. In Heilongjiang Province, meanwhile, an avalanche of redundant workers from a bankrupt state-owned textile plant had washed on to the tracks protesting that redundancy pay of $25 a month was not enough. The Chinese authorities were reported to be clearing up one of the blocked lines using pickaxes and dynamite. How they were getting rid of the rocks and mud I didn't hear.

Undeterred, the train passed through groves of camphor trees, glades of tower blocks and the city of Hailar, renowned for its medium-density fibreboard. Travel is a dangerous business, as many travel writers before me have eagerly pointed out, in detail and often with a degree of accuracy. Some have almost been bitten by snakes, one or two have got frighteningly close to being menaced by distant squirrels, a number have heard pirates spoken of in cocktail bars and at least one has come perilously close to getting his head jammed in the Grand Canyon. Clearly, when it came to jeopardy my own journey was as nothing compared to those of the many brave wordsmiths who have battled across the Andes mounted on a saddle-backed hog, paddled up the Orinoco in a vol-au-vent case, or floated across the Red Sea under a balloon filled with their own hot air, yet it would not do to underplay the genuine menace that at times fired a warning shot across my bows.

One such incident, which still stalks my dreams, occurred just outside Zalantun. While waiting for some pictures of red-necked phalaropes to download, I had gone to open a tin of ground Italian coffee and noticed just in the nick of time that the inner rim was extraordinarily sharp and jagged. Clearly, had I absent-mindedly run my finger round it while the Mocha Express was coming to the boil and I was listening out for the football scores, a nasty cut could have resulted, one which, should I have had a family history of haemophilia and not been able to call an ambulance due to some unspecified problem with the local telephone system, might have led to a very serious situation indeed. By luck and my own preternatural instinct for survival I got through, but several hours later, when the full weight of the calamity that might have been dawned on me, my legs turned to jelly, my teeth began to chatter and I had to lay my head in the lap of a diminutive Ewenk pensioner and beg to be comforted with hair stroking and soft-voiced tales of how Borhan chose the names of the months and the camel became jealous of the rat and danced in ashes.

A few moments later, after the kindly old Ewenk gentleman had alerted the security guards, they arrived and, in their roughly concerned way, dragged me to a different compartment slapping me vigorously to calm my nerves. I paid them handsomely for their counselling and their families and their colleagues too.

Soon after, darkness began to creep unbidden across this antique land. I dozed beneath a coverlet of horsehair and sweet Chinese red wine, occasionally peeping from the window at the Daqing oilfields where the pumping engines rocked back and forward like devout believers at Friday prayer and every fence, hedge and tree was supported by a buttress of plastic carrier bags.

Daqing held a special place in the history of Chinese communism. It was here in 1960 that Mao Zedong had launched the big push to make the People's Republic self-sufficient in energy. Seventy thousand tons of equipment and forty thousand workers had poured into the area to bore for oil. Amongst them was Zwang Jinxi, leader of drill team number 1205. In temperatures that fell as low as −30°C, Zwang and his crew worked flat out until, after five days, they struck the first major well in what was to become the nation's biggest oil reserve. Zwang's endeavours earned him the nickname 'Iron Man Wang'. He was raised to the status of revolutionary hero, or, as the Chinese Communist Party preferred to style it in their pithy fashion, 'object of the official emulation movement'. He joined such figures as Canadian thoracic surgeon Norman Bethune and Chen Yonggui, mastermind behind the Dazhai collective farm Iron Girls' peasant worker teams. Wang featured on millions of posters, teeth gleaming in a manner that suggested long-term use of cabamide peroxide whitening gel and something shaggy on his head that was either a fur hat or an inspiration to Mötley Crüe's hairstylist.

In Daqing City (which billed itself under the none too reassuring strapline 'Super large in size, empty in the middle!') I went and had a look at Wang's statue. After the oilfields Wang carried on working and battling against the elements, class enemies, erroneous ideas and those cow monsters, snake demons and clowns that were entrenched in ideological and cultural positions. Unfortunately he couldn't get the better of the biggest revisionist of them all and died of cancer in 1970. There had been other red heroes since, not least Zang Hua, a medical student who was suffocated by fumes while rescuing a peasant from a manure pit in 1982, but somehow I couldn't help feeling that when it came to the official emulation movement there just weren't the characters in the game any more.

Harbin was known as the Ice City. It was the coldest place in China and spent an inordinate amount of time trying to persuade the International Olympic Committee to let it host a Winter Games. I had come hoping for Chinese après-ski. I imagined mulled rice wine and an owl fondue, but it turned out the ski resort was actually 200 miles away. I had to make do with a meal in a national duck restaurant and a glass of fizzy beer that tasted of zinc. Afterwards I relaxed at a resort villa where staff and guests communicated in the international language of billiards and karaoke.

'It was once said "If the Chinese took up skiing they would win an Olympic medal",' one of my fellow guests informed me joyously, 'And now we have taken up skiing!' Whoever had said that had probably been under the impression that China would produce a winner simply because of the conflation of the huge population and the law of averages. In China, though, they tended not to leave things so much to chance, as had been evinced by their swimmers. At the World Championships in Australia vials of HGH had been found in one Chinese competitor's luggage, another had tested positive for a steroid masking agent and a member of the freestyle squad had been discovered to be a bottle-nosed dolphin. She would have got away with it too if a crafty Australian official hadn't held a fish up above the pool during the second length.

Harbin had once been one of China's most cosmopolitan places and the main thoroughfares were a veritable museum of European architectural styles ranging from Byzantine church to Rotterdam shopping precinct. Nowadays the city was celebrated for its annual winter festival of ice sculpture. This featured the world's largest man-made ice and snow garden, a 120-metre-long ice model of the Great Wall of China and several thousand ice lanterns that Harbin's senior ice lantern consultant assured me were 'the best in the world'. Luckily it was June.

Instead I travelled in a horse-drawn carriage and upon an Austrian-style gondola. I visited the Flood Control Memorial Tower and the Second Ring Highway of Harbin, which, I was told, is not just something to look at but also serves a function. The Pearl Museum was of more than passing interest. Along with their use in jewellery it demonstrated how pearls had been used in medicine, and not just to treat engorgement of the wallet. Pearls, it seemed, could be dissolved and then drunk by people in need of boosts in calcium, or used to treat acid stomachs. They were also thought to be an aphrodisiac. This reminded me of how Cleopatra, when presented with a black pearl by some suitor or other, had dissolved it in a glass of wine and slugged it back in one gulp. The Egyptian queen's action is usually seen as proof that she was wanton and voluptuous, but to my mind the only thing it really shows is how bloody awful the wine must have been in those days. I mean, what kind of wine dissolves stones? 'Parafino, the Italian Chardonnay that makes rocks melt.' It's hardly an advertising slogan, is it? I tried to find out more details, but putting 'Cleopatra black pearl' into the search engine produced precious little information about Ptolemaic Egypt and rather more than I needed to know about nipple jewellery and clear-crystal clit clamps.

The train for Vladivostok left promptly on Wednesdays. It took me to Mudanjiang. Here wooden tongue depressors, grinding tools and rubber goods attracted interest, but the major tourist attraction was the engine repair shops, where thirty steam locomotives a month were bashed back into working order. Here hordes of camcorder-wielding men from Solihul and Kansas City eagerly recorded the clunks, bangs and hisses and the air was filled with talk of tender locos, good noise, well-kept Y222 rakes, tidy 35Y yards and the promise of live steam action in the Jing Peng Pass.

Live steam action of an entirely different stamp was probably available in the border town of Suifenhe if you looked for it. Suifenhe was an obscure point on the global trade map, but that didn't seem to bother the locals. The place had the atmosphere of an Old West boomtown without the wholesome scent of horse manure. The air was 35 per cent alcohol by volume and so full of wild hormones even the clouds had sprung breasts. You could get pissed and pregnant just by taking a deep breath. Sizeable Russian clusters, unbuckled by the delight of discovering the only country on the planet that made them feel rich and wasn't a long-haul flight away, reeled up and down the lanes and alleys throttling the last remaining life out of soul classics Michael Bolton had left for dead and snogging one another when the vodka ran out. Chinese women with tattooed eyebrows and make-up so thick it wasn't so much pancake as pizza offered translation services and waved fake negative AIDS test certificates. The whole place was so sleazy it made Berlin during the Weimar look like Salt Lake City during the Osmonds. When a barber in Suifenhe offered customers something for the weekend he meant two teenage opium fiends and a trained snake. I stayed at the Economic and Trade Mansion. The economics were of the madhouse, the trade rough, the mansion so unsettlingly murderous I suspected the 'I' was a misprint. Still, I felt at home. After all, as the Chinese say, the lips of the donkey do not fit on the horse's mouth.

7

'Lots of Twelve-inches Build a Course'

Suifenhe to Okinawa

Vladivostok. If there was anywhere on earth that sounded more Russian I couldn't think of it. Vladivostok. The very name conjured forth visions of springing Cossacks, choirs of Volga boatmen and rows of mummified, tarantula-browed generals standing on a dais in the snow staring blankly at passing missiles. To my mind Vladivostok was to Russia what Don King is to big-haired American bull-shit. It was the acme, the pinnacle. It was also, I was told by numerous experienced visitors, the pits.

I found this to be a harsh judgement. True, the place had been battered by the ill-winds of economic collapse; the main local industries were fish gutting and logging, the major export wood chippings and a popular local snack was sour pork belly fat. And I acknowledge that the local government changed so regularly the mayor's office was fitted with a revolving door, the trams were on strike on odd days of the week and the power shut down whenever two households attempted to watch TV and boil the kettle at the same time. Certainly the summers were wet, the winters brutal, the city frequently sacked by cyclones. All right, the citizens were 4000 miles from Moscow and the nearest capital city was Pyongyang. Okay, you were advised not to get in a taxi if there was another passenger already in it, or to get on crowded buses, or to spend too much money in a single shop in case your spree should alert loitering muggers. Of course, my hotel offered a security guard hire service and recommended I eat at a restaurant called Kapitan Kuk that served Australian ram ribs and Fosters lager. And, yes, I admit there was a puppet theatre, but all this aside Vladivostok still seemed worthy of a place in the pantheon of romantic distant destinations you just might visit one day if you won the lottery. After all, how many cities boast a music festival called Vladirockstock?

Vladivostok means 'Possess the East'. Unesco has listed it as one of the world's ten most prospective cities and sea romance veils its fantastic delights. Many travellers have tried to capture the port's charms by comparing it with other great anchorages. Vladivostok, it has been said, is like Naples without Vesuvius or San Francisco without the Golden Gate. To my mind it was more like Gothenburg without the meatballs.

I spent my first morning at the Oceanarium, a floating fish well that was home to fur seals, white whales and a school of gleeful porpoises. I think I could guess what lay behind their exuberance.

The Soviet military had once employed a large number of dolphins and white whales. Then, when the USSR fell apart, the funding ran out and the redundant mammals were sold off. Most of the navy whales and porpoises were part of Sevastopol's prestigious Black Sea Dolphin Division. They had been trained in the main by a former submariner named Boris Zhurid for a variety of tasks, some so bizarre as to be barely credible. Most of them were used for locating mines and retrieving stray torpedoes, but some were taught to attack enemy frogmen with harpoons, or with a dart that pumped CO_2 into their adversary until he exploded. The elite group – the, as it were, Navy SEALS of porpoises – had actually undergone a course in parachuting, the idea apparently being to drop them into enemy waters to recover or destroy secret military hardware. Under expert tutelage the dolphins had learned to skydive from 10,000 feet, or to free-fall from helicopters hovering above the sea.

Another group were programmed for something even more dangerous than this. They were trained to attack enemy ships or submarines (they could recognise them by the propeller noise) with explosive charges attached to their heads. They were kamikaze porpoises. If the dolphins at Vladivostok were jumping through hoops a little more brightly than was normal it could just have been the relief of escaping from a suicide mission.

After the Oceanarium I delved into the city's rich heritage, visiting a submarine, the Hall of the Seamen's Culture Palace and admiring the pollack catch at the fish quay. Later I dined in a waterfront restaurant on marine souvenir salad washed down with Zolotoy Yakor beer. The decor was Korean Middle Earth.

I detoured on my way back to the hotel to pass the offices of the Far East Shipping Company. The grandfather of Yul Brynner had once owned FESCO and the future King of Siam himself had been born in the house that now formed part of their headquarters.

I am a great fan of Yul Brynner, not least for his performance in *The Magnificent Seven* in which he takes on a horde of Mexicans lead by Eli Wallach's Calvera. It is a measure of Calvera's sadistic cruelty that throughout the entire movie he spares the life of Horst Buchholz. Yet Brynner is unfazed, despite the fact he is approaching the task with three major disadvantages. Firstly, he and the gang are outnumbered by 10 to 1; secondly, the village they are protecting has no natural defensive features except for some irritating mariachi music; and, thirdly, and most worryingly, his character is named Chris. Unless there is a B film in which Victor Mature plays a gunslinger from Tombstone called Trevor, Christopher is surely the worst name ever for a six-shooter-toting Old West tough guy.

It would not be so bad for Christopher if the rest of The Seven was made up of hired guns named Nigel, Colin and Gordon. But, no, he finds himself surrounded by Vin, Lee, Britt and Chico. You sense at any moment they are going to start teasing him. That they don't is down to Brynner's awesome charisma and air of command. That and the fact that his baldy head keeps distracting them.

The next day was Monday. After a breakfast of international standard I went down to the passenger quay to catch the ferry to Japan. Unfortunately it had sailed on Saturday. There was supposed to be another one in a week, but nobody was confident. 'Schedule subject to change without notice' warned a declaration above the timetable. 'Sailings dependent upon cargo' cautioned another. There were other ferries to Japan from various parts of Primorsky Province but the running times were just as debatable.

Had I been a regular traveller I would have been trapped in Vladivostok. I would have gradually had my spirit crushed by the Siberian vastness. I would have

ended up loitering around in internet cafés with pot-
bellied geeks with crumbs in their wispy beards who
introduced themselves as Tanya, teenage nymphette eager
for experience. I might have found work on the local
English-language newspaper writing headlines about child
abuse, heroin addiction and the fact that Primorye was
now self-sufficient in potatoes, melons and gourds. I could
have contracted a persistent irritating cough and, mindful
of the high local TB rates, been seized with panic when
one day over lunch in Pizzaland I sputtered into my
hankie and noticed flecks of red in my sputum. I might
have sat in Vladivostok's hospitals listening to the metro-
nomic bleep of life support systems and morphine-crazed
yelps of terminal patients, only to be informed by a doctor
with the staring, saucer eyes of a troglodyte that tests
revealed no sign of blood but considerable evidence of
tomato, onion, oregano and pepperoni. Had I really been
there all this might have happened, but since I was only
virtually there I had another choice. I could simply delete
two days of notes, arrive forty-eight hours earlier, catch
that 18.00 ferry for Fushiki and still have time to explore
the GUM shopping centre.

And so it was. Unfortunately this means that I will not
be able to tell you about my train journey from Suifenhe
with a group of Chinese oldsters who were going to Russia
on their bi-weekly forage for mushrooms, ginseng and
frogs. Or of the moment at the border in Grodekovo
when the Yantar-1 control system detected a Manchurian
cobalt-sponge platinum trader whose body was emitting
five hundred times the permitted level of radiation. Nor,
I'm afraid, will you hear of how, on arrival in Ussuriysk, I
discovered that a man-eating Siberian tiger had killed
three hunters in the region and might have menaced me

too had I got there a mere five years sooner. The story of what happened when I pressed 'Click Here' for my chance to win 50 pounds of lobster will also have to wait. But then that, like Conan Doyle's Giant Rat of Sumatra, is a tale for which the world is not yet ready.

It was a tough decision, but as I stood on the deck of the MV *Antonina Nezhdanova* with the briny breeze slapping my face like an insulted fop, I knew it was the correct one. We slipped out into the Eastern Bosphrous at nightfall. The music of the port cooed a melodic adieu and the sparkling nimbus of the harbour lights bade lambent farewell until someone in Aleutskaya Street plugged in a hairdryer and plunged the city into darkness.

The FESCO ferry was a grumbling leviathan with creature comforts that were still at the cold-blooded stage of evolution. Better a diamond with a flaw than a pebble with none, however. And, besides, the blustering engines did their job, propelling us through a poppling slush of spawning firefly squid and out into the ———. The ——— had formerly been known as the Sea of Japan but lately there had been moves to drop the name in the face of hostility from North and South Korea (hatred of the Japanese being the only thing upon which the respective governments could agree). The Koreans called the sea that lay between them, Russia and Japan the East Sea, claiming the Sea of Japan tag illustrated Tokyo's arrogance and continued sense of superiority. The Japanese countered by producing documentary evidence suggesting that it was eighteenth-century Italian missionaries who had first named the Sea of Japan, not them. The Koreans responded with maps showing that the sea had previously been known as the Sea of Korea, Sea of China and the Oriental Sea. 'The Korean Government,' said a spokesman from the South Korean information ministry, 'deems it inappropriate to name the sea after just one country because it is historically unjustified and causes discord.'

The Japanese Maritime Institute responded huffily: 'The situation is ridiculous. Imagine if Madagascar suddenly declared that the Indian Ocean should be called the Madagascan Ocean.'

To try and pacify both sides, the International Hydrophonic Bureau proposed that on future maps the sea should not be named at all. Personally I thought they could have done something more positive. Renaming the sea the Getalife Straits, for example.

We arrived in Japan just after dawn on Monday. The port of Fushiki, a vague outline of flare stacks, oil tanks and hardcore breakwaters, slumbered beneath an early morning sky the colour of a tramp's vest. A dark clump in the background could have been mountains or the hovering fug above a distant city. Fushiki is a minuscule metropolis that has taken on the central role in handling Japan's burgeoning second-hand car trade with Russia. Dealing with passengers is an afterthought, which probably explains why the customs post and passport control was located amongst the optics, soda hoses and stale beery whiff of a lounge bar.

The Russians had travelled to Japan for one purpose only – to buy up as many second-hand electrical good as they could get their hands on and then scarper back to Siberia before the Japanese cost of living could raze their life savings. The local population, whose spirit and financial ability blossomed under the sea scent, were mindful of this fact and celebrated the arrival of the Russian ship by clearing out their attics and their garages and setting up stalls in the dockside car parks. The scene beyond the customs building/bar was like some monstrous car boot fair. I made a cursory inspection, elbowing my way past elfin Mukluks with fridge-freezers balanced on their backs, pockets stuffed full of calculators and toasted sandwich makers, but nobody seemed to have a copy of Milton Bradley's *Samurai Swords* complete and in good condition (some bumps to box corners, signs of adhesive tape on top-right seam, one *Ronin* figure repaired with polystyrene cement shows minor bubbling round ankles) and so I moved on into the mysterious East unhindered by comforting 1980s boardgames.

Those people who have visited Japan have found a landscape of smouldering, snow-ponchoed volcanoes and bashful cherry blossom, where sleek white locos zip through the paddy fields like hi-tech eels and pet rocks caper beneath the knee-high canopy of the bonsai forests. They speak of gardens made entirely of stones and gravel unbroken even by the occasional artfully placed shrub, cactus or crisp packet; of towering cities, winking with neon and abustle with white-faced ladies and stern-faced salarymen who queue at all-night vending machines to buy chilled underpants, conceive children in love hotels and sleep in filing cabinets. Those of us who have actually taken the trouble not to visit Japan have discovered quite a different country altogether.

The train, for example, is faded Venetian-red and as streamlined as a garden shed. I am no expert, but it looked to me like it might have been bought second-hand from Belgium. Passengers were scant, there was not a bowing geisha, salt-throwing sumo wrestler, Elvis impersonator munching on a bilious-coloured poison fish or hyper-tense golf-swing-practising CEO to be seen. In fact my fellow travellers consisted entirely of a youth with hair dyed the colour of a Yorkshire terrier who was brandishing a can of beer and busily singing the Scorpion's riff-tastic hit 'Another Piece Of Meat'. Clearly, then, there was no need for those uniformed fellows in white gloves I had been assured would be on hand at every station to cram commuters into the carriages. This was a grave disappointment. After all the dumplings I'd eaten so far I needed one of them to help me get into my jeans.

In Toyama it was the season of fresh green. They have been beating copper in the city since 1623. Toyama has the highest per capita number of home owners in Japan. The population are the third highest earners in the country but only the tenth highest spenders, which makes them the number one Japanese savers. The city was a large car park with intermittent blotches of office and living space. I couldn't see any people. They were all at home counting their money. I ate hot soups of carp, grouse and vegetables, followed by a nourishing game of bingo.

I had been told that my next stopping point, Takayama, had a multitude of craft shops. Luckily it proved to be nowhere near as horrific as this made it sound. The town was said to be one of the most traditional in all Japan. It was a treasure trove of carved wooden houses with lacquer furniture and porcelain tea sets where an atmosphere of priceless quietude, trammelled meagrely by the Air Jordan soles of the twenty-first century, prevailed. All of the buildings had paper walls, but crime rates remained mercifully low.

I busied myself at sake tasting and Nintendo. Ladies of general invitation wore their hair in the mara mage-style, monks blew shellfish, young people spoke the language of flowers and the sound of the Yamanga drums rumbled in my stomach. I feasted on local delicacies that did not feature in the guidebooks. All the town's hotels were 13.8 miles away, so I slept standing up in a wheelie bin fending off the remonstrance of the local constabulary by claiming I had mistaken it for a youth hostel. In a 1997 poll 54 per cent of Japanese people said they envied cats, but the rhinoceros beetle remained a more popular choice of pet.

The next morning I took time out from my busy schedule – investigating the truth behind Australian rugby league star Aaron Moule's claim that he was retiring from the game to pursue 'my eternal thirst for reading philosophy and psychology' – and took a taxi to Hida village. In Hida the local farmers were famous for plying their cattle with beer. This was said to make the flesh tender, pale and flavourful. And it meant they were more likely to kiss you, too.

In Hida there was a large golden-roofed building with a fish tank in the middle of it. This was the world shrine of the Shukyo Mahikari. Mahikari was the traditional cult cocktail of the sinister and the senseless, apparently blending Zen Buddhism and neo-Nazism with koi carp. The new religion was said to have been founded by an Imperial Army officer, Yoshikazu Okada, who had prepared for his future role as the Heralding Messiah by helping to organise the Nanking pogroms in which two hundred thousand Chinese men, women and children had been killed. On his death his adopted daughter had succeeded him as God's representative on earth. The Mahikari were alleged to be militaristic anti-Semites with links to the Aum terror group. It was reported that they believed the world would end in an inferno sometime soon and that only they would survive. Though the fact they had carried on soliciting cash donations suggested that the conflagration was also going to spare certain high-quality retail outlets as well. What else they thought and did I cannot say because most of the information about the Mahikari was to be found on the homepages of a man who apparently didn't have a space key andsoitwaswritten asonecontinualflowofwordsthateventuallygaveyouathump ingheadache.

I made my way eastward in the direction of Nagoya. On the outskirts of this untidily recumbent metropolis, in the town of Tokoname, I made an unscheduled stop. Japan has a number of fantastic specialist museums. Sadly my itinerary meant I could not visit the Sapporo Sewerage Science Museum, the Kiseki Museum of World Stones, the magnificent establishment in Kasaoka City which pledged itself to broadcasting the many splendours of the horseshoe crab, or the Tobacco and Salt Museum in Tokyo. This latter was a particular loss as it was staging a special exhibition entitled 'Ashtrays – Art, Craft and Humour'. Still, I felt that the Kiln Plaza Museum in Tokoname might make up for any disappointment with its justly lauded collection of historic toilets.

Kiln Plaza was not the only Japanese museum devoted to the toilet, I should add. There was also the World Toilet Exhibit on Shikoku Island, which boasted as its centrepiece a solid gold lavatory that was said to have cost half a million dollars. This, though, seemed to me to be mere vulgar ostentation compared to the tasteful, delicate nineteenth-century porcelain vessels to be found in Tokoname.

The presence of toilet museums in Japan is hardly a surprise. Toilets are something of a national obsession. There are websites and books devoted to the topic. Tokyo's public loos have their equivalent of the *Michelin Red Guide*. The National Toilet Symposium has been held here for over two decades, drawing hundreds of water-closet experts from around the globe. Japan's Hideo Nishioka, meanwhile, is said to have the most comprehensive collection of toilet tissue in the world. Where this lavatorial fixation came from is hard to say, though the fact that Japan's original indigenous population are called the Ainus may have very little to do with it.

The latrine was not always the object of such intense focus. For centuries citizens of the Land of the Rising Sun were happy with holes in the ground and seaweed. The 1980s were the dawn of Japanese advanced digital toilet technology. This was when the country's number one toilet maker, Toto Ltd, perfected a programmable lavatory seat that transformed the humble WC into a hi-tech combination lav-and-bidet called the Washlet and marketed it with the catchy slogan 'Even your bottom wants to stay clean!'

Since then Japan's toilets have undergone many upgrades including the addition of heat-controlled bowls, sprung seats designed to help eject arthritic pensioners from the pot and 'Sound Princess', an audio-cistern that mimics the sound of flushing to cover up unsavoury noises. Prices had risen accordingly and it was now by no means uncommon for the Japanese to pay £3000 for a loo. Basically, though, it all boiled down to the same thing. The Japanese toilet not only carries off waste products, it also washes your bottom and then blow-dries it for you. I tried to virtually use one, but the nearest I could get was a US company which promised that if I stopped by their retail store they'd let me test-drive any Japanese toilet and throw in a massage free of charge. To tell the truth I was rather, well, relieved. The whole experience sounded a bit weird and it wasn't helped by the dubious decision of Toto

Ltd to give their toilets women's names. If I had a burning desire to have a Jasmine or a Chloë shoot water and hot air at my bum then, frankly, I wouldn't tell a plumber about it.

Situated in the epicentre of the Japanese Rhineland, Nagoya was a city actively preparing for a future in which lifestyle, technology and culture worked together to create harmony. This was a pleasant thought as in most other cities I had visited lifestyle, technology and culture tended to spend most of their time beating the shit out of one another, while environment stood on the sidelines sobbing, 'Leave it, Cultch, he ain't worth it.'

I spent a morning in Nagoya's Brazilian quarter, looked at Japan's first TV tower, admired the Kinki Nippon Tourist Company and wandered the Imaike entertainment district, which was seedy but had spunk. After a glass of wine that would not only have dissolved a pearl but the shell it came in, I watched pets being walked by virtual owners and made my escape. In a local government poll in the 1970s the citizens of Nagoya had chosen the camphor as their city tree. I suspect they looked back on that as a highpoint. It is a waste of time trying to bite off your navel.

Much more to my liking was Owase, a recreational-style beach resort to the south-east of Nagoya on the Kii Peninsula. The Owase Lively Village was still at the foundation stage, leaving the ambience just on the wakeful side of somnolent. The bay was a boomerang of white sand, on one side gently nuzzled by a warm black current, on the other courted by handsome, cypress-scalped knolls.

In a creeping, tepid rain I took advantage of home-made goodness-using time-honoured techniques and picnicked on the beach with a goodly supply of dried

horse mackerel. Afterwards I scuba-dived in an underwater flower garden of radiant invertebrates. Soft coral,
veined and puce, swayed mellifluously, bulbous sea
anemones beckoned with mustard-yellow fingers, electric-
blue sea squirts winked and twinkled and playful sponges
buffeted my flanks. All the town's hotels were 23.9 miles
away so reluctantly I caught the train to Tanabe, a town
named after a speed racing exhaust system, and found a
bed in a hotel where ecological concerns and liquid soap
were in diplomatic negotiations.

I had been carefully following a rail itinerary picked
for its scenic majesty. The next part of it took me westward. Refreshing breezes swept the orange country and
mystery and tradition abounded amongst a bounty of
seafood. You don't get clams from a ploughed field.

The outline of Wakayama was a green rectangle
fronting a turquoise sea, nimbly trimmed with emerald
mudflats. Sixteenth-century fortresses with roofs that
curved like samurai armour lurked on wooded hills, rain-
bows arching overhead. The town was regarded as the
historical and cultural heart of Japan. It had been inhabited since earliest times when the ancients first began to
hunt with sticks and pottery. Nowadays Wakayama was a
contented hive of calmness and fulfilment, famous for
bamboo fishing rods, Gobo dolls, pile fabric, bath salts
and insecticides.

I took a hot spring bath that enhanced my inner and
outer radiance and afterwards went to watch some traditional river fishing. A trio of men in a 13-foot boat and a
team of cormorants held on leather leashes carry out this
eldritch rite. The craft pushes out into the river after dark
in search of *ayu*, or sweetfish, a Japanese breed similar to
smelt and known locally as 'the queen of the freshwater

stream'. Lamps are lit and held over the water and this, along with the beating of a drum, attracts shoals of *ayu*. Why the fish are attracted by light and drumming is not known. Presumably they think it's a nightclub. When the fish have appeared the cormorants are released into the water to catch them. Whenever one manages to get an *ayu* in its gullet the fishermen pull them to the surface by their leash and force them to disgorge it.

The cormorant is not the loveliest bird in the world. Its name comes from the Latin for sea crow, it is denounced in the Bible as an abomination and its excrement is so toxic it kills the trees it roosts in. All of which makes you ponder what sort of person would want to eat something a cormorant barfed up. The answer is the Japanese royal family. The imperial household is traditionally presented with gifts of sweetfish caught this way. No wonder Emperor Hirohito always looked so cross.

Mind you, for the sweetfish themselves being eaten by a cormorant is a pleasant reckoning compared to one of the alternatives awaiting them. In the caves and crannies of Japanese rivers lurks a creature so disgusting even hardened zoologists wrinkle up their noses when discussing it – the giant salamander. *Andrias japonicus* is one of the world's largest amphibians. It grows to five feet in length and weighs the same as a husky. It is big, lumpy, fat-tailed, squat-toed and covered in sticky mucus that gives off the odour of a peppered condom. A survivor of prehistoric times, it has not evolved in twenty million years (insert your own Ted Nugent joke here). The creature feeds at night, lying blotchily on rocks, gazing ignorantly at the world with tiny, lidless eyes and sucking anything that passes too close into its giant, wart-spotted mouth. Beetles, snails, snakes, mice and sweetfish – it isn't fussy. If the

choice were between the giant salamander and a cormorant, most animals would fling themselves into the
beak of the sea crow without hesitation. The giant salamander is now rare. Since 1951 the Japanese government
had strictly protected it. Once mountain peasants ate
them; now they were forbidden even to touch them. I
can't help thinking this must have come as a huge relief.

The gentleman sitting next to me on the Osaka-bound
train had white hair tinged with nicotine that curled up on
his head like a contented polecat. He was reading a bowd-
lerised version of a *Bondage Fairies* manga comic. In the
tradition of these things dark and angular strips hid male
members. On his wedding night the Victorian art critic
John Ruskin, brought up on a diet of classical nudes, had
infamously been so shocked by the sight of his wife's pubic
hair that he had gone into a nervous decline. How much
greater, then, must be the surprise and disappointment of
the Japanese maiden when she discovers her boyfriend
does not a have a large black oblong down his pants?

There were three people sitting across the aisle – two
women, both in their late thirties, and a man of the same
age. They were surrounded with bags and luggage as if
they were coming back from their holidays. One of the
women leant forward eagerly, her mouth flapping open.
Opposite her the other woman wore a kindly encouraging
expression. The man, meanwhile, who I took to be this
woman's husband, stared straight ahead. His eyes had the
blank, glassy look of a soldier who has been in combat too
long. I had no idea what they were talking about but I
could guess.

The talking woman said, 'So I said to him, I said, "You
stay here with your precious tropical fish and your plasma
TV if you want, but I'm going to get some sun and sand."

He said, "You wouldn't dare go on your own." I said, "Oh, now, wouldn't I, buster!" I was straight on the phone to the travel agent. Booked it just like that. He said, "What'll you do for company? You'll be lonely. You won't know anyone." I said, 'Don't you worry about me. I'm a good mixer. I'll make friends, you just see if I don't." And the first night in the hotel I met you two, didn't I?'

'Yes,' the other woman said with a weak grin.

'Well, I'll be back home in,' she checked her watch, 'thirty-five minutes and I bet he'll be glued in his chair watching *Iron Chef*. "How d'you get on," he'll say, "did you miss me?" I'll say, "Miss you? Miss you? I didn't have time to miss anybody. I hooked up with this lovely couple first night at the hotel. They were a bit shy at first but I really brought them out of themselves. Such good company. Got on like a house on fire. And they insisted – *insisted* – I went everywhere with them after that." Eee we had some laughs, didn't we? I bet you never thought you'd see your Hidetoshi limbo dancing in a coconut brassiere, did you?'

'No,' the other woman said.

'"Two weeks we spent together," I'll say to him. "Hardly out of one another's sight morning, noon and night. Beach, swimming pool, disco, day trips to the pearl fisheries. And never a cross word. *Never a cross word, mind*." And he can put that in his pipe and smoke it! I mean, don't get me wrong – I love him dearly. Love him to bits. But sometimes you've got to stretch your wings, or your relationship goes stagnant. You know what I mean?'

'Yes,' the other woman said.

'Eee well,' the woman said as the train began to slow, 'this is me. Wonderful holiday. Wonderful holiday, luvs. Thanks to the pair of you. Wouldn't have had half as much fun if I hadn't bumped into you and I dare say you'll be saying the same. I'll see you again. See you again, I'm sure.' She gathered up her cases and bags and, waving, alighted from the train.

We pulled out of the station. The quiet woman waved one last time and then turned away from the window. Silence fell. Then after a moment the woman said, 'Do you think we will see her again, like?' Her husband took a deep breath, 'I fucking hope not,' he said.

I had no time for Japan's second city, Osaka, and continued westward, through Fukuchyama – home to the Kitakinki Tango Railway and a ladies' live steaming festival. At Tottori there were pear trees, a fantasy of wind and dunes and the multitudinous braziers of the cuttle-fishing boats sparkled on black water elliptical and poetic as a haiku. While gazing at them I was approached by Larry Irvine who asked, 'Harry Pearson, would you like to prolong your life by twenty years?' I replied, 'Yes, but how would I know that I had?'

Larry was peddling a perfectly natural substance produced by the pituitary gland that made fat and wrinkles simply fall away. The way Larry told it, if you fed this stuff to an elephant within a week it would look like an aspirin. The perfectly natural substance was human growth hormone. I had come across HGH before because it was widely used by professional cyclists. Which probably explained why their shirts and shorts were always so tight.

As I already stand six feet five inches I didn't really see that I had much need of growth hormones. In fact, since I had been struggling for years to find a decent off-the-peg suit that didn't make me look like Jerry Lewis, what I really needed was not something that would make me bigger but that would make me shrink. I told Larry I would pass on the human growth hormones but would be very interested in some human diminishing hormones. Larry said he didn't know much about HDH (or at least that is how I interpreted his lack of response) and so I told him.

The amount of drug abuse that goes on in sport is well documented, but one of the undiscovered scandals is the widespread use of human diminishing hormone by jockeys. Developed in the USA in the 1960s, HDH was originally intended to help retired defensive linemen adjust to a normal life. 'These guys were so big they literally struggled to fit in to normal society,' said my source. 'It was painful to witness. One minute they were heroes, the next they were just oversized lunks who kept getting trapped in revolving doors. HDH was supposed to help with the transition to ordinary life by making them littler.'

Unfortunately it wasn't long before word of the drug's astonishing effects had started to spread. Soon it was all the rage amongst artists, media types and musicians (followers of the 1980s Washington Go Go scene will recall Trouble Funk's epic salute to HDH, 'Let's Get Small') but it was among horse-racing folk that it took hold in a big way.

'Suddenly,' my source revealed, 'size wasn't important. Anybody who could ride and could get his hands on HDH could become a jockey.' At first the drug was used sparingly but, as is the way, the demand for success led to greater and greater amounts being ingested. 'I've seen hulking construction workers shrink themselves to the size of a cocker spaniel in the hope of catching a trainer's eye,' my source recalled. 'Unfortunately they usually only succeed in catching his kneecap. Getting smaller is all that counts. They don't consider the risks they are running.'

And the risks are considerable not least because of the drug's infamous side effect – monumental flatulence. To any normal person farting like a sheep let loose in a turnip field would simply be embarrassing, but when you've shrunk yourself down to three feet nine and 20 pounds it's downright dangerous. No figures exist as to the number of young men and women whose bloody remains have been scraped off the stable ceiling but it must be hundreds.

I told all this to Larry. From his silence I judged that he was shocked. I haven't heard from him since.

Matsue had maintained the atmosphere of the castle town days and its alternative nickname was 'The City of the Tea Ceremony'. A Japanese Venice, there was water everywhere. Thirty thousand hydrangea blossoms decorated the temple gardens like a genuflecting horde of *washi* balls. I enjoyed the seven exotic flavours of Lake Shinji-Ko and stayed at a hotel that promised 'some English services are available'. With a twinge of homesickness I availed myself of a clumsy, disinterested waiter and a receptionist who, since her boyfriend's departure from the premarital bed, had been forced to spend entire weeks with a telephone to her ear plaintively mumbling the words 'I know he is, but I can't get him out of my mind, Di' over and over again. Every time you asked for anything she groaned and made a noise like a camel freeing its dentures from a particularly intransigent toffee. It took her so long to retrieve my room key I kipped most of the night on an improvised hammock strung between the pot palms in the lobby.

I pressed rapidly on towards Kagashima. Japan passed

by in a blur of lacquer work, wooden shoes and plum
sauce. At Kitakyushu there was a large railway station
and what appeared to be a pyramid of Ferrero Rocher
chocolates so gigantic even the ambassador himself would
have dropped his bundle when he saw it; at Fukuoka they
were weaving crests and improving Chinese scissors; at
Kunamoto the buckwheat noodles had accrued a reputation of national renown. To tell the truth, though, I wasn't
really watching. I had got the hump with Japan.

Maybe I had been expecting too much. Any country
where you can go into a department store and buy jelly to
feed to stag beetles is bound to generate a high degree of
anticipation. But after Asia and the old USSR, Japan
seemed overarranged and artful. There was nothing hap-
hazard. Everything, from the monasteries to the
mountains, appeared to have been placed just so according to some finer aesthetic sensibility. It looked great, it
worked superbly, but even experiencing it virtually gave
you the unnerving feeling that you were making the place
look untidy. Japan was the land of the tea ceremony and
I was more a bag in a mug, milk, two sugars and a
Burton's Wagonwheel type.

I arrived in Kagashima feeling about as comfortable as
a bongos player in a chamber orchestra and caught the
ferry to Okinawa. From there it was forty-eight hours by
boat to Taiwan and the mad promise of Monkey
Mountain.

8

The Duck's Quack Does Not Echo

Okinawa to Manado

Okinawa is 67 miles long, has a population of 1.28 million people, 40 US military bases and more than 3.5 million visitors a year. The inhabitants are the longest lived on the planet. This is because on Okinawa there is simply no space to lie down and die.

When you could elbow a bit of leeway, the subtropical paradise revealed itself to be a vivid kaleidoscope of blooming flowers and blossoming Volvo dealerships. The locals conversed in a most speakable dialect, only the old wore textiles and pig's ear in vinegar caught the eye, nose and throat of the peripatetic gastronome. On the Pacific shore a stand of blurred palm trees provided refuge for a unique woodpecker and masked a sun-fondled beach on which tourists queued up to sit down. In the seas beyond clown fish tripped over one another and fell into buckets of whitewash. Okinawa is the home of karate. Luckily there is not enough room to kick anyone.

I travelled to Khaosiung on the Arimuta Sangyo Company ferry. According to the only information I could find this anonymous vessel left Naha in Okinawa at 7.30

on Friday and docked in the Taiwanese port at 6.00 on Sunday. 'Journey time 16 hours' it said on the timetable. Either somebody couldn't do his maths or the Japanese had abolished Saturday, possibly as some sort of daylight-saving measure.

As the ferry crossed the ———— on its way to our first port of call, it passed above what may have been the ruins of Japan's answer to the Lost City of Atlantis, Yonaguni. According to the Japanese, Yonaguni was built fifteen thousand years ago, making it the world's oldest metropolis. Divers were currently exploring it to try and find out how it had come to sink below the water. My guess is that eventually they will find a petroglyph reading 'Another week and still no sign of that bloody plumber'.

We docked twice on our southward journey. Hirara was a list of discount hotels and two horizontal black lines on a white field where visitors engaged in forest recreations and sporadic bursts of meditational archery. At Ishigaki-Jima the green was deep and impregnated with singular wild stock. After that we hit the open seas and entered the Bashi Channel. This notorious throttle point on the Pacific highway is regularly rattled by typhoons and hurricanes made ever more furious and violent by climatic change and the fact that their names – Edna, Eileen, Bernadette – were far less cool and sexy than those of Japanese toilets. Happily it was the season for neither, nor did the legendary tsunami threaten. Instead, the main danger to our ship was running aground on a reef of re-financing offers. We passed the largest of these deadly floating mortgage-bergs just south of Oluanpi, its lethal, submerged small print (for only a third of the mortgage is visible above the surface) brilliantly illuminated by the Taiwanese island's 1.8 million-watt lighthouse. Standing

21.4 metres tall, this beacon can proudly claim to be the only armed lighthouse in the world.

Arriving freighters totally overshadowed Kaohsiung, Taiwan's largest port, although that may just have been my perspective. The city had been founded by aborigines who had been disturbed by the violence of four hundred-year-old pirates. It was a lively place of persistent cloud where brothels lurked behind barbers' shops, butcher birds hid in thorn bushes and the full beauty of the Jungjeng bridge could only be appreciated from beneath.

Taiwan was a paradox. It had been founded by Chinese nationalists led by Chiang Kai-shek in 1949 and had been battling for international recognition ever since, to little avail. It was not a member of the United Nations or the International Olympic Movement. It had no diplomatic representation in any major foreign country. It was a nation of twenty-three million people that officially did not exist. It might have been unnerving for the population, but the locals were too busy making 60 per cent of the world's notebook computers to fret about it overmuch.

The democratically elected Taiwanese government did worry, though. They worried about the failure of the West to acknowledge that their country was not part of main-land China; about the scheming of Beijing and the long-running dispute over the ownership of the Spratly Islands, an archipelago that was claimed by Taiwan, China, Malaysia, the Philippines, Vietnam and possibly, though no one was quite sure on this point, Brunei. Most of all, though, they worried about betel nuts.

Betel nuts are the fruit of the tropical palm. They look like green olives. Chewing betel nuts is said to give you a buzz equivalent to drinking six cups of coffee. They also give you fresh breath, scarlet gums and the expectorating capacity of a randy Bactrian camel. Two hundred million people use them worldwide. Pavements in many Far Eastern countries are so splattered with red goo they look like the ceiling of the Jockey Club after a beanfeast.

Proponents of the betel nut say it sharpens the mind and the reactions and promotes a sense of wellbeing. Opponents say it encourages laziness, moral laxity and sexual promiscuity. Supporters point out that it is Taiwan's number two cash crop, that it is easy and fast to grow and provides thousands of jobs. Detractors counter that its shallow roots and thin foliage are producing an environmental catastrophe of soil erosion and water run-off. Fans say it is a panacea that cures headaches, stomach pains, venereal disease, rheumatism and schizophrenia. Enemies say it gives you oral cancer.

According to the Taiwanese authorities betel nuts also contributed to swifter and more dramatic deaths. Or at least the people who sold them did. In Formosa the retailing of betel nuts has traditionally been entrusted to young women. They sit in glass booths at the sides of the roads plying their trade. In recent years in an attempt to attract customers the betel nut girls, or spicy sisters as they were known, had taken to wearing clothing so skimpy it might have been fashioned from offcuts of confetti. According to the government in Taipei the scantily clad sellers were directly responsible for hundreds of men crashing their cars into telegraph poles.

To stop this magistrates had recently passed a law that compelled the betel nut beauties to cover up 'the three Bs' – bosoms, buttocks and bellybuttons. This intervention was met with howls of outrage from the sellers, the customers and car-salvage operatives. Not content with that the government also declared its intention to destroy all

betel palms growing on publicly owned land and to
increase the duty levied on them. As one incensed entrepreneur told the BBC, 'They are trying to tax our nuts out
of existence.'

I checked into an establishment that might have been
named in my honour, the Gink Hotel, and betook myself
to a nearby restaurant. Here the menu featured Salmon
Head Pot, Hell's Treasure, Steamed Pigs, Stinky Tofu and
Mountain Rat. At least I assume it was the menu. The
waitress may simply have handed me a Frank Zappa
discography by mistake. Undaunted, I plumped for fried
crickets followed by chisan popsicle and washed it down
with papaya milk. Along with the coconut the papaya is
the only fruit that suckles its young.

At a nearby table an elderly local with the drooping
jowls of a basset hound and glossy hair highlighted with
an aubergine rinse was tucking into a dish of snake. Many
Chinese restaurants served specially prepared snake
dishes. Historically these were credited with increasing
male potency. Nowadays many chefs made sure they did
by stirring Viagra into the sauce. It was an invigorating
melding of the traditional and the modern, kind of like
one of those CDs that fuse drum and bass with the bagpipes.

In a post-prandial malaise I sauntered along the bank of
the Love River. This waterway is the soul of Kaohsiung.
Sadly these days you could pronounce the letter 'R' in
front of that description. Open sewers flow into the Love
River. This is not only a fact; it is also the title of a best-
selling country and western album. When it was released
in Taiwan *Wayne's World* was called *The Rambunctious and
Clever Ones*.

Back at the Gink I found a message waiting for me.

Referee Marc Geraert of Ypres ended a West Flanders League game between FC Wijtschate and Vladslo prematurely to save Wijtschate from further punishment. The team from Heuvelland were losing 16-0 at the time. 'I felt so sorry for them,' Geraert explained. Wijtschate are used to it, though, having conceded 132 goals in just fifteen games. 'All our players are farm boys,' explained a club spokesman.

The following day, mindful of Kaohsiung's offer to change my life in a wonderful way, I took a taxi into the surrounding countryside. Here white cattle with the flapping dewlaps of dowagers grazed on herb-encrusted buttes and pagodas like stacks of ceremonial sombreros cast whimsical reflections on the mirrored surfaces of the lakes. The hills were alive with the sound of monkeys. For this was the home of the Formosan rock macaque.

Macaques have been described as the second most successful primate on the planet after man. This of course all depends on what you mean by successful. No doubt the macaques look on their failure to spend hour upon hour scouring the internet for jokes about Osama bin Laden and then downloading and texting them to friends as a sign that the top spot is rightfully theirs.

Macaques come in many forms including the crab-eating macaque, the booted macaque, the pig-tailed macaque and the proboscis monkey, a large-nosed breed that spends its time frolicking happily in Japanese hot springs apparently oblivious to the fact that it bears an incredible physical resemblance to Richard Milhouse Nixon. Formosan rock macaques have pale, pinched faces, nervous, twitching eyes and grey hair. En masse they look like a coachload of feral pensioners.

Recently the macaques, like betel nuts, had been falling

foul of the authorities. Having learned by observation that humans normally carried food in plastic bags, they had taken to leaping out of the undergrowth beside footpaths and snatching them off passing walkers. According to the Taiwanese government the result of this activity was that the monkeys had become obese and begun suffering from hypertension. 'They have become spoiled and lazy,' said a government spokesman, sternly pointing out that the macaques appeared to have ditched their traditional method of getting about by leaping from tree to tree and had taken to ambling along boarded pathways instead, possibly stopping every once in a while to complain that their feet were killing them and to show pictures of their grandchildren to complete strangers.

Before setting off on my journey around the world I had resolved to use air travel only as a last resort. Getting from Taiwan to Manila by sea was problematic, but, spurred on by the dismal spectre of a meal on a tray of prechewed slop and that moment in the duty free shop when you will yourself to buy a bottle of twelve-year-old malt whisky or VSOP cognac but somehow emerge clutching a bottle of Green Izarra – the astringent herbal liqueur from the Basque country that has a bottle the shape of a goat's scrotum and the aftertaste to match – I discovered a Japanese freighter that plied a triangular route from Chiba to Kaohsiung and back again via the Philippines capital.

Owned by Orient Overseas Container Lines, it was a 16,000-ton cargo vessel of stolid aspect. It did not carry passengers. A number of solutions suggested themselves. I could apply for a job on board as a deckhand or cook and jump ship when we docked in Manila Bay, or stow away in a lifeboat enlisting the aid of a kindly boson who would bring me scraps to feed on during his watch. Both had a certain manly appeal, but after due consideration I opted for another alternative. I hired a 20-foot container from a man I chose to think of as Mr Lau. Mr Lau's hairdo – spiked on top, long at the back – did not so much resemble a mullet as a kipper attempting to hide under a hedgehog. I assume it was trying to get away from the noise of his shirt. Mr Lau had the aspect of somebody recently expelled from charm school. I surmised that in the 1960s he had travelled extensively in ladies' under-wear, but then the bottom had fallen out and he had reinvented himself as a lifestyle trader.

Mr Lau showed me his range of containers, pointing out their youth and sturdiness. I reminded him that Belgium didn't introduce the driving test until 1973. He indicated that his prices compared favourably with those of other companies in Kaohsiung and Taipei. I recalled that the Romans farmed hedgehogs for meat. He indicated that his hire charge was inclusive of all state taxes and port duties. I countered that live pigeon shooting was once an Olympic event. Eventually I hammered him down to the asking price and still had change out of the fact that Swedes had driven on the left until the 1960s.

I filled my newly acquired steel container with a cor-duroy sofa, a 48-inch plasma-screen TV, a satellite dish and ten family packs of Cheesy Wotsits and had myself loaded aboard as cargo. As we skirted the Luzon Strait I settled back and switched on the television.

TV, it has been said, trivialises everything. During my journey I had met plenty of evidence to back that sugges-tion up. One night on a cable channel I had watched a programme called, *I'm a German Celebrity Get Me Out of Here!* It turned out to be a documentary about the Battle of Berlin. Don't ask me who won. I switched off after they voted the alsatian out of the Bunker. I mean, the Goebbels' kids I could understand. The kids were irritating. But the alsatian, what had it done? I tell you, people could learn a lot about loyalty from that mutt.

Thankfully Philippines TV was of an altogether higher order. Here viewers could stretch themselves intellectually with shows such as *Rosary Crusade*, *UFO Baby*, *Berks* and *Master Cooking Boy*, or relax with the high-quality daily soap *Sana'y Wala Nana Wakas*, featuring television's most memorable love team Jericho Morales and Christine Hermosa and a theme tune by Sharon Cuneta, the singing megastar who was just a couple of vowels away from severe embarrassment.

By the time my container ship was chugging past Olongapo and into the tranquil waters of Manila Bay I had become quite addicted to Filipino soaps. So much so that I had even taken to texting in my answers to the multiple-choice daily trivia quiz. Ano ang title ng episode na pinagtambala ni John Prats at Heart Evangelista ngayong enero?

A Flat týre.
B Burger joint.

Well, you don't have to be a genius to get that one right, do you?

An efficient bridge crane swiftly unloaded my container. Japan and the Philippines had still officially been at war as late as 1951 but the old wounds had been healed by decades of diplomacy and Pokémon.

As I stepped on to the quayside I staggered and fell. After so many days at sea I had lost my land legs. I found them down the back of the sofa and was soon walking normally again. Not that it was necessary to walk in Manila, a motorised megalopolis of eleven million souls where public transport came in sundry shapes and forms, flowing down the thoroughfares like Technicolor treacle. I hopped aboard a public utility jeep. The jeepney is a polychromatic pantechnicon with the ground clearance of a turtle and seating that lurches to the Draconian side of Spartan.

As we bumped and bored our way into the heart of the city my senses were assailed by the Far East. The streets of Manila hummed to the sound of vulgar commerce and throbbed to the beat of the techno drum. We passed colonial Spanish churches of ample proportions, a procession of suckling pigs wearing sunglasses and a group of women dressed in flame-coloured Crimplene body suits who pointed at the rooftops in a primordial ritual of mysterious purpose. In the hostess bars of Angeles City teenage girls in shiny bikinis danced with sag-gutted European men old enough to be their husbands. In the parks peacocks with the gaudy plumage and strident calls of bookmakers' molls made a vivid nuisance of themselves amongst the mango trees. The rowdy air was a hearty broth of exotic scents – sweet rambutan, fragrant bougainvillea, sweating nuns and cockroach repellent – and so humid you didn't so much breathe it in as drink it. Manila holds the world record for the most rainfall in a twenty-four-hour period with a fabulous 38.5 inches on 17 October 1967, but the atmosphere could slurp that amount of fluid out of the population in a few sticky minutes.

The Philippines is made up of 7107 islands. In terms of landmass it is slightly smaller than Italy, but its coastline is twice as long as that of the United States. It is the world's largest producer of coconuts and hemp. Philippines hemp pulp is used to fashion sausage skins, tea bags and, of course, Manila's most precious gift to the globe – the brown envelope.

Manila's second most precious gift to the world was the yoyo. *Yoyo* means come come. The Philippines was probably not the yoyo's point of origin but it had been around on the islands for centuries. In 1521 Ferdinand Magellan had witnessed Filipinos sitting in trees with rocks on string, which they threw at passing animals, reeling them back up if they missed. Later they got down out of the trees and beat the Portuguese explorers to death with sticks. That of these two activities it was the former that became an international craze stands as vivid testimony to the basic decency of humankind.

The yoyo enjoyed a vogue amongst European gentry at the fag end of the eighteenth century when it was known as the battledore, but it was a Filipino, Pedro Flores, who introduced it to the United States. Flores had arrived in California to make his fortune in the 1920s, a joyful and exuberant era when an entrepreneur with smarts and pizzazz could become a millionaire overnight simply by attaching a ball to a bat with a rubber band. Unsurprisingly, Flores made a bundle with the yoyo.

I took a billet at a drive-in hotel offering bed, breakfast and an oil change at a pulchritudinous price. Next morning I visited Fort Santiago, famous for its flowering trees, homing pigeons and torture chambers. By now it was becoming plain to me that the Philippines was no ordinary place, but a bijou cornucopia of fabulous cameos. On its islands can be found the world's smallest fish, littlest falcon, tiniest shell, most diminutive monkey and shortest volcano. Perhaps not surprisingly it is also home to the Hobbit House, a Manila music club staffed entirely by midgets.

The perfectly proportioned population of the Philippines are romantic and artistic and much given to winning beauty contests, cockfighting and transvestism. Filipino women pride themselves on being glamorous, lovely and talented. Modesty is another strong suit. In recent times their rulers have generally been characterised by stack-heeled shoes, bouffant hair-dos, tinted glasses and Swiss bank accounts. Luckily for them the Philippines is rich with natural resources that lend themselves nicely to embezzlement. It was here, after all, that a fisherman had once chanced upon a pearl even a broad of Cleopatra's gargantuan appetites would have struggled to swallow. It weighed 14 pounds.

The previous President, Joseph Estrada, had been impeached and charged with taking £209 million in bribes and kickbacks, a substantial slice of which he had taken to the off-licence and invested in strong drink. Estrada expressed his contempt for proceedings by turning up at court in his bedroom slippers. The trial collapsed.

On Calauit Island, south-west of Manila, another former President, Ferdinand Marcos, had let loose hundreds of animals purchased from East Africa; there were zebra, giraffes and impala. He claimed it was part of a zoological experiment, but rumour had it he had really done it as a gift for his son, Ferdinand Junior – known as Bong Bong – so that he could indulge his fondness for shooting big game without straying too far from home. Bong Bong was said to be greedy, power mad and generally a credit to the British public school system that had educated him. He had recently followed the family tradition by entering politics.

The Marcos family could afford to indulge their whims. They were accused of stealing $1.6 trillion worth of gold from the Philippines during their twenty-year reign. One of the items snatched for them by the police was a gold Buddha weighing over a ton. The Buddha belonged to a man named Roger Roxas who claimed to have found it in a secret tunnel behind a hospital in 1971. The Japanese military commander in the Philippines, General Yamashita, had apparently hidden the statue in 1944. Unable to carry it with him when the Imperial Army retreated, the general evidently planned to return for it when the war was over. The Allies thwarted his plans, however. They hanged him.

A US court ordered the Marcos family to return the Buddha to its rightful owners, the Roxas family. The returned statue turned out not to be made of gold at all, but of gilded bronze and lead. The Roxases protested that the Buddha had been switched, saying they knew it couldn't be the original because that had had a detachable head filled with diamonds. Whatever the rights and wrongs of the case, I can't help feeling that the Gautama's message of rejecting worldly goods and living a life of asceticism had got lost somewhere on its way across the South China Sea.

On a warm morning I boarded the ferry that would take me from the capital to Mindanao, bewitching motherland of the pomelo. This was not an undertaking for the faint of heart. Philippine ferries went down more frequently than the average British heavyweight. There were one hundred accidents a year. Many of the boats were old tubs that had been taken out of service running to and fro between Liverpool and the Isle of Man, refitted and set to work in the Sulu Sea. Conditions on the Pacific Rim were considerably more volatile than those in the Irish Sea and quite a lot of them sank. There was a huge amount of water for them to disappear in, too. Until recently the Philippines Trench was thought to be the lowest point on earth, then Michael Bolton released his cover version of 'When A Man Loves A Woman'.

I had rented a stateroom on the ferry for the 560-mile journey to Davao del Sur. Decked out with mirrors and upholstered in fawn suede it was like the hidey-hole of a louche Bond villain, the sort of place where you felt over-dressed if you were wearing anything more than orange Terylene trunks, a short, black, silk kimono, a couple of Pina Coladas and a sadistic grin. Luckily I had packed for just such an occasion.

We passed along the endlessly writhing coastline. The Visayas Islands, like glittering green jewels, beckoned the voyager to come sport with them. From jungly slopes could be heard the reliable noon-day call of the kalaw bird, the sweet troubadour warbling of the wood thrush and the warrior scream of the Philippines monkey-eating eagle, a massive bird with the back-combed quiff and beaky, intense look of Barry Manilow trying to open a child-proof bottle.

Mindanao was home to the world's largest flower, the Titan arum, or Stinking corpse lily, a two-metre-high phallic spike that opened to reveal a scarlet interior and emit a stench of putrefaction that could be detected half a mile away. The repugnant odour helped the plant to propagate by attracting thousands of flies and an equal number of foreign botanists. The insects spread the pollen from male flower to female and the scientists transported the 15-pound corms all across the globe. The Titan arum could now be found from California to Kew Gardens. Thus did Mother Nature weave her intricate and subtle pattern of creation.

Davao del Sur, where our ferry finally came to rest in a flurry of horns and tossed ropes, was touting itself as the ideal retirement location for US citizens. The weather was warm, the air fresh, the water pure and the cost of living lower than a snake's armpits. According to the literature the local population were 142 different tribes and races, Muslim and Christian, in harmonious blend. Unfortunately the Moro Islamic Liberation Front didn't seem to have read it. They had been fighting for independence for the past three decades. The war had cost a hundred and twenty thousand lives. Now terrorist cells trained and sponsored by al-Qaeda had joined the MILF. Rocket-propelled grenades were fired at passing ships. Bombs exploded with gory monotony. As if to prove my point, one went off in the market square of Koronadal City on the morning of my arrival, killing thirteen shoppers and wounding hundreds more.

This was virtual Mindanao. Colourful Bagobos displayed their extraneous crafts. Sun-browned children dived overboard to the music of the two-stringed lute. Gardenias blossomed, Semtex boomed. Orchid farms and plywood factories abounded. Truly was the internet a world of contrasts.

I didn't tarry long in Davao, passing a single, surly night in the Insular Hotel before boarding an 18,000-ton Mitsubishi-built cruise ship with immense inside passage capacity. I had no ticket but breezed past security posing as the relief entertainer. That night in the Battakundi Lounge I like to think I entertained the assembled throng

of incredulous pensioners as Gumphrey Bolt, the banter-
ing butler. My catchphrases, 'Your nuts, M'Lord' and
'Your crackers, M'Lady', went down a storm. If I'd had
time to pick up all the coins that were hurled at me I'd be
a rich man, I can tell you.

My destination was Bitung on the northern shore of
Sulawesi, a short hop, step and a jump along the
Kepulauan Archipelago in the Celebes Sea. Sulawesi was
an island shaped like a monkey dangling by its tail. It had
been called Celebes by the Dutch, a name that may or
may not have arisen from the confusion caused when a
Netherlands naval officer putting ashore on the island for
the first time asked the local blacksmith 'What is this place
called?' and received the reply 'Celebes' which is, more or
less, the Malay word for 'forge'.

Sulawesi was one of the eight Spice Islands. The others
were Seram, Batchian, Banda, Ginger, Sporty, Scary and
Posh. Relatives of anybody who didn't see this punch line
coming are advised to contact an undertaker immediately.

I must confess that I was rather nervous about visiting
Indonesia. The situation in the country sounded hairier
than a Grateful Dead concert. There were murderous terrorist groups, volatile volcanoes, dozens of poisonous
reptiles and a long and notorious record of puppetry.

There was also a hint of savage weirdness. Two years
before I arrived, for example, Indonesia's brutal security
chief, General Wiranto, had been forced to resign after
reports that he had sanctioned death squads on East Timor.
He was now making a living as a nightclub crooner, touring
the archipelago promoting an album of love songs, *For You
My Indonesia*. Watching him perform must have been like
turning up in a pub and finding Josef Stalin doing 'Sorry
Seems To Be The Hardest Word' on the karaoke.

My fears proved unfounded. Bitung was a charming town set amongst fertile hills and rippling xylophones. Its principal attraction was a 12-metre-high replica of the Eiffel Tower that stood in the middle of a roundabout at a busy road intersection in a defiant 'come and get me' gesture to drunk jeep drivers. As a counterpoint, an hour out across the bay on Lembeh the Indonesian government had built a monument to celebrate victory over rebels on Irian Jaya back in the 1970s. One hundred metres high and flanked by a gigantic pair of plaster thistle heads, the Trikora Tower looked like a one-eyed snake on a pogo stick.

The unedifying edifice was surrounded by groves of swaying coconut palms. Palm oil was one of the region's biggest exports. The high level of saturated fatty acids in palm oil and the fact that food manufacturers in the West insisted on squirting it into practically everything they processed meant that many dieticians blamed it for the rocketing incidence of obesity and heart disease. To hear doctors tell it palm oil was a weapon of mass destruction more insidious than sarin and more lethal than mustard gas. Palm oil did have another use, though. It could power the internal combustion engine. It was cheap, renewable and environmentally friendly. Unfortunately cars running on it tended to balloon in size and have a stroke.

I took a taxi along the coast to the old port of Manado (or Manado-do-do-push-pineapple-shake-the-tree, as it had been known during the days of Dutch occupation). The provincial capital was a place of rich delights. So laid back it could touch its heels with the top of its head, Manado was blessed with few inhabitants. Made wealthy by a yearly harvest of cloves, it had an air of opulence and mulled wine.

I took a room at the splendidly named Ritzy Hotel. Here the Sulawesi Sea was my swimming pool and my sun deck. The shore was a jumble of disrobed heights and flocculent flats. The turquoise waters around Bunaken coral gardens were alive with cantering pygmy seahorses, spooky ghost pipefish and schools of frolicking scuba divers; while the mimic octopus attempted to pass unnoticed by imitating Marlon Brando and standing next to a boulder. In the evening, as the buttery fingers of the retreating day star gently strummed the mellifluous bay, I dined in a fish restaurant on stilts. After I had fallen into my grilled tuna jaws for the second time the management forced me to get down off them and sit in a chair.

After dinner, as I strolled along the white sands, a woman named Diane bearded me. As far as I could judge Diane had the peppy, full-of-beans look of a West Highland terrier that's just rolled in a cowpat. Diane had a new weight-loss scheme to promote. It worked by harnessing the natural synergies of unsaturated fats and the hydro carbons produced by chargrilling literally to burn cellulite away. I told Diane I was already on a very good scheme, the Mafia Diet. You eat what the fuck you want and if anyone says you're fat, you kill them.

9

Gumi Bilong Kok

Manado to Port Moresby

The MV *Nggapulu* arrived at Bitung from Jakarta. Its destination and, not entirely coincidentally, my own, was Jayapura on the perpetually revolting island of Irian Jaya. We were scheduled to take in Servi, Biyak, Ternate and Sorong along the way.

The MV *Nggapulu* was a new and pristine vessel, keeled and fitted in the yards of grisly Hamburg. I had an A-1 cabin with a writing desk and German lavatory. In honour of Indonesia's colonial past the dining room melded Javanese and Dutch styles. Having had experience of restaurants in the Netherlands I presumed this would mean the food would be plentiful, spicy and delicious but that you'd have to cook it yourself because the members of staff were far too important to bother with such trivialities. Later I decided I was wrong and found the service impeccable and the dishes not in the least bit clog-like.

Most of my fellow passengers were retired folk, whose burgeoning buttocks and oscillating bellies bore testimony to a tendency to take the term 'all-day breakfast' literally. More than once I heard some old bird respond to the waiter's inquiry 'Would you like the menu, sir?' with an enthusiastic 'Yes, siree, and better double up on the desserts, I feel mighty peckish today.'

They were a cheery breed, however, and never more so than when confronting the downturn in all civilised values that had begun when they went through the menopause and had been gathering pace ever since. To sit on the foredeck with the hot salty spray splattering your cheeks like the excited yarn of a hungry man was to act as a magnet for tales of insubordinate sales staff, chiselling shopkeepers and woolly-headed law enforcers who didn't seem to grasp the reformative powers of a few dozen firm smacks over the ear with a sand-filled sock. I was trying to patent a device for just such eventualities. It was called the Talkman. Using advanced computer and audio technology, the Talkman would analyse another person's conversation and make suitable responses such as 'Really. 37p, that's outrageous', 'Eee she never, the little madam?' and 'Hanging's too good for them, I say' while the wearer snoozes peacefully or reads a book.

I paused but briefly in Jayapura for I was running several months behind schedule. The port, as I can recollect it, was a happy cavalcade of concrete prefabs with corrugated tin roofs, where washing hung on balconies over a rust-red river, the pavements were covered with straggling piles of squid-like Batavian endives and the streets hummed to the adenoidal whine of swarming mopeds.

The monument on Lembeh had led me to suspect the place might exude a feeling of incipient menace, but the only genuinely threatening thing I encountered in Jayapura was the drinking water. This was not to say that conflict was not to be found elsewhere in the region. Irian Jaya means Glorious West Guinea in Indonesian but the locals preferred the more prosaic West Papua. They were predominantly Melanesians and had no affinity with the Malays of Java, Borneo and Sulawesi. Indonesia's former rulers, the Dutch – who knew Jayapura as Hollandia – had acknowledged that fact, hanging on to the colony long after Indonesia gained independence. They eventually handed it over to the administration in Jakarta on the understanding that it would remain autonomous. West Papua, though, is home to the Grasberg mine, the world's largest gold deposit and the third biggest source of copper on the planet. The Indonesian government was about as willing to risk losing that as a Mongolian is his best hat. Bitterness and bloodshed ensued.

I spent the night in a hotel on pylons that jutted out across the harbour and the following morning, after some good-natured back and forth in our respective languages, secured a berth aboard a dinghy belonging to a cadre of local brigands who were earnestly smuggling vanilla pods into Papua New Guinea to dodge the excise duty. We dawdled along the vine-tangled coast, trolling for black bass, in the hope of putting the Indonesian Navy off our delightfully sweet scent. When our inflatable skudded past the lighthouse and the solar-powered beam that marked the border near Wutung we knew we had been successful. Shortly afterwards we put ashore near a wrecked WWII Japanese landing craft on the white sands of Vanimo Beach.

I bade farewell to my rough-necked but golden-hearted shipmates and strode off up the beach avoiding the onrushing herds of surfers seeking the perfect wave. Why do surfers always run? Do they think the sea is going to disappear suddenly into the distance like a departing bus? Whatever the answer there were plenty of them at

Vanimo who might have provided the answer – had it been possible for a man of my well-honed indolence to catch up with them.

Papua New Guinea was big-wave territory, pounded by breakers that at times reached homicidal force (a tsunami that struck the coast a little to the east of Vanimo in 1998 was estimated to have killed three thousand people), and it was attracting more and more groovy surfing dudes from around the world.

It is well known that all sports involving boards are cool, cutting edge and populated entirely by shaggy-haired young men in baggy clothes who talk knowledgeably about goofy foots, stale fish, the Zen-like harmony of cutting fresh powder and the reasons why, no matter how much you wash, your bellybutton always seems to smell of cheese.

Surfing, sailboarding, skateboarding and snowboarding have all established themselves down the years as bastions of the counterculture. Oddly, though, ironing has so far failed to take a hold, this despite the presence of streamlined boards, lots of hi-tech peripherals and the frequent attempts of parents to get their teenagers involved by picking up the laundry basket and calling, 'Yo, let's go crease some big white stuff, bro!'

Though it is alternative in so many ways, surfing retains one traditional aspect – women tend to be only peripherally involved, usually as spectators. Many reasons have been advanced for the essentially masculine nature of the sport, but my view is that it all comes down to the fact that the original boards fashioned for the Hawaiian nobility were made from the wood of the wiliwili tree (yes, really).

I checked in at a hotel of comforting vintage. Here ceiling fans revolved like lazy propellers, circulating warm air and chopping and dicing bush flies around the deceptively spacious lounge. That night after a pleasing dinner I was visited by the sort of moth my partner imagines every moth to be – one with the wingspan of a pigeon, antennae the size of fern fronds and a body like a furry frankfurter. The Hercules moth is the world's largest. Cast in many variegated shades of brown and fawn it not so much flutters round the light bulb as uses it as a punch-bag pap-pap-pap! I imagine that if one got in the closet it would munch its way through a two-piece suit in a matter of minutes, burp and say, 'What, no waistcoat?'

I would like to have seen the Hercules moth in my room pitted against a swarm of the Siberian mosquitoes, and probably could have done if I'd been able to locate the right sort of sporting webcast – 'Stand by for raw insect-on-insect action coming later, but first, from a secret location in Alabama, it's fiiiiiiiiighting tortoise time.' (The Alabama attack tortoise, incidentally, is a formidable creature capable of deceptive speed and blessed with jaws capable of crushing a little gem lettuce. It also displays a marked degree of cunning, shunning the frontal assault and instead preferring to stun its victim by rushing to the top of the nearest tall building and diving off on its head. The resulting sound has been likened to that of somebody cracking a chicken brick with a pair of maracas.)

I had imagined I would be able to get a bus out of Vanimo across the central highlands and on to the southern coast. This was a piece of massive self-deception right up there with Barbra Streisand's when she took the role of the $500-a-night hooker in *Nuts* (as a friend remarked, 'If she offered me $2000 a night then maybe we'd be getting somewhere near a negotiating position'). Papua New Guinea is roughly the size of Western Europe and has a road network that's about as developed as a baboon's sense of etiquette. This is hardly surprising since 29 per cent of the country is more than 1000 metres above sea level and most of the rest of it is rainforest or swamp.

There were two ways out of Vanimo – a Fokker Friendship to Port Moresby or a twice-weekly ferry that went along the coast to Madang, 'the Prettiest Town of the Pacific'. From Madang there was a road to PNG's second city, Lae, and from here, on my atlas at least, a broken red line worked its way south to the capital. Whether this was an unmetalled road or a smear of strawberry jam from a long-forgotten teatime scone I could not rightly tell, but I determined to find out.

The ferries from Vanimo to Madang, like most of the sea-passenger services in PNG, were operated by Lutheran Shipping, a name that seemed a little surprising until you learned that the local evangelical branch of the Lutheran Church owned it. It sounded like the sort of vessel that would carry no backsliders, but I managed to scramble aboard somehow.

We pulled out from Vanimo jetty and set a course east, hugging the channel between the swampy shore and the Schouten Islands and onwards into the Bismarck Sea. As that name, a range of mountains called the Hindenbergs and a highest point named Mount Wilhelm attested, the northern slice of Papua New Guinea had once belonged to the Germans. The Kaiser had taken control of it in 1884, his government grovellingly christening the new ter-ritory Kaiserwilhelmsland in his honour. Having spent much of their time securing a homeland in Europe the Germans had come to the empire-building game several centuries after the British, French, Dutch, Spanish and Portuguese and by then there was not much of the world left to grab. In the nineteenth century, though, having colonies was regarded as a status symbol amongst European monarchs rather akin to having lions on your gateposts. So Germany snatched northern Papua, part of Samoa, Namibia (or Luderitzland as it was catchily titled), Togo, Cameroon and Tanganyika. This was not as good as India, Cuba, Martinique, Java or Macao, but at least they did better than fellow late arrivals, Italy, who ended up with Libya and Eritrea.

During the First World War, Australia, which had been administering the southern section of the country on Britain's behalf since 1905, marched in and booted the Germans out. In 1976 the country was granted its independence. It was now an enthusiastic democracy in which no fewer than forty registered political parties wooed an electorate of less than two million.

My fellow passengers were an avuncular bunch. The women applied rouge to their entire faces from forehead to chin and sang songs of love, death and travelling by lorry. The men wore P-Funk afros and accompanied them on jaw harp and a variety of drums, the largest of which was known as bikpela bilong sing-sing.

The peoples of Papua New Guinea speak many different languages. Figures vary but it is somewhere between 700 and 817 (in PNG authoritative answers were as rare as rocking horse manure. Even population figures fluctuated between 3 and 5.1 million). To overcome the communication problem many people speak pidgin as their primary tongue. Pidgin is defined as any polyglot, non-indigenous tongue used for communication – Swahili and MTV being the two major examples. The pidgin in Papua was a kind of formalisation of native pronunciations of English words (cake was kek, New Guinea Niugini and so on) with lots of compound nouns that only really made sense after you knew what they were. Gras bilong ai, for example, was grass that belongs to the eye, or eyebrows, and pen bilong maus was pen that belonged to the mouth, in other words lipstick. From that you can probably work out what gumi bilong kok might be, but my guess is you will struggle with hap laplap bilong wasim plet and ol pikinini bilong rop wain.

Our devout ship gurgled along the coast past the inlet of Septik River, the little town of Wewak and the volcanic hump of Karkar. Mangrove swamps fringed the shore, and upturned dugout canoes lined the beaches like the discarded shells of enormous nuts. In the encroaching foliage sentinel pigs snuffled and grunted. The rainforest of Papua and West Papua covered an area the size of Mexico. They were described as the Lungs of Asia. Nobody could tell me where the heart of the continent might be, but an emerging consensus was that the Malaysian steel town of Ipoh was worth a shout if you were looking for the fundament.

We arrived in Madang some while after we had set off, time being of little account in a country where less than 2 per cent of the population owned a TV set. From the harbour I took a Public Motor Vehicle to the regional capital of Lae. PNG's PMVs were adapted Mitsubishi buses. Due to the truculent nature of the local highways many now had suspension which, to borrow a joke from Arthur Rimbaud (and, let's face it, how often do you get the chance?), had begun to enter the realms of the ideal. A kindly Papuan had earlier advised me 'To hesitate not in telling your stories to fellow passengers'. I heeded his words with gusto. As we bounced and jarred our way eastward I amused and entertained all on board – six men, three women and a large, bristly sow – with such success that many were suffused with newfound energy and felt able to disembark several dozen miles from their destination and walk the rest of the way.

Lae was home to the regional volleyball giants. The aroma of coffee beans and the sugary fragrance of frangipani were a constant factor of life on the streets, while in the surrounding country portable sawmills were playing an increasingly important part in forest management.

On the day of my arrival Lae was *en fête*. Men painted with white skeleton bones did totemistic dances and women in grass skirts smiled contentedly, as if oblivious to the invention of the strimmer. The palpable excitement was understandable. It was Pay Friday for public-sector workers. Rust-acned pick-up trucks piled high with beer crates rumbled into the suburbs; punch-drunk VX landcruisers growled past on their way to Planet Rock, Morobe's premier nitespot and pool hall. I took shelter in my hotel, a building of pleasingly robust aspect and twenty-four-hour security. Pay Friday had a reputation for turning rough. In a country where there are guards at the supermarkets, the police are armed with M16s and rugby league is a passion, roughness is best avoided.

The following morning I dodged through the vomit and broken teeth and made my way to Papua New Guinea Market. Here buka baskets were plentiful but biscuits were under construction. I was looking for souvenirs but much of what I found was a mite unsettling: snakespine necklaces, skull racks (well, you know how it is: you shrink those heads and then you never know quite where to put them, do you?) and penis gourds that would have inspired incredulity even in the copywriters behind the 'Do you want to turn your old man into a big boy?' ads.

Eventually I plumped for a bush twine bandicoot, which at least looked as if the person who made it had never eaten anyone.

Afterwards I went to find the place where the great aviatrix Amelia Earhart and her navigator Fred Noonan had last been seen alive. That was in 1937, Lae was a ten-year-old goldrush town and the two Americans were on the final stretch of a record-breaking round-the-world flight.

Earhart had first come to prominence in 1928 when a publicity agent acting on behalf of sponsor Mrs Amy Guest had selected her from a list of applicants to become the first woman to fly across the Atlantic. Mrs Guest, a wealthy US expatriate living in London, was determined to find 'the right sort of lady' for the honour. She was worried that without careful management the historic milestone might fall to an ill-educated, vulgar or sordid female – the distaff equivalent of pilot Jack 'Pal' Smurch in Thurber's story 'The Greatest Man in the World', who arrives home to a hero's welcome after a non-stop circumnavigation of the globe, but has to be pushed out of a hotel window by the Vice-President when he reveals himself to be a foul-mouthed womanising drunk.

The publicity agent plumped for the ex-nurse from Kansas (in more ways than one – later he dumped his wife and married her) and Amelia became the darling of at least two continents when her Fokker F7 successfully made the trip from Newfoundland to Wales.

As the heroine embarked on a celebratory tour of the US there were mutterings that it had all been a fix – not least from supporters of the two male pilots, Wilmer Stultz and Louis Gordon, who had taken turns flying the plane on that voyage. Accusations of what would now be called tokenism dogged Earhart ever after and, some say, may have contributed to her fateful end. Earhart did her best to prove the doubters wrong. In 1932 she made the flight across the Atlantic solo in a Vega 5B. And shortly after that she became the first pilot male or female to make the trip from Hawaii to California by air.

In 1937 Earhart set out on what she said would be her final 'stunt long-distance' flight – a round-the-world trip that would stick as near to the equator as possible. Her comment proved to be tragically prescient. In May 1937 she and Fred Noonan headed east from Oakland, hopping down to Brazil and from here across the Atlantic to Senegal and on to Khartoum. Karachi, Rangoon, Bandung and Darwin had all been passed when they arrived in Lae.

Here, 22,000 miles into her journey Earhart ditched her parachutes (most of the homeward journey was across the sea) and had the direction finder on her Lockheed Electra fixed. At midnight she and Noonan set off on the 2200-mile trip to Howland Island in the Pacific. Last radio contact came at 19.30 hours when the US Coast Guard cutter *Itasca*, which was stationed off Howland specifically to give guidance to the aircraft, received Earhart's radio message telling them that she was approaching but running low on fuel. She was never seen or heard from again.

Within a couple of hours US naval vessels and aircraft were searching the ocean in the area indicated in her last message. But despite the involvement of 9 ships and 66 aircraft, neither the Lockheed nor its wreckage could be found.

Earhart's fame and the sudden totality of her disappearance inevitably led to conspiracy theories of Bilderberg proportions. Amongst the front-running theories are that Noonan was an alcoholic who sent them miles off course; that the pair were on a spying mission for President Roosevelt and were shot down and captured by the Japanese who later forced Earhart to broadcast to US forces as 'Tokyo Rose'; that the couple had fallen in love during the course of the journey, ditched the Lockheed deliberately and lived happily together on a remote atoll for decades afterwards (you can almost see them there, sipping banana daiquiris while Glenn Miller and Elvis do a floorshow); or that the US Navy's search was badly organised and, despite costing around $4 million, missed the duo and their aircraft completely, and that the radio log of the *Itasca* was later altered as part of a cover-up and an officially sponsored whispering campaign about Earhart and Noonan's incompetence was authorised by Roosevelt himself.

That afternoon I visited the offices of the jauntily monikered Bas A Nova Company and asked about the possibility of getting a car and driver to take me to Port Moresby. The man behind the desk assured me that there were no roads linking the north and south portions of the island. By now I had given my atlas a thorough wipe and could see that the dashed red line linking Lae with the capital had been made by the cartographer's pen rather than some errant conserve.

'Are you certain?' I asked. The man said that he had lived all his life in Lae, some forty summers, and in that time as far as he knew there had not been nor was there now a road across the Bismarck Highlands. It is always unpleasant to have to get on your high horse with someone, but in this case it seemed fully justified.

'You are wrong,' I told him forcefully. '*The Times Comprehensive Atlas of the World* says there is a road there. *The Times Comprehensive Atlas of the World* is authoritative. It is the atlas of record. If it says there is a road there, there is a road there, whether there is a road there or not. And I want you to take me along that road, whether it be real, or no, in a four-wheel-drive vehicle with air conditioning and a radio tuned to a local station that plays the hits of Lionel Ritchie continually twenty-four hours a day with brief interruptions for news, weather and commercials for pile ointment and discount carpets. Do I make myself clear?'

An hour later I was heading south through the town of Wau with a breeze in my hair, a smile on my lips, a song in my heart and the beginning of a melodious chortle in my left kidney. It was a long time since I had ridden a bicycle, but I was beginning to enjoy it.

I ascended from the stifling plains, where the climate had swaddled me like a gigantic microwaved hot towel, into the friskier air of the mountains, pedalling through a land where flora, fauna and culture concocted a vibrant mosaic that languished untouched by the passing aeons and was a goldmine for the scenic photographer. The impervious forest was full of damp-nosed marsupials, spiny vermin and boring mites. The turgid bogs home to blood-sucking leeches and razor-fanged crocodiles. Bats as big as fox terriers noisily masticated plantains and flapped their black and leathery wings. Carnivorous, slack-bellied lizards sucked the juice from multi-eyed spiders. Men with bright yellow faces, scarlet moustaches and bone nose jewellery peered from clots of eight-foot-tall bristling grasses looking for heads to hunt. Mere words cannot accurately describe the sensation of being in so magical a place.

When darkness fell I took shelter with some men of a nameless and ancient tribe. My place of repose was a shaggy topped and authentic dormitory. In the highlands the tribesmen lived in primitive conditions in communal houses, worshipped the Duke of Edinburgh as a god and subsisted on a diet of rats and sago – so not that different from boarding school really.

Thankfully eating people was no longer compulsory. Up until the 1950s the Fore people of PNG had practised ritual cannibalism. In part of the funeral ceremony known as kukum na kaikai they ate the dead relative. Apart from providing plenty of opportunities for jokes along the lines of 'Your father doesn't seem to agree with me', 'I never could stand mother's taste', 'My brother-in-law's always made me sick' and so on, it also offered a welcome change of diet. One of the other main sources of meat for the tribal people was cave bats. They hunted them with lassoes made from rattlesnake skin. Which meant that before you got the chance to catch and eat a bat you first had to kill and eviscerate a rattlesnake. Compared to this cannibalism suddenly doesn't seem so bad. Scoffing your granny is not a pleasant thought, admittedly. But at least grandmothers don't hang upside down in dark holes surrounded by mountains of their own mouldy droppings. Well, okay, but not all of them.

The following morning, feeling surprisingly clean and hygienic and fortified by a breakfast of sweet potatoes, the lifeblood of the highlands, I remounted my bicycle (a top-of-the-range model complete with streamers, wicker pannier and horn that played 'Dixie') and pushed on through a squeaking herd of my host's fiscal hogs in the direction of Kerama, the village children chasing behind me, the sound of their flip-flops slapping the hard earth like the applause of an ironic mob.

The dangers of travel in Papua New Guinea are greatly exaggerated, inevitably by the deskbound, the lily-livered, the bungalow dwellers and the spunkless. That is not to say that mortal peril does not lurk behind every tree stump, or complimentary tropical fruit platter – it does. This, after all, is 'The World's Last Frontier', braved by a meagre twenty-four thousand visitors (one hesitates to mention the 'T' word in this rugged context) a year. Truly did PNG live up to its boast of being 'the last place people have never been to'.

Tribal warfare still plays its part in the life of the highlands. There are complex cultural reasons for this but mainly it was to give the men something to fill their days. The Melanesian women are practically workaholics. They farm, chop wood, transport heavy loads on their heads, cook, clean and look after the kids, which leaves the blokes with little to do save turn their hair into prize-winning flower arrangements and lasso the odd bat. Clearly, then, they were in need of a hobby. They could have taken up watercolours, tapestry or marquetry, but instead, like so many men across the world, they settled on kicking the shit out of one another.

I had been told that they did concern foreigners in their combat; that it was not unknown for a melee to stop in mid-thrust to allow a European to pass through the battlefield unmolested, like a blind man with a guide dog wandering across a council rugby pitch. Those short on spirit, courage and experience tended to fret about such matters. Noting that the tribesmen carried an arsenal of hardwood shillelaghs, fire-tempered spears and poison-tipped arrows, they would worry that collateral damage was inevitable.

Well, so what! For, after all, the warriors were not without conscience. They took responsibility for any accidents they caused. In a recent incident, for example, a member

of the Konoumpka tribe had killed a man from the
Kondika. After negotiation the Konoumpka agreed to pay
the grieving clan compensation of 50,000 PNG kina, 157
pigs and a cow. This was travel insurance enough for me,
though I couldn't help wondering if my own clan would
have space in the garden for that many pigs.

At lunchtime I paused at the top of a mountain pass of
Presleyan majesty to refresh myself with a cocktail of
crushed papaya and Pisang Ambon, the green banana
liquor of Indonesia (there had been a duty free shop on
that cruise liner). The sky was as blue as a baby's eyes and
as clear as his conscience. From somewhere far below
came the pounding rush of a barbaric waterfall. Yet even
here, so far removed from the wandering hands of moder-
nity, the hounds of sales were on my traces.

As I sat swigging my drink, gnawing an iguana drum-
stick and reminding myself that a spate of collapsing
lampposts in the Croatian capital of Zagreb had been
blamed on the high ammonia content in the urine of local
dogs, a chorus of bird calls, monkey whoops and BT
Yahoo's metallic thunk alerted me to the approach of
man. A minute or so later the glutinous mass of the sago
palms disgorged a fellow in a red boiler suit.

Mike O'Reilly had, I surmised from his manner,
cropped ginger hair and the intense staring eyes of a religious zealot who's just spotted a boy crumbling
communion wafers into a cardinal's hat. 'Is your septic
tank a ticking time bomb?' he growled in a style that
frankly brooked no demur. I should think Mike had a
voice like gravel in a cement mixer and I sensed that he
was one hell of a tough guy, the Red Adair of waste management. I imagined that in his line of work you needed
nerves of pre-tensile steel and an attitude so cool it would

freeze nitrogen. 'Get back, folks, there's a fair chance she's gonna blow,' Mike would say as he calmly approached a rumbling cesspit, monkey wrench in hand, toothpick slotted into the corner of his mouth. Which was good, because that was just the sort of man I needed. As I explained to Mike, I *was* worried about my ex-septic tank. I feared that, if not quite a ticking time bomb, it might well turn into some kind of lethal land torpedo.

The problem was, I told Mike, that it is one of the old above-ground bunker-type septic tanks made from brick and concrete and with a manhole on the roof. This tank had been replaced about six years before with one of those routine giant fibreglass specimen bottle things they bury under the ground, but it was still there and as far as I knew it was still full. I say as far as I knew, but the fact was I did know. It *was* full – I was just trying to blot it out because knowing it was there put me off my dinner. The reason we had had to have the new septic tank put in was that the old one had ceased to function. Or, as the Scotsman who came to empty it said, 'The pump cannae suck that lot up. It's as solid as the Rock of Gibraltar.'

So there it was sitting on the other side of our garden wall surrounded by elder trees, a nine-feet-square cube of compacted and antique dung. Which would not have mattered much except that it was perched precariously on the lip of a redundant quarry at the bottom of which, separated from the quarry floor by an ill-maintained drystone wall, was a railway line. My fear, I told Mike, was that rain and roots would gradually erode the ground around the septic tank until one day it came loose from its moorings and slid down the slope like some mad methane-powered bobsleigh and crashed into the side of the 8.54 Stranraer to Newcastle train. Imagine, I said to Mike, the newspaper headlines: 'Dozens Injured by Sliding Wall of Stinking Slop', 'Terror of Passengers Caught by Careening Crapball', 'Firefighters in Breathing Apparatus Struggle to Free Commuters From Toilet Waste Typhoon – Air "Still Lethally Combustible" says Chief'.

Think about it, Mike, I said. The loss of life and the irreparable damage it would do to Britain's already ailing public transport network. I mean, would anybody dare get on a train again if they thought that at any minute they could be derailed by a thundering tsunami of sewage?

As I said, Mike was plainly a rugged individual, but I'm afraid this vision had scared even him. I never heard from Mike again. My only hope is that he hasn't suffered irreparable psychological damage.

From then on my journey was, quite literally, all down-hill. I freewheeled with my feet in the air and the pedals flying past endless terrain, hornbills of great magnitude, Christian missionaries and native peoples who had thirty-six words for banana. By mid-afternoon I was whizzing down the highway into Port Moresby.

A survey carried out by The Economist Intelligence Unit recently ranked Port Moresby as the world's most difficult city for a foreigner to live in (Melbourne and Toronto tied for best). Problems included temperamental electricity, periodic water rationing, erratic telephone connections, carjackings, muggings, burglary and murder. To add to that there was political unrest. Papua New Guinea was poor and desperately in debt, political corruption was endemic. The previous year the army had briefly mutinied over proposed defence cuts and a few months later students, incensed by proposed economic reforms, had rioted. Cars were torched, shops looted and the police shot three people dead. The country was ranked 133rd out of 173 in the Human Development Index. The parliament building looked like the prow of a sinking freighter. Port Moresby was a place of bougainvilleas and barbed-wire entanglements.

It also appeared to be another of PNG's many dead ends until I discovered the Hypermax crew finder. This splendid site acted as a kind of lonely hearts' column linking up ships with sailors in all four corners of this funny blue and green cuboid we call earth. Using it, I was quickly able to locate a yacht that was sailing from Moresby to Cairns the following afternoon and present myself to its captain for inspection.

The skipper of the vessel, which I shall call the *Quavering Prince* for reasons previously elucidated, asked me to detail my crewing experience. I told him I had none, but that I was a professional wordsmith of fifteen years' service. I had noticed, I said, that the sailing fraternity made sporadic and scattergun use of the shortening powers of the apostrophe. Thus boatswain became bo'sun and the forecastle the fo'c'sle and so on. I felt I would be able to spend my time profitably aboard his yacht applying the naval apostrophe (or na'phe as I had begun to style it) more rigidly, thus slicing the time taken to issue orders by upwards of 30 per cent. The skipper plainly thought I was a right ars'le but since I would cost him nothing in terms of space or food, he agreed that it would be churlish not to take me.

(By the way: hap laplap bilong wasim plet and ol pikinini bilong rop wain – a dishcloth and a grape.)

10

'Behold the Turtle!'

Port Moresby to Socorro Island

On the shores of James Bay in northern Ontario it was −40°C. A savage wind whooped and hollered across the tundra. Go out in it for two minutes and you felt as if it had sawn open your skull, lifted the top and placed a pack of frozen turkey nuggets in your brainpan. Icicles hung from your eyelashes, earwax crumbled, your feet seemed to swell to the size of shoeboxes and your socks felt as if they were filled with polypropylene. By midway through your second shiver you'd be cryonically frozen and the locals would stand you in the corner of a lean-to log store and wait for the ground to soften.

There was nothing for it but to hunker down and wait until spring surfed in on a wave of hope and midge lava. I had hired a little cabin made of earth and wood for the purpose. It came furnished with a pot-bellied stove, kerosene lamps, a minimal electricity supply generated by a zinc-bladed wind turbine and rumbustious odours.

Months trapped indoors by the weather with only virtual company and I might have gone down with cabin fever, or at least its British equivalent – shed fever. In the spring visiting trappers would have discovered me wild-haired, mad-eyed, reeking of creosote and sorting bags of screws into colour-coded margarine tubs.

I passed my time happily enough scanning the local press and engaging in email games with my friends such as the popular 'Matrimonial Challenge'. This is a game of skill in which contestants must gauge the honeymoon destination of the happy couple from snippets of information gathered from the wedding reports in a local paper (the ones that usually come under the headline 'Slack-Jawed Fellow Weds Girl With Chubby Arms'), such as the groom's occupation, length of ivory silk tulle in the bride's train, name of the maid of honour. It is a game requiring intuition and knowledge of popular trends but I have found out that by shouting 'Dominican Republic' at every opportunity I can always finish in the upper percentile.

It was also a time to repair my equipment before the final push. This was not something for which I had any relish. Computer companies were determined to demystify their products and make them user-friendlier. For some reason – possibly, let's speak plainly here, because they were largely a bunch of socially demobilised sad-sacks in cargo pants – they had decided that the best way to realise this aim was to dress everything up in the kind of cutesie-wutesie imagery elderly thespians use when talking to their pet Pekineses. The result was that at some point over the coming weeks I knew there'd come a moment when I'd find myself on the phone to technical support listening attentively as an operative told me, 'Now point your winkie at the muffin and double-click. When the jell-o jar icon comes up open it and select baby-Boo. Have you got him? OK now, is he a squeaky bear or a bouncy bear?'

I confess that spending the winter in Canada was not

part of my original plan. The real traveller who circum-
navigates the globe is forced to do so in one direction,
whereas the virtual traveller can adopt an altogether less
obvious strategy. I had thought to travel around the world
in opposite directions simultaneously and meet myself on
Pitcairn Island.

But when I had mentioned my idea to a friend he had
remarked sternly, 'There is a fine line between a concept
and a gimmick' and that in his opinion I was jumping
over it with both feet yelling 'Geronimo!' in a high-pitched
voice, and so I had abandoned it in favour of a more sensible course.

I will not bother you with details of my vessel's voyage
through the Great Barrier Reef, home to countless bizarre
and beautiful killer jellyfish. Suffice it to say it was full of
alarums, hearty laughter, hornpipes, grog and barked
orders to 'Raise the furbelows, stow the Austrian blinds
and steady on the dado rail, helmsman.' The depths were
regularly plumbed.

We put ashore in Cairns, that most welcoming of cities,
at seven bells (EST + 18.37hrs). The climate was neo-
subtropical with a refreshing twist of lemon. The quayside
thronged with bronzed Australians who were, of a piece
and all at once, easy-going and ruthlessly combative. This
may seem like a paradox. It is not. The Australians com-
partmentalise. They are relaxed when it comes to
barbecues but fiercely competitive about games. The
British are the exact opposite. We struggle to beat anyone
at tennis, but when it comes to burning sausages and acci-
dentally setting fire to garden furniture we are so focused
there is literally no one who can live with us.

In Cairns tourism was unavailable and you were advised
to try again later. Nevertheless, I was still able to enjoy an

outback experience with platypus viewing surrounded by five thousand avocado trees, and the city's waterfront esplanade insistently beckoned me to take a stroll.

Australia is a land of wonders where lush rocks, rolling dust and majestic clouds of flies combine to create reverberant tapestries on an epic scale. Here you will find the Babindu Boulders of the Cassowary Coast, Valentine's Performing Pigs and the company that pioneered the trade in flavoured peanuts. The English commonly deride Australia's lack of culture but that is mere prejudice. Australia, after all, boasted the Sydney Opera House, Peter Carey, the Pedigree Meaty Bites Yard Dog Championships, Misky the Frisbee-Catching Wonder Whippet and the world's oldest gum-leaf playing competition.

There was also the Coober Pedy All-Australian Beer Belly Championships. When local politico Russell Hinze had presented the prize to the winner (120 bottles of beer, what else) a few years ago he commended competitors on their bloated physiques with the words, 'This just goes to show we're not a load of bloody queers.' Could even Florence in its Renaissance pomp have offered anything to match it?

Sadly, there was no time to explore this lustrous *olla porida* of refined and demotic ingredients. For far off in the distant past I heard the muffled hammering of a deadline that had finally worked free of its bonds and begun banging on the door of the cellar into which I had bundled it several years before. So instead of drifting down through Queensland in search of a crocodile that hadn't been wrestled by anybody called Steve, Rick or Shane, I began my journey to the New World. Using crew finder I signed up as kitchen boy on a tramp steamer. For six months we sailed around the Pacific islands with our cargo of old newspapers begging the price of a cup of tea off passing merchantmen.

My shipmates on the MV *Muddy Biscuit* were a bunch of sturdy composites. My direct boss, 'Cookie' Ping, was a foul-mouthed Malaysian Chinese with a Scouse accent, two glass eyes and a habit of throwing meat cleavers at evacuating rats. The first mate, Mr Hernandez, nursed a dark secret. So dark in fact that even he struggled to make out what it was. An enigmatic and brooding Swede, Captain 'Moose' Larsson, skippered the vessel; his despairing moans boomed out through the blackness of the long tropical nights like an existential foghorn. It was not a happy ship. Grievance hung in the air as irremovably as the scent of boiled cabbage in a bedsit. Only two things prevented mutiny – Larsson's incipient Nordic brutality and the vast and empty ocean, stretching before us every day, endless, unchanging, without hope or meaning, like a long and godless future. Them and the boson's Judy Garland evenings.

Tiny and widespread, the islands of the Pacific are dotted about like breadcrumbs, the occasional pea and the odd discarded dog chew on the vast blue linoleum of the seascape. They are all the same but marginally different. Topaz waters, a hook of white sand, mangroves crawling with mud crabs, a volcanic peak, grey jowls scrofulous with vegetation, palpitating palm trees, hibiscus, rhododendrons and such like blowsy shrubs, charming people with flowers in their hair, half a dozen colonial verandas, a copra-crushing plant, feral pigs, unemployment, Christianity and the hovering headline 'Trouble in Paradise' are the prevailing characteristics. The differences, such as I was able to discern them during my brief forays ashore, I will briefly elucidate.

In Noumea, New Caledonia, the locals spoke the language of the flowers. And French. The island had the biggest lagoon in the world and some of the cleverest crows. Chlorine and soft drinks are major local industries.

The guano-rich island of Nauru is the world's smallest republic. It is just eight miles square and home to four hundred banks. The road is also the airport. Nauru used to be known as 'The Kuwait of the Pacific'. Kuwait made its fortune out of oil, Nauru out of fossilised shit (some readers may wish to make a joke about Status Quo at this point).

On Norfolk Island the locals were celebrating their first murder for 150 years. Two million square miles of empty sea surrounded the island. It had been discovered by Captain Cook who had named it after the Duchess of Norfolk presumably because, like her, it was beautiful, vacant and completely out of touch with the modern world. The original inhabitants had come from Pitcairn in 1856. They were proud of the fact that they spoke with eighteenth-century Cornish accents, apparently oblivious to the fact that everybody in Cornwall speaks with an eighteenth-century accent. The Pitcairners believed in universal suffrage, compulsory education and their right of self-determination. At some point the island was taken over by the Australians who only believed in the first two. The Norfolk Islanders were not happy about it, but being of British descent confined their rebellion against Sydney's colonial oppression to pacing up and down in the garden going 'Tsk, tsk, tsk. Bloody typical!'

Suva, capital of Fiji, is the hub of the Pacific. A bubbling fish kettle of ethnic diversity, its ninety thousand inhabitants spend their time in the refulgent botanical gardens arguing about sugar cane quotas. A lot of the local crafts are imported from China.

We docked at Mata Utu, the largest town of Wallis and Futuna, a few hours after the New Zealand container ship *Sofrana Bligh*. There are thirteen thousand people living on the archipelago, fifty hotel beds and no opticians. News happens every three to four months, but it had been nearly a year since the last outbreak – when the islands' only newspaper, *Te Fenua Fo'ou*, had been shut down by the most important of the French possession's three kings for printing stories linking him with a corrupt politician. Manioc is cultivated to feed the pigs. The major export is stamps.

Nine islands make up Tuvalu, which means eight in the local tongue. Tuvalu was formerly the Ellice Islands. It got divorced from the Gilbert Islands in the 1970s to become the world's second smallest country. We docked at the capital, Vaiaku, on Funafuti just in time to enjoy one of the fortnightly twists at the Lagi Hotel. The nation had the sheen of prosperity about it. This was because its internet domain suffix of dot tv was currently earning it several million quid a year in rentals. Most of this had been spent on roads. By the time you read this there will be cars to drive on them too in all probability. It costs $20,000 to join the United Nations.

On the way east from Nukulaelae we crossed the international dateline and immediately switched from being ahead of the times to being behind them. There was no evidence of this in Tokelau, which has belonged to New Zealand since 1925 and has a population of 1431, none of whom has apparently bothered to design a national flag. Tokelau is made up of three atolls, one of which is called Fakaofo. We did.

Samoa used to be Western Samoa but has since become more central. It has a lot of coconuts, low wages and a twenty-minute prayer curfew every evening. If you want to know the time of the next bus you must ask a policeman. The inhabitants are generally wider than they are tall and most of the trousers on sale in the shops are actually Bermuda shorts for fat people.

In Pago Pago food and entertainment are children born of the same womb and happy hour goes on for twice as long as you might expect. Sensible and intelligent, the locals hold an annual holiday to celebrate the mating season of the reefworm and strongly disapprove of short trousers. American Samoa is one of the centres of the tuna-canning industry. Tuna is nicknamed 'the chicken of the sea' and is the USA's favourite sandwich filling.

On 'The Rock', as Alofi Niue was affectionately known, relaxed hours were the bread-and-butter of every day. There were no rivers or streams, the island was two-tiered and littered with intimate coves and their equally cosy womenfolk. On high days and holidays the brassiere and moustache were sported in splendid conjunction. Even a novice can catch the big fish here, though my own efforts were unsuccessful. 'To catch the fish you must first think like the fish,' an angling site told me. 'Ask yourself, if you were a fish what would you be thinking?' 'How do I burp under water?' I replied.

Fifteen nubbins of stone with the landmass of Greater Manchester spread over an area the size of India, the Cook Islands have no international disputes. This is hardly surprising as even the most ill-tempered of governments would be hard pressed to fall out with such a place. Aitutaki, the blue lagoon, is so beautiful even recalling the time I didn't spend there is enough to bring the glisten of dew to my world-weary eyeballs. Aitutaki was originally called Utataki Enua O Ru Ki Te Moana, which is longer than the island itself. Captain Bligh discovered it. The name was later shortened, possibly after several naval signalmen suffered cardiac arrest when semaphoring the original name from shore to ship. In 1990 Cook Island's weightlifting star Mike Terui was forced to withdraw from the Commonwealth Games after he broke his hand punching a pig. Mike thus joined middle-distance star Steve Ovett (ran into a church) and 10,000-metres runner Carl Thackeray (collided with a cactus) in the list of athletes suffering from acute SIS (Stupid Injury Syndrome).

Penrhyn, or Tongareva, is one of the Northern Cook Islands. It is a pure atoll, each of the string of islands connected just beneath the surface of the water. When Europeans first arrived here they found the inhabitants of each of the islands living quite separately, despite the fact that at low tide it was possible to wade from one to another along the submerged lava beds. The islanders took this singular attitude for one simple reason: surrounded by ocean, unvisited for century after century, they had gradually and understandably come to the conclusion that Tongareva was the only inhabited world in a deserted blue universe and, since the idea of a united planet is an anathema to mankind, had split themselves into tiny nations proclaiming their profound differences from their neighbours when to the outsider they all appeared very much alike.

We ventured on through the further eastern reaches of Kiribati, past elusive Starbuck Island that snuck under most lines of sight thanks to a highest point just 15 feet above sea level; Vostok Island, discovered in 1820 by Captain van Bellinghausen and named in honour of his ship, the exact spelling of whose name remains uncertain to this day; and Flint Island, which was home to a colony of brown boobies, the birds having selected this remote spot after suffering continual harassment from questing sailors eager to restock their ships' supply of fresh double entendres.

French Polynesia was quite literally shrouded in legend. The Tahitian metropolis of Papeete, with its marinas, luxury yachts and five-star resort hotels, was like an advert for Bacardi. The interior of the island, meanwhile, was all cascading waterfalls, giant ferns, coconut palms, papaya and everything necessary for a shampoo commercial. During the day aquamarine lorries chug past a cathedral with a spire that looks like a moon rocket from a 1950s comic; at night the urban scene is an enterprising pot-pourri of Polynesian, Mahu, gay and transvestite who get down to the latest sounds – in all probability high-octane BPM with house, garage, speed, thrash and handbag-wrestle all thrown into the mixer by DJ Dr Drunk and his Disco Jodhpurs. (I may no longer be young but I like to think I still grasp whence the young folk are coming. Recently I bought a CD by rapper Eminess. He's a bit like Eminem except that if you don't like any of the tracks you can take them back and exchange them for a pair of underpants or a prawn sandwich.) Pearls and tattoos are popular gifts while rolling food trucks are the favourite place to eat.

At Pitcairn Island we put ashore on the ship's boat. The local community police person warned us not to bring any honey, honey products or bee-keeping equip-ment with us as the island's bees were free from disease and were keen to stay that way. There were more pressing worries on Pitcairn, however – nine male islanders, a quarter of the population, faced charges of sexual assault. The investigation had been going on for three years. If the men were convicted and jailed it was likely that Pitcairn would cease to be viable as a community. That it was still one owed much to the dogged resilience of the descendants of first inhabitants, the escaped mutineers from HMS *Bounty*. The Pitcairners had left their tiny home en masse twice, the first time to relocate to Tahiti (they returned shortly afterwards, having found it godless and a tad gaudy) and then to Norfolk Island. Even Norfolk Island proved a bit fast for some of the die-hards and within a few years they had made the 4500-mile return voyage to Pitcairn. Nowadays the mainstays of the local economy were bone carving and feeding visiting detectives and the contractors who'd been brought in from New Zealand to upgrade the island's courthouse and prison.

Easter Island was also known as Rapa Nui and the Scared Island, or possibly the Sacred Island – opinion is divided. Though it is a tropical paradise much of it looks quite a lot like the North Yorkshire moors. It is the world's most isolated inhabited island and belongs to Chile, though it is as far away from Santiago as London is from Baghdad. There are 2700 people living on Easter Island; they enjoy dancing, music and wearing plastic coconuts on their chests. Land Rovers and horses are the commonest forms of transport and quite a few of the local shops look like pigeon coops.

The island's most famous inhabitants are the Moai. The Moai are gigantic stone heads with pendulous ears and an earnest yet thoughtful look that suggests they are trying to remember the name of the female assistant from *Ironside* for a pub trivia quiz. They measure upwards of 20 feet and the biggest weigh around 80 tons. There are six or eight hundred of them on Easter Island depending on who you talk to. Quite why these figures differ so markedly is hard to say, because it's not as if the Maoi are forever darting about the place to confuse anybody who's counting them. The Chileans are a proud and independent people and would probably be reluctant to admit they can't do it themselves, but my suggestion is that they settle the vexed question of how many heads there are by calling in outside help. The man they need is Peter Desailey. When I was in Cairns, Desailey had astounded the crowd at Hay, New South Wales, winning the final of the Australian Sheep Counting Championships by accurately counting an amazing 277 sheep. His opponent was one out with 278. If anyone can nail the Maoi figure once and for all, Pete is the man.

Nobody is really certain when the Moai were made or by whom, or how they were moved to their locations on the cliffs overlooking the sea and erected. Neither is anyone sure just what they were for. Possibly they were religious, or maybe they were designed as a deterrent to potential visitors. If it was the latter then they were ineffective, because it seems that the people who built them were wiped out by Polynesians sometime in the sixteenth or seventeenth century.

The fact that carvings of a creature that is half man and half bird have been discovered on Easter Island has inevitably led to speculation that the heads are somehow connected to travellers from another planet, probably great ogres who would have bought them to display on the knick knack rack saying 'Look at this! It's so tiny! How do they carve the little faces?'

The Isla Sala y Gomez are uninhabited, mainly by Germans.

It took us many weeks to reach the Galapagos Archipelago. We travelled across a seascape so awesome in its vast emptiness that at times it was tempting to believe we had been cast adrift in the mind of a radio DJ. We were followed on our wanderings for several days by a waved albatross that glided elegantly over the *Muddy Biscuit*'s obtuse stern trail. The waved albatross is a fascinating bird that hatches from an egg the size of a Coke can, has a reach comparable to that of an NBA star and can stay in the air for two years at a stretch, mentally toughened for such endurance by a chick-hood diet of regurgitated fish.

Despite the opportunity it provided for such pointless avian facts, I couldn't help worrying that the bird's presence might be an ill omen. A virtual jack tar of naval lore surfaced to put my mind at ease, after a fashion: 'The albatross is not unlucky of itself. It is only unlucky if you kill the albatross,' it said. 'Especially for the albatross,' I added.

As I watched the 22-pound bird swaying and bobbing on the currents the old salt continued, 'Of other evil portents there are many to trouble the sailor,' he intoned gloomily, 'a red-headed or flat-footed person met on the journey to the harbour, stepping aboard with your left foot forward, priests and flowers, curlews and cormorants all presage disaster, death and a last resting place in Davey Jones's locker. And what of your own benighted vessel? Did she not set sail on the first Monday in April, that infamous, blood-stained day upon which Cain slew his brother Abel?'

'No, it was Tuesday,' I said.

I felt the fellow glower. 'Hearken ye to my words,' he might have said. 'This vessel is marked. That bird,' pointing at the albatross with a finger as gnarled as a horseradish root, 'is not the only thing that is following us!'

And with a groan that would have sent shivers down the spine of a dictionary he disappeared back into the search-engine room.

The fellow was right, of course. The vast winged bird was not the only thing that pursued the ship. Ever since I had left Berlin my every move had been dogged by a red button marked 'Prizewinner'.

'Congratulations' read the sparkling legend that hovered above the ruddy bleb. 'What will happen if you push the magic button? What will you win?' By now I knew the answer. There was only one thing you could win on the internet – a vacation in Orlando.

At some point between Takayama and Nagoya the number of free holiday weeks in Florida I had picked up during my trip clicked over into its second year. By the time I had arrived back in England I would be able to spend thirty-six cost-free months in the Sunshine State, splashing about in a swimming pool beneath the dazzling rays of the local teeth. The prizes were being issued from the USA, a country where murder was punishable by death, so you'd think forcing holidays in the Sunshine State on innocent people would be worth a couple of dozen jolts from an electric cattle prod at least. Yet the FBI did nothing. What message does that send to the kids?

The Galapagos Islands are home to some of the most fascinating animals on earth. So isolated were the creatures from reality that they had not yet learned to be afraid of man. However, I did manage to startle one or two by jumping out from behind a boulder and yelling 'Boo!'

We anchored in Academy Bay and took the boat into the settlement of Puerto Aroya on Santa Cruz. The island was all rock and cacti. Here I patted the ageing head of a massive tortoise and chucked a frilled marine iguana

under his scaly chin. The exact names of the plethora of
birds I saw are lost in the fog of memory though I believe
there were a flock of swallow-tailed poltroons, a nesting
pair of unleaded petrels, a host of bobble-headed noddies
and the odd nasty tern.

The Galapagos Islands are owned by Ecuador who had
tried to persuade the world to call them the Archipelago of
Colon with conspicuous lack of success. The trinket shops
offered tasteful models of the animals I had seen. Or at
least some of which I had seen. One quadruped that had
eluded my gaze was a strangely disjointed equine in black
and white. I studied it closely and it soon became clear
that the Galapagos Islands must be the last remaining
wild habitat of the pantomime horse. I asked a number of
people to guide me to the place where I could see these
handsome creatures frolicking, or doing a traditional
conga with a bucket stuck on a front hoof, but the locals –
mindful of the wellbeing of these shy beasts and the fact
that they were still prized as a delicacy in Belgium – were
resistant even to the most persistent inquiry, fending me
off with silence and the odd reminder that internet stalk-
ing is a crime.

Ten days after leaving Santa Cruz we dropped anchor
near Ile Clipperton, a coral island about the size of a
shopping mall that was claimed by Mexico, owned by
France and disowned by humanity. I was sent ashore with
a treasure map they said had once been the property of
John Clipperton, the marauding eighteenth-century buc-
caneer in whose honour the island was named. The fact
that it was drawn on a Tiger beer mat should perhaps
have alerted me to its provenance even before the sound-
ing of the ship's horn and the rattle of its anchor chain
did. The *Muddy Biscuit* disappeared across the horizon

without so much as an ironic wave from my former crew-mates.

I was marooned. Frankly it did not come as much of a surprise. There had been an unpleasant atmosphere on the ship for quite some time. And it wasn't just emanating from Cookie Ping's vest. It is a sad point in a man's life when even his imaginary friends refuse to talk to him.

But there was little time for moping or recrimination because at that very moment a man whose problems put my own into perspective approached me, the soles of his elegant brogans moving across Ile Clipperton's friable shore with the delicate crunch of an Italian contessa eating an amaretti biscuit.

Prince Adogogo was the son of a tribal chief in Togo. The government had killed his father (whether by simple gunshot or bludgeon or by some more sadistic method involving overcooked Brussels sprouts and Eddie Murphy videos, I was unable to ascertain, the Prince being still too numb from grief to furnish such details) and now all the family wealth – about $37 million in gold and precious gems – was being held in a Swiss bank whence it could only be released using my credit card details. An unlikely tale you may feel. Perhaps. But I had been on the internet for nearly six months and had come to realise that it is by such Byzantine schemes that matchmaker fate brings men together.

His Royal Highness wanted money. Unfortunately my credit rating was so low it could crawl under a broody duck. However, I had something better than mere cash to offer him. I had a vision. I could give the luckless African noble the once-in-a-lifetime chance to invest some of his family millions in a gadget that was going to be the Filofax of the new millennium. Prince Adogogo, I said, listen to this: if you're one of those folk who find eating a bowl of pasta a nightmare then the Pasta Fasta is for you! No more expensive cleaning bills, no more angry dates with linguine down their cleavage, no more three-hour-long meals that leave you hungry, angry and splattered with vongole sauce from crown to waistband. When confronted with a bowl of Italy's finest simply whip out Pasta Fasta! It's the handy, pocket-sized, battery-powered food vacuum. Setting one sucks up the pasta. Setting two blows it straight into your mouth. No mess, no fuss, no 'Gee where did you get that tomato-coloured tie' misery. And Pasta Fasta also puts an end to those I-can't-use-chopsticks-but-I'm-too-embarassed-to-ask-for-a-knife-and-fork Chinese restaurant blues too! It's another life-changing idea from Chronco. Patent pending! At the time of writing the Prince was still considering my offer.

A troop of amiable Teutonic scuba divers rescued me from the shores of Clipperton Island and deposited me 700 miles further north on the Islas Revillagigedo, where man and manta ray meet and say, 'How the hell do you pronounce that?'

Socorro, the largest island of the archipelago, was shorn like a Red Army recruit. Sheep were everywhere, munching, burping and busily destroying the local eco-system. The dry forest was full of unique wrens, tree lizards and parakeets which busied themselves at an assortment of domestic tasks most of which involved chewing flies. The Germans were eager to swim with the mantas, vast flat fish that swooped through the oceans rippling and flapping like unanchored lino on a draughty floor. I could have accompanied them through the plankton-rich upwellings, but recent experience had soured me to human company and I made my excuses and left.

11

The World Capital of Capitals of the World

Socorro Island to Denver

I hitched a lift aboard a ketch returning from the Marquesas. From what I could judge the seventy-year-old owner, who was as likely to be named Count von Hummel as anything else, was a Mexican by birth whose family had arrived from Trieste with the ill-fated Emperor Maximilian in 1864.

Brother of Emperor Franz Joseph and brother-in-law of Princess Sissi, Maximilian spent his brief spell as ruler of Mexico compiling a three thousand-page guide to the etiquette of his new court only to be shot in a most uncouth and disorderly fashion by the supporters of Benito Juarez, a lawyer who couldn't match the Habsburgs for manners but had the sharp durability of gravel, which in war generally proves more useful. The von Hummels had swiftly recovered their equilibrium and went on to make a fortune from farming kidney beans. The count had recently diversified into Chinese eggplant with considerable success.

The count was distinguished of brow, with the nimble build of a tap-dancer and a habit of wearing his jumper

like a scarf. He asked what I could offer by way of pay-
ment for the 400-mile trip across the Sea of Cortez to his
native hearth. Since by now I had come to realise that the
one true currency of the internet was trivia, I tossed him
the fact that 95 per cent of all fauna in the Brazilian
rainforests is sloth and that cornstarch is a natural anti-
dote to iodine poisoning and told him to keep the change.
Impressed, he ushered me aboard. I spent the two-week
voyage in conditions of some luxury, sleeping in a hammock
slung between the wizen and the lineker. The ketch, the
name of which must remain a secret to protect the innocent and because the photo was too blurred to make it out
and making stuff like that up is tough and tedious work,
could not have been further removed from the *Muddy Biscuit*
if you had wrapped it in brown paper and posted it to
Moscow. The crew were silent and smiling, the vessel sleek
and spotless and none of the food had been mechanically
reclaimed.

As is traditional, the count's paramour was much
younger and taller than he. A bikini-ed ex-model, she
spent her days leaning against the rail with her head tilted
back and her face tracking the sun like the flower of a
Jerusalem artichoke. Occasionally she rubbed a honey-
coloured hand through her blonde hair. She had obvious
highlights, though I thought it best not to ask what they
were.

The Sea of Cortez was a safari park of aquatic vitality.
The fins of preposterous hammerhead sharks sliced the
cyanic water, sailfish leapt exuberantly and an olive ridley
turtle swam obliviously amidships, lost in her quest for
krill and the answer to who exactly Olive Ridley was and
what she had done to merit having a marine reptile
named after her.

We docked at the opulent marina in Puerto Vallarta. Once but a humble fishing village, this was now a world-class resort where visitors enjoyed the timeless experience of nature with the comfort of modern plumbing. The cosy streets of the city squirmed idly amongst the blossoms of history. The colonial plasterwork had a frivolous aspect and the Church of Guadalupe wore a jaunty crown. On the Malecon crowds of folk, friendly and diverse, rubbed themselves with cactus juice to protect against the glare of the spotlights in Carlos O'Brian's disco. So magnificent and celebrated were the sunsets they seemed to occur at least six times a day.

I took a taxi to one of Puerto Vallarta's innumerable beaches. The vehicle was one of the new breed designed in France and thrust down the highway by compressed air. The engine made a low thrumming noise, which left me feeling vaguely disappointed as I had hoped for something more like the gleeful razz of a loosed balloon. The air-powered taxis had been introduced to try and help thin Mexico's fast-coagulating smog, but there were doubts about their efficacy. They had to be charged with electricity, a process that took four hours. And some environmentalists felt that having cab drivers hanging round in a service station mini-mart eating microwaved pies and reading girlie mags for that length of time would do more damage to the planet than diesel fumes.

The beach was reached through a sheath of condominiums. On the shore chrome-haired men with sad moustaches and serviettes tucked under their collars wandered the gilded sand singing songs of romance and cockroaches, fireworks popped and cascaded in the ebony sky while donkeys with flowers in their ears smiled coquettishly from the shadows of the sweating palms.

Out in Banderas Bay (the seventh largest on earth) humpback whales crooned and schools of porpoises bludgeoned intrusive sharks to death with their rock-hard noses, so that young women in iridescent thongs could cavort in the creamy surf, their limbs unbitten save by the immaculate bridgework of a Californian software billionaire. Not that the odd gory attack would have been out of place. In Mexico sex and death are inextricably intertwined. This is either profound or crass, depending on how you look at it and incredibly messy whatever way you do.

I spent the night in a special-category hotel. I was not entirely sure what this meant but if the other guests at breakfast were an indicator it seemed you could only get in on the orders of a judge. I made my way to the bus station with a spring in my step and a portmanteau of tortillas under my arm and boarded an elite coach to Tepic.

The three-hour journey took me across the northernmost part of Jalisco Province. Jalisco means 'The Sandy Place' but that moniker offered the vista only rough justice. We swished past rows of blue agaves, vast pineapple-like plants with leaves so sharp they could impale a horse, that were turned into tequila, which could fell one. Mexico passed by in a swirl of colourful ceramics and improbable shades of blue. Dripping air-conditioning units jutted out from the sides of buildings like aluminium goitres, bellicose nomads danced, extraordinary art was visible in all its modalities and pretty, laughing señoritas in straining cheesecloth filled every nook and cranny that wasn't already tenanted by a lounging gecko.

We arrived at Tepic, a city endowed with a large degree of urbanism, just in time for lunch. The Mexicans have been cooking for seven centuries which means that if they were English the cabbage would be just about done. I dined splendidly on fish stuffed with 'previous' butter and coconut sweetmeats at a well-regarded table beneath the pine trees, fountains and lampposts of the central square. The restaurant had a patio atmosphere and fine views of the cathedral with its notorious tower of three bodies.

Tepic is the capital of Nayarit. Touristically speaking, Nayarit is one of Mexico's most lovely provinces. Its huge rich pastures sponsor cattle, bovine, ovine, equine and goatish. The vast flatness is cut by mountain chains and bisected by the Tropic of Cancer; the platinum coast is gently massaged by the softest of waves. In this geographically blessed location the plush soil bears fruits of unequal flavour. 'You are afraid of the defunct yet use a shroud as a coverlet!' was a local expression that begged to be thrown into the action.

At Tepic station, a buzzing concourse of variable humanity, I caught one of the twice-daily trains to Mazatlan. I was travelling on the Mexican Central. This was the backbone of the Mexican rail system. Unfortunately the train moved more like an invertebrate. The journey northward took several days. In fairness, I should say that this did include several long halts to allow the crew to remove build-ups of barnacles and another after we had collided with a deaf heifer, the driver explaining that his failure to brake was down to the fact that the moss growing on the windscreen had obscured his view.

Sluggard though the journey was, it was made bearable by my fellow passengers. I was delighted by their jollity and zest. After all it must be hard to remain upbeat when your country is $191 billion in the red and its fifth major export partner is the Netherlands Antilles. Unperturbed by economic circumstance they strode up and down sharing Mezcal from a bottle fashioned from a bull's foot, refrying beans, strumming guitars and encouraging the communal singing of folkloric songs. One told of a group of workers travelling to Pennsylvania: 'On arriving in Milwaukee/The Italian women asked us/"Where are you Mexicans from?"/We replied, those of us who could speak English,/"We are from the state of Chihuahua and have a contract with the government."'

Hearing this could only make me feel a little homesick, for its verses closely echoed those of a popular fifteenth-century English folk tune, 'Bonny John the Supply Teacher' with its evocative chorus, 'The Geography class asked "Where is Miss Reeve?"/ Bonny John replied, "She is off on statutory maternity leave."'

Mazatlan is a city with diverging personalities, carefully nurturing the visitor while never forgetful that it is the prawn capital of the world. A prawn's heart is in its head and it rejoices under the genus name of *Penaeus*. Nevertheless, I ate a bountiful quantity in a seafood restaurant with prices to suit the shallowest vest. He who lives with hope dies happy is a Mexican proverb with which fans of *Thirtysomething* may wish to argue.

The climate of Mazatlan is semitropical. What the other half is no one would tell me. It was overhung by the Sierra Madres and famous for its colourful fiestas and illustrious roundabouts. The ubiquitous Mexican chortling lasses were on every corner, their merry peals blending with the booming hype of property developers and the semiautomatic bursts of hooded gunmen. Keychains make an interesting departure gift for diligent hotel staff and will often be appreciated more than cash.

The next day I boarded the northbound train once more. We travelled across Sinaloa Province where the abundance of sea tempered the climate and the pressure was 29.82 inches. Sinaloa was a privileged land of rich submarine aqueous mantels, irrigation ditches, international tattoo parlours, prickly jungle and stereos. I broke for a lunch of strained fish with lime in the state capital, Culiacan.

I was unable to find my next port of call, Cuidad Obregon, due to a search error and moved on instead to Hermosillo, 'City of Oranges'. The capital of Sonora bills itself as 'Quite different' and it is, especially from Stevenage. The city sports a ball gown of illuminations and stares forthrightly at the future. Cash crops fuel the local economy, vegetables are free, beer is of the barrel and the roast beef celebrated in ballad and verse. The most fascinating thing about Hermosillo, however, is that it remains permanently on the cusp of day and night. This affords tourists and visiting media professionals limitless chances to capture its colourful desert twilight for posterity. Nothing in Hermosillo – not the fractally eroded buttes, the giant digital cacti, the daedal flourishes of the Spanish colonialists or the reflective modernism of the autonomous university – can be seen without the backdrop of apricot-fading-into-blueberry sky. It is a state of affairs at once marvellous, yet eerily monotonous, though my view may be coloured by the fact that my night in a horizontal complex was disrupted yet again by gaggles of Mexican womenfolk who chuckled throatily outside my window.

The next day I continued my long journey through a landscape of yellow flowers, chirruping bats and wide men in excitable ties. At Nogales I crossed the border into the United States. I left Mexico to the accompaniment of a valedictory clarion of maidenly laughter which in truth

I barely heard. I was on edge. My nerves twanged like banjo strings. This was the part of my journey to which I had least looked forward. The USA was a blighted land, strip-mined to oblivion by thousands of greedy British authors. Now all that remained were vast heaps of worthless slag on which the occasional English travel writer could be seen scrabbling desperately in search of one last payload of fat people jokes. What could one say about the United States that hadn't been said already a thousand times? Well, that it is an incredibly small country populated by thin, sarcastic atheists who walk everywhere would be a start, I suppose.

In fact, I must report that during my long and arduous haul from the Mexican border to the 49th Parallel I did not see a single overweight person. All the Americans who crossed my path were as finely honed as Japanese aphorisms. The women exuded wellbeing and strode about the place, arms swinging as if they had just skimmed a discus the Olympic qualifying distance. The menfolk, meanwhile, were perpetually engaged in shovelling snow, wrestling with golden retrievers or simply resting a foot on a conveniently sized rock and staring into the middle distance of prosperity, hardwork and easy-fit jog pants. All of them wore the look of people fulfilled through physical exertion. Indeed, by the end of my journey across the States I had begun to suspect that the average US citizen could achieve orgasm just by lifting a log basket.

Nogales was a city divided by a fence. Practically everybody who lived there was a legend and mammoth bones were piled up on every street corner. Apart from that it was largely weather and golf.

I headed northward across Arizona. The US national census showed that between 1990 and 2000 the average

Arizonan had aged by two years. This was a blow to anyone selling wrinkle cream but it shouldn't encourage complacency. The rate things were going in 2150 the whole population would retire.

Arizona is home to the world's tallest fountain and its largest sundial. The state gemstone is turquoise. The state fossil is petrified wood. The official state neckwear is the bola tie. The state amphibian is the Arizona tree frog. As yet there doesn't seem to be a state textured interior-wall covering but that is probably only because the debate about the relative merits of Artex, anaglypta and flock is still raging in the legislature.

Arizona is a vast landscape of red rocks, golden-leaved trees and Titan missile silos, silent save for the mewing of raptors and the occasional bang of an exploding septic tank. We passed by ostrich farms, state park dumpstations and the town of Coolidge where a protective steel umbrella erected over a Mesozoic ruin was costing tax-payers $38,000 a year to paint. 'Thanks for coming. Don't forget to come back soon!' the citizens cried to even the most fleetingly glimpsed visitor.

I arrived in Tucson in mid-afternoon and immediately flagged down a taxi to take me to Biosphere 2, a giant glass ark that looked as if it came straight out of a 1950s sci-fi novel. The Biosphere 2 project had begun in the early 1990s. Funded by a Texan oil billionaire it was a sealed ecosystem that contained several mini tropical land-scapes including a rainforest, a coral reef, a savannah, a marsh and a desert. It also contained a human habitation area and a farmed zone. The biosphere was the most tightly sealed structure ever built. Its electricity was gen-erated by solar panels and the internal weather system controlled by computer. The animal population consisted of insects, fish, reptiles, chickens and eight human beings, four men and four women. The idea was that the biosphere would be occupied for one hundred years by 'biospherians' working in two-year shifts. These teams would grow, harvest and gather all their food. Unfortunately, problems with crop failure led to the human aspect of the experiment being abandoned in 1995 when the second group came out several months early looking dangerously malnourished. Biosphere 2 was one of the most advanced scientific experiments of the late twentieth century and set out to answer important questions about sustainable farming, recycling and the feasibility of setting up colonies on other planets. However, there was only one question the general public really wanted answered: did any of them have sex? And the answer delivered loud and clear by everybody at Biosphere 2 was 'Mind your own business'.

After my visit to the biosphere I did not have much time to dally in Tucson. I spent the night in the upscale eastside, dining in a western eaterie where the 'strictly no necktie' policy added to the wacky fun. The next day my plans were thwarted when the History of Pharmacy Museum told me I was forbidden to enter. This proved to be fortune draped in the vestments of disaster, though, for it allowed me to go to the Otis H. Chidester Scout Museum instead. Otis had been the oldest continuously active Scout in the US (Tucsonans plainly had a thing about continuity – the city also boasted 'the USA's oldest continuously owned family restaurant') serving for eighty-four and a half years before the woggle. A game old bird with a scouting shirt buried beneath an epidemic of embroidered patches, he stared out from behind owlish glasses with the look of somebody about to burst into a hearty chorus of 'For He's A Jolly Good Fellow'. Otis had pioneered the idea of the Printing Merit badge and helped invent the sleeping bag. Fittingly, he had died on Lord Baden-Powell's birthday.

After that uplifting yet strangely poignant experience I boarded the train again, heading north to Phoenix. The landscape was the same unchanging jumble of mesas, buttes and mountains in varying shades of orange ranging from processed cheddar to condensed tomato soup. The colours gave the countryside a funky seventies retro feel, but I couldn't help feeling that in a few years' time it would look very passé and cheesy. Wildlife was said to be abundant here but the only fauna I caught sight of were fibreglass dinosaurs and the occasional gaggle of genuine college students eager to play naked. It is illegal to shoot cacti in the USA.

Phoenix was a fast-growing, sprawling city that was popular with active seniors aged fifty-five and over. The Breck Shampoo Hall of Fame had shut down, but luckily the Mystery Castle was still offering guided tours. The Mystery Castle is solid testimony to US vim and ingenuity. A builder, Boyce Gulley, constructed it from scrap materials. If he had been British he'd have got a few pallets and doors and knocked up a treehouse. Because he was American he didn't stop until he had a mansion with eighteen rooms, thirteen fireplaces and an underground pub. His daughter still lives in it.

Phoenix was also the last resting place of Miracle Mike, the Amazing Chicken. Mike had died in the autumn of 1946, which was quite a feat since his owner, Lloyd Olsen, had chopped his head off in April 1945. That had happened at the Olsen family farm in Fruita, Colorado, when Mike, a Wyandotte rooster, was just five and a half months old. He shook off the loss of his brain without much fuss, put on weight and was soon so famous he made *Life* magazine. Mike was insured for $10,000.

Mr and Mrs Olsen took the rooster on a US tour, exhibiting him in Atlantic City, New York, Los Angeles and San Diego and charging 25c admission. Then, coming back from San Diego, disaster struck. In a motel in Phoenix Mike choked to death. Feeling guilty about his failure to save the unfortunate cockerel, Mr Olsen told everybody back in Fruita that he had sold it to a carnival operator in California and that it was being displayed nationwide. As a result of this little white lie many people still believed Mike was alive as late as 1949.

Mike's departure from this earth was sad, but at least he had a better time of it than some of the inevitable copycat headless chickens that pursued the same directionless course. One no-brain Coloradoan rooster named Lucky lived for eleven days before fatally colliding with a stovepipe.

I changed trains in Williams. The schedule allowed me time for a meal. I ate huevos rancheros (not served with potato) washed down with orange juice (no refill) while enjoying old-time music and a selection of James Dean memorabilia. Williams stands athwart Route 66, experiences all four seasons and is The Gateway to the Grand Canyon. The Grand Canyon wasn't on my route. This was a disappointment not least because all through my meal (Please inform staff you wish to split the bill *before* ordering) I had been deluged with publicity for Marvelous Marv's Grand Canyon Tours, which, from what I could judge from the pictures, promised not only an insightful journey around one of the world's natural wonders in the company of Marvelous Marv (something of a natural wonder himself) but also regular glimpses of flying saucers.

Flagstaff is known as The City of Seven Wonders. It is named after a flagstaff. This may seem a little prosaic, but it is better than some of the alternatives. Across the state-line in New Mexico stands The City of Truth and Consequences, which took its appellation from a 1950s radio quiz show.

I hadn't been planning to stay the night in Holbrook, but when the train halted there a big sign 'Have You Slept In A Wigwam Lately?' flashed up. Clearly this was an opportunity not to be missed and so I checked into the jus-tifiably renowned Wigwam Village Motel and my very own tepee. Sleeping in it was quite like being on the Great Plains with Sitting Bull and Crazy Horse except that it was air-conditioned and made out of concrete and there was no boiled dog on the menu. Still, you can't have every-thing.

Just after Lupton we crossed the state border into New Mexico. New Mexico is a land of faraway wonders where 360° panoramas yell aloo-hoo to the natural lover of adventure. The state motto is *Crescit Eundo*, 'It grows as it goes'. This is one of those phrases that at first seems to make no sense whatsoever but, after careful thought and consideration, is revealed to make *absolutely* no sense what-soever.

The train drummed on through Gallup, a vibrant com-munity famous for the rich abundance of its Native American crafts including baskets, rugs, jewellery, neon signs and hollow-stem auger drills. Gallup was in the grip of controversy. Highway 666 ran through it, its satanic implications causing havoc amongst local evangelists who were campaigning for it to be changed.

We sizzled on through Grants, once designated 'Carrot Capital of the World' until Cellophane wrapping saw the title usurped by California. In many ways the latter part of Grants' designation was no surprise. In the Far East every city seemed to be 'The Pearl of . . .' – 'The Pearl of the Gobi', 'The Pearl of the Pacific', 'The Pearl of that Peninsula of Borneo that Sticks Out at a Vaguely Obscene Angle but for Which There Is no International Recognised Name', and so on. In the USA every city or town seemed to be the 'World Capital' of something or other. Rocky Ford, Colorado, was 'The Melon Capital of the World'; Sumner, Kansas, was 'The Wheat Capital of the World'; Akron, Ohio, 'The Rubber Capital of the World'; Austin, Texas, 'The Live Music Capital of the World; and High Point, North Carolina, 'The Furniture Capital of the World'. Wisconsin, meanwhile, boasted Wausau, 'The Ginseng Capital of the World'; Bloomer, 'The Jump Rope Capital of the World'; Somerset, 'The Inner Tubing Capital of the World'; Boscobel, 'The Turkey Capital of the World'; Sisley, 'The Canned Ham Capital of the World'; and Green Bay, 'The Toilet Paper Capital of the World'.

New Mexico is the tourist destination of choice for wealthy aliens. The aliens tend to land at night, mutilate a few cattle and then take people away as souvenirs (of course if the people of New Mexico had the sense to carve a few giant stone heads this wouldn't happen). Aliens had abducted so many people in New Mexico that at times there were just three people left to run the whole place. Luckily one in four New Mexicans worked for the government, so nobody noticed.

Sometimes the aliens returned the people they had abducted and asked for a refund because their sister had already got one just like it. Before they did so they completely erased their memories so that all they could remember of the incident was that the aliens who had abducted them wore silver all-in-one body suits and Oakley eyejackets and showed a childish interest in their captives' private parts possibly because they didn't have any themselves.

The biggest alien resort was the area round Roswell 100 miles across the Sacramento Mountains from where I was now. A UFO was said to have crashed at Roswell in 1947. The US military quickly recovered the bodies of the dead aliens and carried out autopsies on them in an army field hospital. This was captured on film that then somehow found its way into the hands of the media. The autopsy film revealed the alien super-beings to be made out of Plasticine. This answered many questions, not least why they only visited earth at night. Obviously if they'd come during daylight the sun would have dried them up and they'd have gone all crumbly.

For some reason, though, the government didn't want anyone to know about the visitors from Planet Play-Doh and so they had organised a cover-up. This involved an endless string of elaborate ruses the most fiendish of which was simply to say 'Prove it' to anybody who raised the topic. Damn but those guys are cunning.

Why the US government was acting in this way was a puzzle. A personal view is that it was due to a puritanical streak that still ran through American society. In much of the country draconian laws govern sexual activity. It is well known, for example, that in some states it is illegal for anybody to engage in what the law defines as 'Jesus-endorsed procreative monkey business' except in the presence of a licensed pastor, while in the Bible Belt an unmarried man can be jailed for three years for wearing coloured underpants. The girdle is still compulsory for female residents of South Carolina and in Tennessee possession of a bellybutton carries a mandatory ten-year sentence. The official sexual position of the state of Arizona is abstinence.

Putting the autopsy findings together with the experience of abducted earthlings, US scientists concluded that the aliens were here for one reason only – to collect more Plasticine so they could make genitals for themselves and engage in acts of godless obscenity. Clearly that had to be prevented. Luckily the fact that the aliens could only move around safely at night helped, because all the craft shops were shut. But if the populace found out, how long would it be before some art store owner looking to make a fast buck introduced twenty-four-hour opening?

In Albuquerque I had planned to souvenir shop at the National Atomic Museum, but it transpired that the gifts I had been looking for – earrings featuring miniature replicas of the A-bombs Little Boy and Fat Man – had been withdrawn from sale after complaints from the citizens of Hiroshima and Nagasaki.

Fortunately, Albuquerque had other delights to offer. The city is home to the International Rattlesnake Museum. As well as an impressive collection of 150 live snakes, including an albino rattler named Marilyn, this boasts an astounding array of snake-related artwork including a wooden skull with a mahogany viper slithering through its eye sockets and earholes. The accompanying caption said that this was an opium casket, but I couldn't help thinking it was actually the biscuit barrel of a very mean old lady – 'Help yourself to a cookie, dear.'

'Waaaaah!'

The museum was keen to dispel myths about the nastiness of the rattlesnake, pointing out that more people in the US die each year from bee stings than snakebites. 'The coral snake has highly toxic venom but a demure manner,' announced one notice board, apparently oblivious to the fact that you could say exactly the same thing about Truman Capote. And you wouldn't want to find him curled up in your boot, would you?

I spent the night in Las Vegas, NM. This was the original Las Vegas, straddling the old Santa Fe Trail, at once proud of its heritage and optimistic about its future. It is a splendid place, one of the nicest I have never visited. There was a museum that looked like the jail from *Rio Bravo*, shops selling boots and saddles, a farmers' market where pick-up trucks displayed massive pumpkins and three-foot-long dreadlocks of chillies and a saloon that invited passers-by to stop in for their favourite libation. Inside the customers were wearing braces and wiping froth from moustaches that would have shamed a Dutch barbershop choir.

Springer was home to New Mexico's only electric chair and also boasted a shoe that had once belonged to the world's tallest man, Robert Wadlow. Wadlow was born in Alton, Illinois, in 1918. He weighed an average eight pounds six ounces at birth but by the time he was eight had rocketed to six feet two inches tall. By the age of fourteen he had become the largest Boy Scout in history. His shoes were size thirty-sevens and were made for him by the International Shoe Company which gave them to him free in return for publicity work. Ironically it was his feet that led to his death when a blister on one of them turned septic and he died from blood poisoning at the age of thirty-two.

Wadlow was unchallenged as the tallest man ever (and likely to remain so since doctors can now treat the sort of pituitary gland malfunction that led to his childhood growth spurt), but the world's tallest living man tag was currently the source of some controversy with two rivals battling for the title. A Tunisian, Radhouane Charbib, at seven feet eight and three-quarter inches was the current holder. He was feeling the pressure from Hussain Bisad, a twenty-seven-year-old Somali refugee who had fled his own country after being shot in the knee by robbers and was currently residing in Neasden. Mr Bisad was officially the tallest living Somali at seven feet seven, but said that he had since grown two inches. Radhouane challenged him to get measured and the outcome of his date with the tape was eagerly awaited. Mr Bisad was laid back about it, saying he was extremely happy living in London despite not being able to fit into phone boxes or use the underground. Though given what phone boxes and the underground are like this may actually be *why* he was happy living in London.

In Raton (celebrated in song by Townes Van Zandt) recent rain had eased firework fears and we crossed the state line into Colorado. Despite the fact that its name means Red, Colorado was distinctly less roseate than the previous two states. In fact it wasn't red at all. I regarded this as rather an advantage to Colorado, especially when it came to selecting accessories.

Colorado announced itself as home of the world's largest flat-topped mountain and the USA's oldest wooden merry-go-round. Apart from that it was breathtaking scenery morning, noon and night. By the time I got to Trinidad I needed an oxygen tent.

I was happy to stop off in Trinidad where the Carnegie

Library had an unusual two-ply tin roof and Safeway had replaced the old red-light district. But I spent the night in Pueblo in a hotel that promised Jacuzzi sweets, but failed to deliver. Local landmark the Bishops Castle was totally decorated with ornamental iron. The next day I was back on the train heading north again along the eastern fringes of the Rockies. Majestic peak followed majestic peak followed majestic peak. This was a distinct problem with the American landscape – there was just too much of it. It went on and on. And on. And on. And on. You saw one rust-coloured chimney of stone outlined against a cloudless aquamarine sky and you said 'Wow!', but by the time you had seen 176 of them you wanted to yell 'Okay, we get the message.'

Denver has a higher percentage of college graduates than any other US city. Its greatest contribution to world culture is the cheeseburger. Denver is a mile above sea level and subject to such low humidity that sweating is impossible for even the fattest opera singers. Antiperspirant is sold here only as a status symbol.

I ate in a huge restaurant that featured indoor waterfalls, caves, climbing walls and regular mock gunfights. The food was nothing to write home about. Unless your parents happen to be health inspectors, that is.

12

A Shelter in Indefinite Wine

Denver to Nuuk

I liked to think I had spent the late autumn in northern Ontario trapping. I was reluctant to kill animals in this cruel manner even virtually, though, and so instead I baited my snares and gins with banana and vanilla and caught several dozen bowls of custard. I sold the skins to a manufacturer of bathing caps for a handsome profit, which I sensibly invested on eBay for a 1963 edition of Waddington's Formula One, the Grand Prix motor racing game that's so rich in nostalgia you can practically smell Graham Hill's moustache wax and hear the high-octane whine of Jackie Stewart. It was mint throughout though the suspicion that two of the dashboards were substitutes gnawed gently away at me like a toothless crone at a ham knuckle. I tried not to let it spoil things. If well cared for, old toys gradually accumulate value. Some regard Formula One as a boardgame. I view it as a way of life and a pension fund all in one.

I took the wheel of the red car and raced over ten laps against a packed grid of five other vehicles. The car I was handling mysteriously came in last. That was always the way. As a boy I had played Subbuteo table football against myself and lost. As I put the champagne back in the icebox I found my mind drifting back.

Drifting back.

Drifting.

The black of night. Clickety-clack clickety-clack clickety-clack. It is the sound of a railway train, or somebody capable of knitting very fast in total darkness. Clickety-clack clickety-clack clickety-clack. I rise slowly from sleep. Reach out and click. A window opens, light pours in, shadows scurrying before it like, in the deathless words of the great Vivian Stanshall, convent girls menaced by a tramp. Through the window I see a dun and limitless landscape, mottled, fibrous and scorched as a well-used asbestos mat in a school chemistry lab, a white clapboard church in the middle distance has a message board mounted across the eaves: 'This programme has performed an illegal operation', it reads, 'and will be shut down. If further problems persist contact the vendor.' The church flickers for a moment and then fades to blackness as a buzz rises and breaks with grim finality.

What I had feared all along had finally happened. And as well as my private email address finally falling into the hands of the cut-price muscle relaxant people, my computer had crashed head-on with oblivion. To be honest, the end had been coming for some while. Every morning when I switched it on that horrible noise that sounds like a thumb running down the teeth of a metal comb went on longer and longer. By the time I got to the US–Mexican border it was lunchtime before it stopped and it frequently burst out again for no apparent reason when I was typing.

Then, just as I was settling myself in a restaurant serving traditional portions of catfish with antique trimmings, it gave one last prolonged creak and disconnected automatically with a discordant electronic 'Thrunk!' When I tried to log on again the Netscape window flashed up just long enough for me to read the Powered by Netscape Gecko blurb before it disappeared again.

I tried phoning the shop where I had bought the Compaq, but when I mentioned the make and the model the sales assistant asked me if 'you've tried pulling the choke out before you turn the ignition'. He was clearly very old for a computer salesman.

I was trapped in Colorado for over a fortnight until a friend offered to bring me one of his office machines. It was an iMac with a broadband connection and, frankly, it was baffling to me. Images and information popped up with the rat-a-tat-tat of automatic rounds. The speed of it all was scary. I felt like an eighteenth-century waggoner suddenly dropped in the driving seat of Michael Schumacher's Ferrari. Things flashed by so quick I could barely register them.

Northbound again. The train didn't continue into Wyoming but rebounded off the state line and ricocheted to the south-west, so I had to get a bus from Greeley, Colorado. Greeley was named after an editor of the *New York Tribune*. The population spent its time falling off horses.

The Greyhound bus lived up to its name. It was sleek, slender and incapable of outrunning an electric rabbit. This was not entirely the vehicle's fault. The speed limit in the USA is very low. This is partly for safety reasons, but mainly to prevent people from leaving. For a law-abiding citizen to get from Kansas City to the nearest international boundary in an automotive vehicle it takes approximately thirty-seven years.

We crossed into Wyoming. Wyoming is the most thinly populated state in the Union. Cattle, sheep and antelopes outnumber human beings. There are five people every square mile, which means everybody has to shout a lot and waiting tables is a job for endurance athletes only. The land is prostrate and voluminous; possessed of an epic, sombre flatness that is the topographical equivalent of Leonard Cohen. Only the odd hillock, gaggle of trees, or amazing offer of 80 per cent off all inkjet cartridges breaks the awesome plains and even a pile of bison dung represents a landmark.

Luckily there are bison roaming everywhere in Wyoming. Big, enormous-headed beasts, they have the huge shoulders and tiny waists and bottoms of a cartoon strongman. Bison are the heaviest land mammal in the US and charge at 30 mph. Old-timers say that if a bison attacks you must never try to outrun it. Sadly they rarely say what you ought to do. Burrowing is one option.

Once, the bison wandered wild and free in huge herds numbering in the millions, but now they are farmed. Bison meat is low in fat, which is a clear advantage in a heart-healthy society. Unless you happen to be a bison, of course.

I debouched in Cheyenne. Cheyenne was the home of Wild West legend though most of the city is now an air-port. Wild West legend has been given a bit of a gloss by fiction. Study pictures of most Wild West outlaws and you quickly see that they don't look a bit like Clint Eastwood. In fact most of them would struggle to see off Emmett T. Walsh in a beauty contest. Far from being glamorous, the average Wild West outlaw had the feral features of a knee-bobbing, table-drumming, cross-eyed crazy who would start a fight in an empty barn. In place of slick trigger-nometry, salty wisecracks and death-defying leaps into the saddles of waiting horses, most of them lived lives of idiotic incompetence and comedic brutality. The James Gang's criminal career, for instance, began when a cousin beat a man to death with a frozen fish. The law enforcers were not much better. Bat Masterson and Wyatt Earp stared out of the photographs with the mean-eyed amusement of a buzzard watching an armoured van speeding towards a deaf badger. Just looking at them made you feel like your skull was fractured.

These days things in Wyoming were on the up. The state had a massive budgetary surplus thanks in no small part to a fivefold increase in the price of coal-bed methane (three words which are possibly the least romantic on earth after 'This is a courtesy call on behalf of Everest double glazing'). Golf had replaced gun-slinging as the hobby of choice and in the local saloon my request for 'a shot of redeye in a dirty glass' met with blank looks and an offer of the cocktail list. I spent the night in a hotel that promised 'an evening turndown'. This was pretty much the story of my life.

The Union Pacific Railroad ran through Cheyenne but it had discontinued passenger services on this stretch of the line back in 1971. Greyhound buses ran to Omaha, Nebraska, but aside from the fact that would mean not getting there until Harry Potter had gone out of fashion, catching the bus seemed a bit tame in the country of Wild Bill Hickok and Annie Oakley. I thought of buying a stolen horse and galloping off across the sagebrush accompanied by the music of Waylon Jennings and a drawling, wry voice saying, 'And in all the trains and banks Harry robbed he never shot or killed anyone', but my attempts to find a rustling website led me only into dark waters. (Did you know that there are people who get a sexual thrill out of wearing brown-paper underwear? Why should I be surprised? The internet is 50 per cent porn and 45 per cent *Star Trek* with an alarming overlap at HornyKlingoncollegegirls.com.) Thwarted in my attempts to put a hot stallion in my shopping basket, I made other arrangements. I walked out of town to a point on the line where a long curve imposed speed restrictions on passing locos and sat down in a stand of cotton oaks to wait. It was time to ride the rails.

Within an hour I heard the lonesome 'Luke! Luke!' of a loco and a forty-car Amtrak freighter chugged into view, its brakes steaming. I ran alongside an open boxcar, threw in my belongings (a ballpoint pen from the German Embassy, a cup of lukewarm coffee and half a Kit-Kat), grabbed the door clasp and hauled myself aboard in a flurry of limbs that to the watcher must have resembled a squid tumbling down an escalator.

Catching freight trains is a great American tradition. During the Depression it is estimated that as many as four million US citizens hitched free rides. Sadly hoboing is now as well organised as every other walk of life. There is a National Hobo Association, hobo radio shows, magazines, CDs, an annual convention and online stores offering hobo supplies. All of them emphasised the positive aspect of the hobo life, how useful they were to society, how culturally diverse, ethnically inclusive, gender empowering and eco-friendly they had become and how very different they were from disruptive and feckless elements such as tramps, bums and writers. The great heavyweight Jack Dempsey had ridden the rails as a youth earning a living in 'last man standing' mass brawls in the backyards of illegal drinking dens. Modern hoboes were more likely to have a Ph.D. in comparative philosophy and supplement their income as a college professor by writing books of verse in the tradition of Robert Service.

I plugged my ears against the incredible rattle and bang of the empty car with sections of Kit-Kat and hunched in the corner watching the door. A freight car door can't be opened from the inside so if you get shut in you're a sitting duck for the bulls. Hopping freights might now be the preferred option of slumming professionals, but it is still illegal to trespass on railroad property.

After Cheyenne more crispbread countryside, then the city of Burns. In the US size is no bar to ambition. Burns has a population of 254 and no surface water. Originally it was called Luther but when the Union Pacific Railroad came through the name was changed to honour a senior engineer. Practically every conurbation on the railroad was named after a Union Pacific employee, as if a little slice of immortality was part of the employment package. Egbert, the next town on the line, had twelve houses and no services to speak of.

As lunchtime approached we crossed into Nebraska. Nebraska had once been known as the Tree Planters' State but in 1945 that designation had been changed to the snappier the Cornhuskers' State, which no doubt gave a big boost to merchandising. Nebraska had the world's largest indoor rainforest and the world's largest porch swing. The state was famous for its porridge-wrestling event. As someone who has wrestled with porridge on seven continents I can say that anybody who takes part has my respect.

We whizzed through the city of Kimball (pop. 2500), which is wet with rain and deserted. The people are all indoors working progressively towards a prosperous future. Their hometown is known as 'The Gateway to Western Nebraska' and 'Missile Centre USA', but it is most famous for its patented flumes. Watering is the big thing in Nebraska generally. Nebraskans are North America's biggest users of centre-pivot irrigation.

The next town of Sidney begged the passer-by to 'stop and stay awhile, we have great things to see!' Amongst these were Scottish dancing, marigolds and a duck. This peppy little place had enjoyed record-breaking economic progress and was also home to Cabelas The World's Foremost Outfitter™. Cabelas Retail Store and Wild Life Exhibit was Nebraska's number two visitor attraction. This was hardly surprising as I can honestly say that I have never seen so much scent-control clothing and performance underwear in the same building.

In nearby Blue Hill town ordnance proscribed women wearing hats 'that might scare a timid person' from eating onions in public. Ogallala was not configured at this address.

North Platte is a city on the move, but where to or when it is going it didn't say. Glenn Miller once lived there and the city boasts the world's largest classification yard.

At North Platte I was joined by a fellow traveller, an old-timer with the crumpled, begrimed and white-bristled look of the last potato in the sack. The old man had brought some broken packing cases with him and we lit a fire in the centre of the car, as far away from the wheels as possible to avoid setting off the heat sensors on the train's brakes.

Grand Island is the premier retail-shopping hub between Omaha and Denver. It has a population of forty-three thousand, quite a lot of which are migratory geese. Grand Island is home to the splendid Prairie Pioneer Museum. This is staffed with re-enactors of the most enthusiastic kind. Everything about them is authentic except for their faces. They are just too healthy looking for real pioneers. Study the visages of the brave families who trailed off across the prairies in the nineteenth century and the clearest thing they have in common is a look of total exhaustion. They are bone weary. Many have heads that are blurred. Most people think this is because they moved while the picture was being taken. It isn't. It's because they were so worn out they no longer had the energy to hold their molecules together. In those days on the prairies people often went to pieces, literally.

In the Nebraskan capital of Omaha fire hydrant parties were scheduled for later in the month. Local attractions included two children's homes, one of which appeared to have run away. The capital of Nebraska was also home to the Gerald R. Ford Birth Place Museum and Betty Ford Memorial Rose Garden. This included a replica of the house in Omaha in which the thirty-eighth President was born (presumably the original was stored in a vault somewhere). Gerald Ford was something of a pioneer. Before he came along most US Presidents veered between the brilliant and dull; the Nebraskan added a much needed comedy element. This was particularly necessary in the wake of Richard Nixon's final term. After all the tension and drama of the resignation the audience needed light relief. Nixon was Macbeth. Ford was the drunken gatekeeper.

After succeeding Nixon and establishing himself as the only President never to have been elected even to the vice-presidency, Ford set off on a dazzling slapstick run worthy of Mack Sennett or Jim Carrey. He fell down aeroplane steps, crashed into fences while skiing, locked himself out of the White House, banged his head when diving into a swimming pool and bounced golf shots off the noggins of spectators. To cap it all, he then lost an office to which he had never been elected in a popularity contest with the hapless Jimmy Carter. The Georgian peanut magnate attempted to follow in Ford's ungainly footsteps. He had one marvellous bit of business in which a rabbit allegedly swam out into a pond and attacked his rowing boat. Luckily the world's most powerful man was able to repel the assault using an oar. When the press cast doubt on the aquatic capabilities of bunnies, Carter was deadpan. 'Rabbits swim and that one was swimming without difficult. I certify to that,' he said. After that he lost his way, possibly due to the interference of God.

Omaha is filled with wooden houses that look like the kind of thing the Addams Family might have resided in. It is a pleasant enough place, but the inhabitants view it as far more than that. Fritz Carlson, a Nebraskan tunesmith and Groucho Marx lookalike, wrote a song about his hometown: 'I'll say it's great in O-MA-HA, O-MA-HA, boost your hometown all day long, and at night when you are sleeping dream of O-MA-HA.'

It was the kind of crap effort that would be rejected at the selection stage by the Norwegian Eurovision Song Contest committee, but in many ways it summed up the self-promotional vigour of small-town USA. Everywhere you passed through in the American interior had an upbeat motto. Sidney offered 'Small Town Values With Big Time Opportunities', while Omaha was 'Where Intellectual Capital Goes To Work'. At first I thought this relentless boosterism was aimed at the outside world, but after a while I started to feel that, like America's flag-waving patriotism, much of it was actually for home consumption. They were geeing themselves up.

I could see why. On the prairie, where a man was apt to feel like an ant crawling round on a sandstone patio, people needed a principle to cling on to. Like British officials dressing for dinner in the most remote outposts of the colonies, there was a need here for certainties and the comfort they bring. The British believed in the power of the Empire, the Americans in the power of the individual. The terror was the same. Out here in the vastness, the fear was that if you ceased to have faith in local zip and know-how within a matter of weeks you'd be living in a cave, eating bats and letting your teeth go yellow.

There was something familiar about it too. Clutz, 'The motoring burg with no reverse gear!'; Snott, 'The word can't isn't in our dictionary!' – the more I read these statements of US provincial pride the more it reminded me of somewhere else I'd been on my trip. After a while it dawned on me where that was. It probably wouldn't do to say it too loudly in Dodge City or Fort Worth, but when it came to trumpeting regional achievements in the face of all reality and with total indifference to the rest of the planet, America is a hell of a lot like Communist China.

In Omaha I hopped a boxcar towards Sioux City. Shortly after leaving Omaha we crossed The Mighty Missouri River into Iowa and turned northwards through Whiting, Sloan, Salix and Sergeants Bluff and a landscape in which wild roses bosomed against mighty oaks and the air was filled with the twittering of goldfinches and the frenetic squealing of excited hogs. The state rock of the Hawkeye State is geode, which narrowly defeated limestone and fossil coral to land the job.

I swapped boxcars in a hump yard in Sioux City on the banks of The Mighty Missouri River. This attractive mini-metropolis promised 'Excellence through community partnerships'. The city had a slightly bleached look and the population were active in blowing the whistle on litter and contacting the City Council's Pothole Hotline. 'Enter the location of the pothole, and weather permitting, we will do our best to get it fixed in a timely manner' said the strapline – and you can't be fairer than that.

Onward I went to my designated stopping point, Le Mars. Le Mars is 'The Ice Cream Capital of the World'. The population were progressive and aggressive and wore the proud expressions of people who had just survived a special celebratory concert by Survivor and the Knack without breaking down and weeping on the shoulders of strangers.

While I ate a supper of boysenberry ice cream, an information window popped up on the screen: yet another secret survey had been carried out to discover 'The Ten Things Women Most Want In A Man'. Number one was, as usual, 'a sense of humour'. I can't help wondering what the natural rationale for this choice is. After all, the fact that men are attracted to breasts is explained by anthropologists as being a subliminal desire to pick a mate who will be able to feed offspring. Likewise buttocks are fat stores and hips for childbearing. Where a sense of humour fits into this scheme is harder to say. Is the woman picking a man who can make jokes because subconsciously she knows that when he goes out hunting the deer will be so busy chuckling at his zany antics they won't notice the pit he's dug and fall straight into it? Ah yes, that Betty Ford: there were always plenty of mammoth chops in her freezer.

The next day I passed through the singular Orange City. As its name implied, Orange City delighted in its Dutch heritage. The townsfolk celebrated their origins by planting tulips, building windmills and arguing a lot. The ornate gables and floral hanging baskets thrilled visitors and many tourists went home clutching a unique souvenir such as a jigsaw or a Dutch street scrubber.

A few hours later, north of Sibley, we crossed into Minnesota and whizzed through Worthington, Wilder and Windom. Minnesota is a busy place. Minnesotans invented the stapler, masking tape and Scotch tape. They had done this so that they could parcel up some of their state compatriots' other brilliant inventions – the pop-up toaster, water skis, puffed rice – and post them to the rest of America.

Minnesota had the world's largest ball of twine and the globe's biggest statue of a pelican. Everywhere in the US had a largest this or the biggest that or the most of something else. Nowhere had a smallest anything. Miniatures don't interest Americans. Unless, of course, it's the tallest miniature.

The Minnesotan city of Mankato promised much but delivered only discount airline tickets and free entry to something called Foreclosure World, which must be the most depressing theme park on the planet. 'What are those funny men doing, Daddy?' 'Well, you see, they're bailiffs and they're taking away the people's home. Look at the way the man of the family is trying to stop them breaking his TV! And his wife is weeping, while the children huddle together looking ashen-faced and developing a psychosis that will lead to alienation and insecurity in later life! Now, what say we go for a ride on the mortgage interest rate roller coaster?'

Minneapolis–St Paul are called the Twin Cities because they were born at the same time, look alike and always seem to know what the other's about to do. I would like to have passed a little time here, but left early when I found I couldn't tell the twins apart and had to address them as 'thingie' and 'the other one' which was embarrassing and probably hurtful too. The authorities had tried to alleviate the problem by dressing the twins in different clothes with name tags all over them, but it didn't help much, so to avoid hurting their feelings further I shipped out on a train bound for Duluth.

We skirted the western fringes of Wisconsin. If all the rivers and streams in the Badger State were laid end to end they would be long enough to circle the globe at the equator. Somewhere in the world there is a person who works that kind of stuff out. And if you wove and plaited all the time he spent doing so you could strangle him with it.

In the Isanti area farmers had been asked to secure anhydrous tanks to help curb meth production and a new state law was causing controversy. The act made it illegal to enter a courthouse with a concealed firearm without the permission of the local sheriff. Most Minnesotans considered this to be an infringement of civil liberties and the kind of mollycoddling the judiciary plainly didn't need. Getting shot during a case was an occupational hazard for lawyers and judges and should remain so otherwise they'd likely get soft and flabby. In Europe they were trying to outlaw the smacking of children.

Braham is the Home-Made Pie Capital of Minnesota. It is a proud little place but the visitor senses a lingering bitterness about the decision of the Minnesota Department of Transport to deny them a traffic light in 1993. The high-school ice-hockey team had once been called the Braham Froyenmen but that epithet had been changed to Bombers because nobody knew what a Froyenman was. It remains a mystery.

Mystery of another sort was to be found a few miles further north at Sandstone, home of the Big Foot Cave. The Big Foot, or Sasquach, was said to stand eight feet tall, have size eighty-five feet, be covered in matted hair and give off a revolting smell of rancid meat. Funnily enough, many of the people who believe in the existence of the beast share two of these characteristics. There are around four hundred sightings of Big Foot a year in the USA, many of them by small children such as Minnesotan Bob McGregor who claimed to have spotted a creature on a building site that was nearly three yards tall and covered in white fur. James Stewart saw much the same thing in the film *Harvey* and they sent him to a drying-out clinic.

In 1967 Roger Patterson and Robert Gimlin had filmed a family group of Sasquach near Yakima in Washington State. This was the Roswell Incident of Big Foot lore. The Patterson footage shows a huge, hairy person with pendulous breasts. Arguments persist over whether it is real, fake or simply an athlete who overdid the steroids and HGH.

In Duluth the balloons were out for a half-marathon and rough-looking merchant ships were disgorging limestone and cement and loading coal. I signed on as a deckhand on a long-gutted slop-coloured freighter bound for Thunder Bay with a cargo of taconite. Lake Superior is 350 miles long and covers an area of 31,000 square miles, but when you've spent as much time as I haven't sailing around the Gulf of ———, the South China Sea and the Pacific, it holds all the raw thrills of a puddle.

We plodded out into the cool clear waters, past a wild, untameable shore of agate beaches. White birch, trembling aspen and tamarack hemmed the lake in their tawny equinoctial splendour, the oranges and fiery golds spilling down the crusty, rock-flecked slopes like marmalade on granary toast. Walleye, rainbow trout and silver salmon sallied skywards in pursuit of midges, belly-flopping back into the lake with the fleshy, aqueous slap of a water bomb landing on the pate of François Mitterrand.

Lake Superior is the biggest expanse of fresh water on earth. It is bigger than all the other Great Lakes put together, which is how it came by its name. Jesuit missionaries tried to rebrand it as Lake Tracy, but it never caught on.

Early the next morning we came alongside the sleeping form of Isle Royale, mist-wreathed and mysterious in the cockshut light of predawn. An insomniac moose had wandered down to the shore to drink. Moose stand seven feet tall and weigh up to 1500 pounds. They have a huge misshapen body and long skinny legs. They look like a grand piano on stilts, though not much. Spotting us, the moose let out a bullish honk. 'That is the sound of a moose,' said one of my crewmates, a veteran with skin so weather-beaten he looked as if he'd spent several weeks soaking in creosote. I thanked him for the information, though since I had just downloaded the sound to Realplayer I knew what it was as well as anybody.

Thunder Bay is a place for all seasons that has been forged by nature and history. Men in top hats brandishing muskets, a demonstration of arc welding and a flock of snowmobiles greeted us as we docked. The locals were understandably excited. The Moondogs had chomped the Border Cats, the crime of the week was breaking and entering and a travelling nudism exhibition had just showed up in town. The latter was housed in a large rig operated by the owner of Toronto's Naturist Store, which must be one of the world's emptiest shops. 'I'm going to a wedding next month and I'm looking for an outfit. Have you got anything suitable?'

'How about your birthday suit?'

'That's an idea. Can I try it off?'

'Be my guest, there isn't a changing room over there . . . What do you think?'

'I like it, but it's a bit baggy round the back. Do you do alterations?'

Canada is an extraordinary place. It is the world's second largest country after Russia, is made up almost entirely of waterfalls and pine needles and yet it has had an influence on the world that extends for many miles beyond its boundaries. Canadians, for example, invented basketball and baseball and practically everything else Americans get up to except democracy and dentistry. In fact, when you have been in Canada for a few minutes it becomes obvious that without its northern neighbour the USA would have ceased to exist centuries ago, worn down by its pathetic inability to produce comedians and ice hockey players, or invent a means of unfastening the fly opening on jeans that didn't involve wrestling with steel buttons until your bladder has burst (a Canadian, Gideon Sundback, came up with the zip fastener). Raymond Burr, Pamela Anderson, Lorne Green, Neil Young, Sam Goldwyn, Jack Warner, Jack Kerouac, Linda Evangelista, Glenn Ford, Mary Pickford, Leslie Nielsen, Dan Aykroyd, Jim Carrey, Yvonne De Carlo – the list of famous Canadians is literally endless. Indeed, as you will judge from this tiny random sample, practically every famous American in history with the exception of Gerald Ford and Lassie is actually a Canadian. Even Elvis Presley came from Saskatchewan, apparently. Luckily for the US the Canadians are far too modest and self-effacing to mention any of this more than about once a minute and so the world remains oblivious to the fact that the world's most powerful nation is actually totally rubbish at everything.

I took an eastbound Canadian Pacific train. We flashed through Terrace Bay in a hail of autumn tints, tumbling surf and offers of Italian-crafted Swiss watches at

unbelievable prices. Ontario is known as the Land of
Shining Waters. There are 250,000 lakes. The state is
famous for cars, eggs and fishing. The Great Ontario
Salmon Hunt is one of the richest fishing competitions in
the world. Unfortunately the £416,000 first prize had
proved too much of a temptation for one angler last year.
He was charged with fraud after judges discovered that his
top catch, a 34-pound fish, contained seven and a half
pounds of lead shot.

The towns along the route of the ol' C P were homely
places that formed the doorway to a plethora of lumber,
rivers, streams, meres and wallows. Canada is all wood
and water. If the country ever catches fire the rest of the
planet will become a giant Turkish bath.

Marathon is a town built on paper, but the navigation
buttons were just for show. Sudbury had northern
Ontario's most comprehensive team of medical professionals and lured the listless tourist with a blueberry
festival, mini-golf and building supplies. The telecommunications centre of North Bay, meanwhile, offered French
onion soup, country-style donuts and a museum devoted
to the Dionne Quintuplets.

Like Robert Wadlow and the headless chicken, the
Quints were a phenomenon of the Great Depression. The
five sisters, Annette, Cecile, Emilie, Marie and Yvonne,
were born on 28 May 1934 at Corbeil, near North Bay.
Despite being a couple of months premature they all survived, thanks in part to regular doses of rum. Fearing that
the quintuplets' father might be going to exploit the girls
by taking them on a tour of the US the Canadian government stepped in and made the children wards of the
state. Despite the fact that they were all perfectly healthy
the authorities built a hospital opposite their house and

kept the Dionne infants there. The parents were shunted aside so effectively that one of the children later confessed that she learned the word doctor before mother.

The hospital was nicknamed Quintland and over the next five years more than nine million people visited it to see the girls make their regular balcony appearances or to view them through a gauze curtain. The Quints were Canada's biggest tourist attraction, pulling in more punters than Niagara Falls. Local businesses profited from Dionne souvenirs that ranged from ashtrays to dolls via penants, handkerchiefs and chocolates. The Canadian government did well out of it too. Having taken charge of the children to prevent them from being used for commercial gain, the authorities are said to have trousered nearly half a million bucks from them. In 1998 the three surviving Dionne sisters finally got some of that money back after prolonged legal wrangling, winning a settlement worth £1.7 million.

At North Bay I shopped in the local mall. If it's dead and you can wear it on your head you'll find it in Canada. The sight of the raccoon-skin caps rekindled a youthful enthusiasm for Davy Crockett. There are two types: without face ($99) and with face ($103). They all have tails, though. Which suggests that somewhere in Quebec there are a lot of raccoon faces going spare. Is it possible, I wonder, to pay $107 and get a raccoon-skin hat with two faces? I thought about asking but, as usual, there is never an assistant around when you want one.

The next day, replete with maple syrup, pancakes and bacon, I hopped aboard the Northlander train for the trip to James Bay. Cobalt was Ontario's most historic town, but the place where I changed trains for the rest of the journey to James Bay was more intriguing. Founded in

1911 after a local gold strike, it had been named after a good-luck symbol. It could have been Shamrock, Rabbits Foot or Horseshoe, but it ended up as something more unusual – Swastika. During the Second World War the state authorities had tried to rename the town Winston but the locals stole the signs in protest and so Swastika it remained. Unity Mitford, sister of the writers Nancy and Jessica Mitford, was a vocal and passionate Nazi and moved to Berlin in the hope of marrying Hitler. Coincidentally, Unity was conceived in Swastika.

From Swastika the *Polar Bear Express* hammered through a landscape of pipe and drum bands, totem poles and orange lodges, accompanied every inch of the way by an irritatingly hearty song that sounded like the sort of thing they used to play on children's radio shows in the 1960s, in between 'Four Wheels On My Wagon' and 'High On The Hill Lived A Lonely Goatherd'. We arrived at the railhead of Moosonee not a moment too soon.

Moosonee was an honest-to-goodness community filled with smiling faces. It was also prodigiously cold. By now the maples had shed their ginger plumage and stood pale and naked against a charcoal horizon fecund with snow. Old women were selling what I first took to be sleeping bags for guinea pigs, but later realised were moccasins from street stalls, their breath hanging in the air above their heads like cartoon think bubbles. The Moose River was turgid and clinking. It was clear that I could not go further north until spring. And so I rented my cabin from a Cree healer and real-estate salesman. I got it for a song and the news that Stirling Moss had twice won the British Lawnmower Racing Grand Prix and that a section of race-horse Red Rum's tail had recently been sold at auction for £529.

It was in the jumbled conclave of Iqualuit that I discovered Aqsaqtuk, possibly the only sport in the world that sounds like a DIY vasectomy. There was a drawing of it by a Baffin Islander (and, yes, I'm surprised he could baff and hold a pencil steady at the same time, too) showing kagoul-clad Inuit encircling a little black dot and looking for all the world like a group of fanatical birdwatchers homing in on a particularly rare warbler.

What was apparently going on was an ancient version of soccer that has been played north of the Arctic Circle since time immemorial on an ice and snow pitch using a leather ball stuffed with moss and caribou hair. The length of the field varies but it can stretch to 10 miles, which severely limits the chances of any end-to-end action. According to some experts it is the sheer size of the playing-area length that accounts for the defensive nature of the game. A personal view is that another major contributory factor to the lack of goalmouth thrills is the fact that the game is traditionally played between teams of men and women divided along marital lines. Any contest that pits Couples against Singles seems bound to end in stalemate. The Couples' attacking strategy will quickly fall into disarray as a misplaced pass leads inexorably to a vicious argument over who last cleaned the toilet; while the assorted spinsters and geeks who make up the opposition alternate between flirting and bitter recrimination. 'That's the second time she's passed to me. I think she's trying to signal something. I think the old Keithmeister magic is starting to work its subtle charms. Oh! Why'd she try to flick that on to Norman when she could see I was in space? What's he got that I haven't? Apart from a new top-of-the-range snowmobile. Honestly, consumer durables, that's all they bloody care about. Well, to hell with her. It's no use waving your

arm at me, you miserable cow. I don't care if you have
worked an opening in front of goal. I'm giving it to my
mate Ricky; he might be fat and have the grooming sense
of the Unabomber, but at least he understands the meaning of the word "Faithful".'

Apart from Aqsaqtuk other popular Inuit games were
head pulling, mouth pulling and ear lifting. In an igloo
space is at a premium. A ping-pong table won't fit.

I had left Moosonee in March ignoring the pleas of my
neighbours to stay on and watch the blossoming of the
lady's-slipper and play another round of The Game of
Nations ('Skill and nerve are the principal requirements in
this amoral and cynical game in which there are neither
winners nor losers – only survivors,' comments former CIA
chief Miles Copeland on the box lid). I shipped out from
Moose Factory on a government icebreaker. The crew, as
you might expect, were a hearty bunch and the vessel
crackled and squawked with the sound of hand-buzzers,
whoopee cushions and off-colour jokes about Demi Moore.
It was a relief when I was put ashore at Inukjuak.

Inukjuak (formerly Port Harrison) is famous as the
home of Nanook of the North, the Inuit hunter who was
immortalised in a 1922 documentary by Robert Flaherty.
I do not know much about Flaherty but the fact that he
was later played in a film by Charles Dance suggests he
was a rotten bastard.

My journey across the ice wastes of Nunavut on a *qamu-
tiik* pulled by six huskies is not one I care to dwell on. Half
a dozen straining dogs that have fed exclusively on raw
meat are not something you should stand downwind from
if you can possibly help it. I will spare you the details, suffice
it to say that by the end of the journey my beard and eyebrows had been bleached white. Mind you, it could have

been worse. If I'd tried to light a cigarette my hair would still be smouldering and I'd be halfway to Uranus.

Flatulence aside, the dogs were excellent companions. Every morning as I emerged from my igloo they greeted me with their broad, open, happy faces, tales wagging and intestinal reports echoing across the frozen tundra like pistol shots. The site of this merry band never failed to raise my spirits. They were as good friends as a man could wish for – hard-working, cheery and steadfast, and they didn't taste half as bad as I expected either.

My sled took me northward into the land of the Inuit. The Inuit invented the anorak. Unlike most wearers they preferred to hunt seals in it rather than rare 1970s bubble-gum cards. I passed through Akulivik, where I spent the night on a *qaat* and was warmed by *qulliq*, and Ivujivik, a settlement whose name means churning and piling ice (especially along the shore). The Inuit language contains 149 words for snow and ice. This is remarkable. And only 227 words less than the English language has for money.

I crossed a landscape in which mountainous bergs sat like gigantic blanched almonds atop royal icing and the air was as clear as a baby's conscience and as crisp as fresh lettuce. Here and there a local huntsman speared a bird with a trident, or stuck his *kakivak* in a passing *char*. Polar bears sniffed the air for seal and photo opportunities, while white tundra swans bumped into one another and honked an apologetic 'I'm sorry, I didn't see you there'.

Daylight was a gaudy band around the dark hat of night. Above my head the Northern Lights flashed and sparked in the indigo sky. I had only seen such a beautiful display in the firmament twice before. Once was in that hotel in Baki, the other when I tripped over a flowerpot on the way home from a New Year's Eve party. At Salluit I crossed the Hudson Straits to Kangiqsujuaq by *umiaq*, fighting off encroaching *orcas* with my *unaaq*.

Kangiqsujuaq had previously been called Wakeham. The name had been changed on the suggestion of indigenous people and the International Scrabble Federation. According to the locals, Baffin Island has it all. And if what you consider all is walruses, polar bears and snow then they are on the button. Not that there was anything to complain of in that. The walrus, for instance, is a fine creature. Up to 13 feet in length and weighing up to 1300 pounds, it needs to eat more than two million shellfish a day to remain healthy. Since a walrus can live for forty years this means that during its life it eats twenty-nine billion molluscs and crustaceans. The indigestion doesn't bear thinking about.

I skirted Frobisher Bay and arrived at Iqualuit in time for tea and *muktuk*. The town has a population of 3500 but many of these are Quallunaats. I spent the night in a prefab with pizza.

The Vikings were an adventurous and fun-loving people who were always throwing parties. And axes. The Vikings made a number of important discoveries. Amongst these were: if you don't shave you get a beard; too much beer makes you sick; hitting someone on the head with a large hammer makes them fall down; and America. Sometime in the tenth century a party of Vikings discovered a land of ice and snow and called it Greenland. The leader of the party was Eric the Red who, if his naming of islands is anything to go by, was probably a pale-skinned, dark-haired man called Arthur.

Since being granted self-government, Greenland has changed its name to Kalaallit Nunaat, which is harder to say but more accurately descriptive. The capital of KN,

Nuuk, is a mass of grim tower blocks notorious for drunkenness, drugs and violence. But an even greater terror
lurked in the interior of this vast and inhospitable land.

Sir Max Beerbohm famously donated a shilling towards
the erecting of the Grace Gates at Lord's, 'not in support
of cricket, but as an earnest protest against golf'. Had the
author of *Zuleika Dobson* been able to foresee the future I
can't help thinking he would have upped his contribution
by several hundred guineas.

In the past decade golf courses have proliferated at
such a rate that nowadays it is surely possible to tee off in
Calais and play all the way to Vladivostok without once
setting foot on any land that isn't under the jurisdiction of
a middle-aged man in a blazer and checked pants. The
massive fairways of the United Arab Emirates have
altered the migratory patterns of several species of bird,
while those in the Far East are munching up the rainforest
and contributing to the melting of the polar ice caps.
Other sports may undermine society by encouraging yob-
bishness, or creating blinkered obsession; only golf has
the strength to give Mother Nature a good hiding.

And even in Kalaallit Nunaat you can no longer escape
this evil menace. It seems that every country on earth now
has a course. I had even stumbled across one in Outer
Mongolia. Greenland didn't actually have one, but it did
host an international golf tournament, the Drambuie Ice
Golf Challenge. This drew thirty-six competitors including a number of lesser-known pros. Rudyard Kipling had
invented ice golf when he lived in Vermont. The
Drambuie Challenge was played across the pack ice using
husky sleds for golf carts. Balls were purple. But in temperatures of −10°C maybe that's not so surprising.

Epilogue

In Kalaallit Nunaat something happened. After a vociferous campaign, the signing of petitions and many angry letters featuring the words 'They've got it in Langley-on-Tyne and there's only four people and a cow living there', British Telecommunications plc finally agreed to let my village have a broadband connection. The effect was stunning.

Iceland whizzed by in a blur of, well, Blur; the Faeroes bounced off my head with a dull splat, the Shetlands had gone past so quickly I couldn't read the name on the sign, Scotland was a multicoloured swoosh of Charles Rennie Mackintosh and haggis. I arrived home with a jolt that may permanently have damaged my spine on the 14.47 Newcastle to Carlisle train.

Apart from the fact that my neighbours now had the capability to receive one-off offers for cheaper Canadian medz faster than the human finger could delete them, nothing much had altered while I had been away. The headline in the local paper proclaimed 'Dad Threw Gnome At Window' and Mr J. B. Robson had given a talk on 'Teapots Old and New'. I staggered out of my office, gaunt no doubt and a little pale. I had travelled over 30,000 miles in a little under three months. Via ship, dugout and rocking jeepney I had wandered thoroughly and seen more than I bargained for. I had visited great cities of manifest erudition and met proud and independent people in vibrant lands so far from the automated bleep of civilisation that to them the notion of moist, quilted toilet tissue with a hint of mint was as unfathomable as a madman's dream.

And now I was home. When she saw me standing in the doorway, swaying slightly from the effects of natural light and fresh air, Catherine raised an eyebrow and offered a quizzical smile. And as I staggered down the corridor towards her she greeted me with those magical words familiar to all internauts freshly returned from an epic voyage.

'Can *I* use the phone now?'